"Robert Weems' pathbreaking overview of African Americans' growing participation in this nation's consumer society stresses both concrete achievements and lasting ambiguities. Deepening our appreciation of consumption's complexities, *Desegregating the Dollar* is essential reading."

—*Philip Scranton*
Kranzberg Professor of History, Georgia Tech

"Sophisticated and straightforward. This is a book scholars and students have been waiting for! A masterful history of African Americans as consumers."

—*Fath Davis Ruffins*
Historian, National Museum of American History

Desegregating the Dollar

*African American Consumerism
in the Twentieth Century*

Robert E. Weems Jr.

NEW YORK UNIVERSITY PRESS

New York and London

NEW YORK UNIVERSITY PRESS
New York and London

Library of Congress Cataloging-in-Publication Data
Weems, Robert E., 1951–
Desegregating the dollar : African American consumerism in the twentieth
century / Robert E. Weems Jr.
p.   cm.
Includes bibliographical references and index.
ISBN 0-8147-9290-1 (acid-free paper). — ISBN 0-8147-9327-4 (pbk. :
acid-free paper)
1. Afro-American consumers—History—20th century. 2. Racism—
United States—History—20th century.   I. Title.
HC110.C6W44   1998
381.3'089'96073—dc21   97-33866
                              CIP

Manufactured in the United States of America
10 9 8 7 6 5 4 3 2 1

Contents

Tables

Acknowledgments

During the course of completing this book, I have been assisted by a number of individuals and institutions. First, I offer a sincere thanks to Niko Pfund, director of New York University Press, for his profound belief in this project. I also want to express my gratitude to the University of Missouri-Columbia's Research Council and the MU Alumni Association for their financial support. Because the core sources of this study are various industry trade journals, I owe a special debt to the staff of the University of Missouri-Columbia's Elmer Ellis and Walter Williams Libraries, the MU Freedom of Information Center, as well as to library personnel at the University of Chicago and De Paul University.

A special thanks also goes out to Faith Davis Ruffins and her helpful colleagues at the Smithsonian Institution's Archives Center at the National Museum of American History. Likewise, I appreciate the assistance of Archie Motley and his staff at the Chicago Historical Society.

Another group of individuals who made an important contribution to this study is past and present members of the National Association of Market Developers. This association of African American marketing and public relations professionals has, since 1953, played a major role in influencing corporate America's attitudes about black consumers. NAMD members who were especially helpful to me include (in alphabetical order) James Avery, Miriam Evans, Yvonne Pearson, Chuck Smith, James "Bud" Ward, Samuel "Sammy" Whiteman, and Ben Wright. Moreover, Mr. Whiteman, who died unexpectedly in December 1996, was the "griot" of the National Association of Market Developers, and his presence and friendship are dearly missed.

Since I first began conceptualizing a historical study of African American consumerism in 1989, a number of my colleagues in academe have given me both useful advice and appreciated encouragement. Persons who were especially helpful include (in alphabetical order) Talmadge Anderson, Sue Porter Benson, Liz Cohen, Robert L. Harris Jr., Robin D. G. Kelley, John

McClendon, Mary Neth, Lewis Randolph, Arvarh E. Strickland, Walter B. Weare, and Gail Baker Woods. A special thanks goes to Winston McDowell, who shared with me materials on the National Negro Business League he gathered from the Albon L. Holsey Papers at Tuskegee Institute.

I also want to acknowledge the efforts of Derek Gabriel and Jabulani Leffall. Mr. Gabriel served as my research assistant during the summer of 1991 as part of the University of Missouri-Columbia's Advanced Opportunity Program (AOP). The AOP, which unfortunately is now defunct, brought undergraduates from historically black colleges and universities to MU to work directly with professors. Jabulani Leffall, a veteran of my various history classes at the University of Missouri-Columbia, is a truly special individual. When I experienced difficulty during the summer of 1996 securing a research assistant, he stepped forward and graciously volunteered his services.

Last, but definitely not least, I'm appreciative of the ongoing love and support of my parents, sisters, friends, and in-laws, and especially that of my wife, Clenora, and daughter, Sharifa.

Although only my name appears on the cover, this book would not have been possible without the people and institutions cited in this public thank you.

Introduction

The history of twentieth-century African American consumerism illustrates the deeper meaning of the maxim "Be careful what you ask for, because you just might get it." African American consumers' historic quest for "recognition" clearly has produced both positive and negative consequences.

Like other groups, African Americans have been directly and profoundly affected by the growth and entrenchment of mass consumer culture in twentieth-century America. Yet, just as the social, educational, and political experiences of African and European Americans have traditionally differed, historically, African and European American consumerism have had mutually exclusive characteristics.

White consumers have expected and received courteous service during commercial transactions. Moreover, advertising campaigns aimed at white shoppers have traditionally conveyed the goodwill necessary to stimulate the purchase of particular products or services.

Black consumers, on the other hand, have a history of being disrespected. During the first decades of the twentieth century, especially in the South, African American shoppers were regularly subjected to "second-class" treatment in retail establishments. Moreover, during this same period, the U.S. advertising industry graphically reflected the callous disrespect that many businesses had for black consumers, as is evident from the proliferation of products whose trade names included such derogatory terms as "mammy," "pickaninny," "coon," and "nigger."

From the standpoint of early twentieth-century U.S. white enterprises, African Americans' overall socioeconomic status warranted the widespread disrespect shown them. At the dawn of the twentieth century, African Americans were primarily a rural, southern, and relatively impoverished segment of the national population. Moreover, any group desire for upward mobility appeared to be thwarted by the existence of American apartheid, popularly known as "Jim Crow." Consequently, American busi-

1

nesses believed they could ignore and disrespect African American consumers with impunity.

Chapter 1 surveys the circumstances that contributed to the birth and development of a viable African American consumer market in the face of
white oppression. It also reveals early corporate attempts to profit from
African Americans' improving socioeconomic status.

Although early twentieth-century institutional racism circumscribed the
life choices of many African Americans, others refused to permit arbitrary
racial barriers to stifle their ambitions. For instance, such books as Booker T.
Washington's *The Negro in Business*, published in 1907, and Monroe Work's
The Negro Yearbook, which began publication in 1912, proudly documented
rising African American home and business ownership, despite the obvious
obstacles to such achievements.

In addition to growing wealth and gains in education, African American
migration and urbanization between 1900 and 1940 contributed mightily
to the group's enhanced status as consumers. The approximately 500,000
rural southern blacks who moved to urban areas seeking war-related jobs
during the World War I "Great Migration," as well as those who followed
them, radically altered the demographic profile of black America. As African
Americans began to proliferate in cities (and major markets) across the
country, a once predominantly rural people with limited disposable income
were increasingly seen as a potentially lucrative market (by both black and
white businesses). Among the first corporations to specifically target urban
black consumers were recording companies and the purveyors of hair and
skin care products.

Chapter 2 examines the impact of accelerated black migration and urbanization, both during and after World War II, on business perceptions of
the "Negro market." As the number of African Americans increased in U.S.
cities, the number of articles relating to the (then) expanding "Negro market" and how to "reach" it increased in advertising trade journals, and the
number of businesses consulting such material increased dramatically.

Between 1941 and 1960, white businesses sought to get their "share" of
the increasingly lucrative "Negro market" in a number of ways. During this
period, major corporations significantly increased their purchasing of advertising space in black-owned newspapers. Moreover, to supplement their
products' enhanced presence in African American periodicals, large U.S.
businesses heavily marketed their goods on "Negro-appeal" radio stations.
Ironically, while these stations featured music and features of interest to
blacks, the vast majority of them were owned by white entrepreneurs. To

further buttress their visibility in the African American community, large companies hired African Americans to serve as "Negro market specialists." These individuals, who represented their employers at such functions as the annual conventions of the National Urban League and the National Association for the Advancement of Colored People (NAACP), were the true African American pioneers in corporate America.

African American entrepreneurs, too, were interested in reaching the increasingly urbanized black consumer market. For instance, those associated with the embryonic Gospel music industry established a church-based, grassroots distribution system to market the songs of notable gospel composers. In fact, Thomas A. Dorsey, regarded as the "Father of African American Gospel Music," owned the company that published and distributed his songs.

Perhaps the period's most dramatic business overture to African American consumers was Branch Rickey's signing of Jackie Robinson to play for the Brooklyn Dodgers. The 1947 baseball season, Robinson's first full season in the major leagues, represented not only a source of pride for African Americans but a box-office bonanza for Rickey and the Dodgers. The Cleveland Indians' signing of the legendary pitcher Satchel Paige in 1948 produced similar profits by enhancing black attendance at Indians games. The subsequent decline and disappearance of the Negro Baseball Leagues as black players and fans began to proliferate in major league ballparks was an ominous foretaste of the impact desegregation would have on historically black community businesses and institutions.

Chapter 3 illuminates the part the search for consumer justice played in the celebrated Civil Rights Movement. African American consumers, long before the mid-1950s, had expressed systematic outrage against discriminatory treatment and outright racist violence. This chapter details the characteristics of the resulting economic retribution by black consumers.

Historically, African Americans have withdrawn their economic support of white-controlled enterprises for a number of reasons. First and foremost, African Americans have staged consumer boycotts to respond to extreme acts of white racist violence. Similarly, blacks have constrained their spending with European American enterprises to protest against humiliating differential treatment based on race, white-owned businesses interested in blacks solely as consumers (rather than as employees), and white companies that used demeaning images of blacks in their advertising. Besides reacting to white indifference, hostility, and violence, African Americans have also withheld economic support of European American businesses in order to better support African American entrepreneurs.

Black gains associated with the Civil Rights Movement resulted from the strategic use of increased African American spending power, rather than from white "moral transformation." More than a generation later, the Texaco Corporation's quick November 1996 public apology to African Americans in response to a threatened nationwide black boycott to protest the company's mistreatment of its black personnel demonstrated the continuing potential and power of organized African American consumer activism.

Chapter 4 suggests a major reinterpretation of African American history during the 1960s. Traditionally, the 1960s have been viewed as a decade during which African American activism, coupled with the liberalism of the Kennedy and Johnson administrations, resulted in both social and economic gains for many African Americans. Yet, when the 1960s are viewed through the lens of black consumerism and white business, the decade featured pragmatic white conservatism rather than altruistic white liberalism. In response to the accelerated urbanization of African Americans, corporations accelerated their quest to reach these increasingly important consumers. This included the expanded use, at the behest of organizations such as the Congress of Racial Equality (CORE), of African American models in print and television advertising. CORE and other civil rights organizations hailed such innovations as civil rights "victories." Nevertheless, corporations, following the advice of the publisher John H. Johnson, their chief black consultant, tended to view such concessions as "enlightened self-interest."

The 1960s also revealed the malleability of American capitalism. Corporate marketers began the decade by developing advertising campaigns that catered to African Americans' perceived desire for racial desegregation. By decade's end, as African Americans moved politically from "We Shall Overcome" to "Black Power," U.S. corporations promoted the "Soul" market to retain the allegiance of black consumers.

Chapter 5 chronicles Hollywood's successful campaign during the 1970s to reach the African American consumer market through the "blaxploitation" film genre. Movies such as *Shaft*, *Superfly*, and *The Mack* not only garnered huge profits for whites throughout the film industry but warped the psyche of an entire generation of black youth with their glorification of drug use, violence, and "street life."

The 1970s also witnessed dramatic gains by white-owned personal care product companies and insurance companies in garnering African American consumer support. White corporations' expansion in these important areas came at the expense of the black-owned enterprises that had historically provided personal care products and insurance to the black community. By the end of the decade, it became increasingly clear that white companies, and not black ones, were deriving most of the profits from African Americans' ever increasing collective spending power.

Chapter 6 surveys African American consumption during the Reagan years. As black social and economic gains associated with the Civil Rights Movement stalled during the eight years of the ultraconservative Reagan administration, class distinctions within the African American community became much more pronounced. This market segmentation prompted corporate marketers to develop more class-specific advertising aimed at African Americans.

Whereas "Buppies" (black "Yuppies," or Young, Urban Professionals) were actively courted by the producers of upscale consumer items and financial services companies, the growing black "underclass" attracted the intense attention of tobacco and alcoholic beverage companies. Considering the economic deprivation associated with 1980s urban black enclaves, as well as the historical use of cigarette and alcohol consumption as short-term "escapes" from reality, it appeared to many observers that the accelerated marketing of tobacco and alcohol in urban black neighborhoods during the 1980s represented a blatant attempt to profit from human misery. Moreover, a closer examination of the operation of cigarette and liquor companies in the African American community revealed their excessive influence over black-owned periodicals, civil rights organizations, and black politicians.

The Epilogue examines the role of African American consumers in today's U.S. economy. African Americans in the 1990s are a far different people than they were at the dawn of the century. Once perceived as primarily a rural group with limited disposable income, blacks today are a free-spending, pronouncedly urban people. Still, advertising and marketing continue to exhibit an ongoing insensitivity toward black consumers.

Even when contemporary black consumers are duly recognized, the consequences are often mixed. For instance, the reemergence of the "blaxploitation" movie genre, albeit in a different form, has captivated a new generation of African American moviegoers in the 1990s. This has been coupled with such recent television atrocities as *Homeboys in Outer Space*, a poorly written transplantation of urban black culture into the cosmos. In addition, an accelerated interest in black consumers by white purveyors of personal care products and insurance has increased the strain on black-owned businesses in these areas.

As the twentieth century draws to a close, increased consumerism has produced both positive and negative consequences for the African American community. The typical African American family today, compared to a similar family a mere generation ago, generally eats a wider variety of food, wears higher quality clothing, drives a more prestigious model of automobile, and listens to a more powerful stereo system. In fact, the collective spending power of African Americans will likely exceed $500 billion before the year 2000. Still, if one were to take a stroll through most urban black enclaves in America, one would be hard pressed to see where increased African American spending has improved the infrastructure and ambiance of these neighborhoods. Thus, the major challenge facing contemporary African American consumers is to develop spending strategies that will stimulate more constructive economic activity within the black community.

Desegregating the Dollar: African American Consumerism in the Twentieth Century seeks to establish the contours of black consumer activity during this century as well as to provide the historical perspective lacking in existing studies of this phenomenon. This panoramic survey of twentieth-century African American consumerism should prove useful to those involved in ongoing discourse regarding blacks' future role in capitalist America.

1

The Birth and Development of the African American Consumer Market, 1900–1940

The first decades of the twentieth century witnessed a dramatic demographic transformation of the national African American community. Between 1900 and 1940, an estimated 1.7 million southern blacks migrated to northern and western cities.[1] This movement, coupled with a simultaneous increase in the number of blacks in southern cities,[2] resulted in a dramatic decline in the number of rural African Americans. During this period the proportion of blacks residing in rural areas dropped from 77 to 51 percent.[3] African Americans' ongoing urbanization, among other things, slowly attracted the attention of the U.S. business community. In earlier years, when blacks were generally perceived to be rural, low-wage workers with limited disposable income, white businesses all but ignored black consumers. The proliferation of contemporary general advertising that caricatured and demeaned African Americans graphically illustrated many white businesses' disregard for the feelings of blacks. Yet as African Americans began to congregate in U.S. cities, spurred by the World War I "Great Migration" and its aftermath, businesses big and small, black and white, began to take the idea of a "Negro market" more seriously. By 1940, a growing number of American corporations began to appreciate the potential profits associated with black consumers.

At the dawn of the twentieth century, the plight of African Americans appeared especially desperate. Although slavery officially ended in 1865, a significant number of blacks, in 1900, were ensnared as peons and sharecroppers in the southern agricultural economy.[4] Moreover, by 1900, the hope and excitement generated by African American political activity during Reconstruction had been transformed into disillusionment by the evolving reality of "Jim Crow" and political disfranchisement.[5]

Because of blacks' apparent powerlessness in the realms of politics and economics, white Americans, and especially white businesses, believed they could, with impunity, denigrate African Americans. This helps to explain the pervasiveness of derogatory images of blacks in turn-of-the-twentieth-century American advertising.

U.S. white business's unabashed contempt for African Americans manifested itself in a variety of ways during this period. First, many companies regularly featured blacks with exaggerated physical features in their advertisements. Other advertisers made widespread use of the term "nigger" in naming products or marketed products that derisively portrayed African American children as "pickaninnies." Finally, turn-of-the-twentieth-century advertising often associated Africans with cannibalism.[6]

The marketing of soap during this period was one manifestation of white businesses' condescending attitudes toward blacks. Soap companies, believing that blacks, if given a choice, would prefer to be white, used ads that implied that regular use of their products could indeed turn the skin of African Americans white.[7] Similarly, white-owned companies that marketed hair and skin care products to African American women operated from a belief that they were beneficently marketing "whiteness" (skin lighteners and hair straighteners) to black female consumers.[8]

Despite widespread economic deprivation, political disfranchisement, and cultural assault from the U.S. advertising industry, not everyone in the early-twentieth-century African American community appeared beaten down or defeated. In fact, contemporary research studies, conducted by blacks, documented the increasing accumulation of wealth by African Americans, despite the obvious obstacles. Moreover, those blacks who amassed assets, during what Rayford Logan referred to as the "nadir" of the postslavery African American experience, formed the cornerstone of an observable black consumer market.

Booker T. Washington's book, *The Negro in Business*, published in 1907, provided an important window to observe turn-of-the-twentieth-century African American economic development. Although most of the book celebrated the accomplishments of individual black entrepreneurs and extolled the National Negro Business League (which Washington founded in 1900), *The Negro in Business* also considered the broader aspects of the black community's economic life. The book's discussion of African American home ownership was especially important.

In 1860 the percentage of African Americans who owned homes was microscopic. Yet, by 1890, Washington reported that 18.7 percent of blacks owned their own homes. Moreover, 88.8 percent of these dwellings were owned free of any encumbrances. By comparison, only 71.2 percent of homes owned by whites were mortgage free.[9]

Between 1890 and 1900 the percentage of African American families who were homeowners increased to 21.8 percent. Of these, 74.2 percent completely owned their residences, compared to 68 percent of white families who owned their homes free of encumbrances.[10] Washington, with undisguised pride, assessed this phenomenon as follows:

> I am unaware that history records such an example of substantial progress in civilization in a time so short. Here is the unique fact that from a penniless population, just out of slavery, that placed a premium on thriftlessness, 372,414 owners of homes have emerged, and of these, 255,156 are known to own their homes absolutely free of encumbrance.[11]

Perhaps the most important documentation of the economic progress of early-twentieth-century black America was *The Negro Yearbook and Annual Encyclopedia of the Negro*. First published in 1912 by Monroe Work, Tuskegee Institute's director of research, this resource, until its demise in the 1950s, provided an impressive overview of the African American experience.

The 1912 edition of *The Negro Yearbook*, among other things, informed readers that the estimated total wealth of African Americans in 1911 was $700 million. Significantly, despite widespread notions of universal black poverty in the South, assets owned by rural southern blacks represented a sizable portion of African Americans' collective resources. Citing U.S. census data, *The Negro Yearbook* reported that, between 1900 and 1910 the value of farm property owned by southern blacks increased by 177 percent, from $177,404,688 to $492,898,218.[12] In addition, this publication noted:

> It is estimated that the Negroes are adding each year to their wealth from $20,000,000 to $30,000,000. They now own about 20,000,000 acres of land or 31,000 square miles, an area almost equal to that of Vermont, New Hampshire, Massachusetts, Connecticut and Rhode Island. . . . Negroes now own and operate 64 banks, 100 insurance companies, 300 drug stores, and over 20,000 dry goods and grocery stores, and other industrial enterprises.[13]

The 1913 edition of *The Negro Yearbook*, besides reiterating much of the data contained in the previous issue, favorably compared the progress of emancipated slaves in the United States with that of emancipated serfs in

Russia. After declaring that "no other emancipated people have made so great a progress in so short a time,"[14] *The Negro Yearbook* bolstered its claims of African American prowess by asserting:

> The Russian serfs were emancipated in 1861. Fifty years after it was found that 14,000,000 of them had accumulated about $500,000,000 worth of property or about $36 per capita, an average of about $200 per family. Fifty years after their emancipation only about 30 percent of the Russian peasants were able to read and write. After fifty years of freedom the ten million Negroes in the United States have accumulated over $700,000,000 worth of property, or about $70 per capita, which is an average of $350 per family. After fifty years of freedom 70 percent of them have some education in books.[15]

The 1916–17 and 1918–19 editions of *The Negro Yearbook* provided important insights into the extent of collective African American consumer power during this period. In 1865 African Americans entrepreneurs were involved in only twelve kinds of commercial enterprises: bakeries, barbershops, blacksmithing, boot and shoe repairing, cabinetmaking, catering, dressmaking, fish and oyster sales, hairdressing, sailmaking, shopkeeping, and vending. By 1915 blacks conducted seventy-one different types of businesses. Two years later, African American businesspeople owned and operated two hundred different kinds of businesses.[16] Given the widespread and rigid policy of racial segregation that prevailed in the United States during this period, the estimated $1 billion in sales in 1915 and the $1.2 billion in sales in 1917 achieved by black-owned businesses were generated primarily by sales to black consumers.[17] (These figures do not take into account the money spent by African American consumers with white-owned enterprises.) In fact, the first available estimate related to annual black spending power, $3,055,000,000 in 1920,[18] suggests that black consumers spent approximately one third of their disposable income with African American enterprises during this period.

The second decade of the twentieth century, besides witnessing the birth of *The Negro Yearbook*, featured the dramatic geographic relocation of African Americans known as the "Great Migration." Between 1915 and 1918, coinciding with World War I, approximately 500,000 rural southern blacks migrated to northern urban areas seeking employment in war-related industries. This proliferation of potential consumers in America's major markets contributed to American business's subsequent interest in reaching black shoppers.

Although Black inter-regional movement during the Great Migration has dominated the attention of historians, a number of southern black migrants did not leave Dixie. While many rural black workers responded to the South's agricultural problems and ongoing virulent white racism by moving North, others moved to southern cities. By 1930, fifty-one of the eighty U.S. cities that had African American populations of at least ten thousand were in the South. Moreover, the number of blacks in southern cities increased by 32 percent between 1910 and 1920 and 41 percent between 1920 and 1930.[19]

An examination of census data for American cities that had black populations of at least ten thousand by 1930 reveals the extent of African American urban resettlement during this period. Table 1.1 lists the eight cities whose black population grew from 60 to 100 percent between 1910 and 1920. Table 1.2 lists the fifteen cities whose black population grew by more than 100 percent during the same decade. Tables 1.3 and 1.4 reveal that black urbanization continued unabated during the 1920s: Table 1.3 enumerates the thirteen cities that experienced an increase in their black population of from 60 to 100 percent between 1920 and 1930, and Table 1.4 identifies the fourteen urban areas that experienced a black population increase of more than 100 percent during the "roaring twenties." Table 1.5, which surveys the dramatic increase of whites in selected urban areas between 1910 and 1930, indicates that the thrust toward urbanization transcended racial and ethnic boundaries.

TABLE 1.1

Cities That Experienced a 60–100 Percent Increase in Their Black Populations, 1910–1920 *

	Number of Blacks in 1910	Number of Blacks in 1920	Percentage Increase
New York, New York	91,709	152,467	66.3
Bessemer, Alabama	6,210	10,561	70.1
Norfolk, Virginia	25,039	43,392	73.3
Columbus, Ohio	12,739	22,181	74.1
Newark, New Jersey	9,475	16,977	79.2
Dayton, Ohio	4,842	9,025	86.4
Beaumont, Texas	6,896	13,210	91.6
Newport News, Virginia	7,259	14,077	93.9

*Other cities that experienced at least a 50 percent increase in their black populations during this period were Cincinnati, Ohio (53.2); Kansas City, Kansas (55.1); St. Louis, Missouri (58.9); Philadelphia, Pennsylvania (58.9) and Indianapolis, Indiana (59.0).

SOURCE: Charles E. Hall, Negroes in the United States, 1920–1932 (Washington, D.C.: U.S. Bureau of the Census, 1935), 55.

TABLE I.2

Cities That Experienced More Than a 100 Percent Increase in Their
Black Populations, 1910–1920

	Number of Blacks in 1910	Number of Blacks in 1920	Percentage Increase
Portsmouth, Virginia	11,617	23,245	100.1
Omaha, Nebraska	5,143	10,315	100.6
Los Angeles, California	7,599	15,579	105.0
Winston-Salem, North Carolina	9,087	20,735	128.2
Chicago, Illinois	44,103	109,458	148.2
Buffalo, New York	1,773	4,511	154.4
Port Arthur, Texas	1,493	3,910	161.9
Toledo, Ohio	1,877	5,691	203.2
Youngstown, Ohio	1,936	6,662	244.1
Cleveland, Ohio	8,448	34,451	307.8
Miami, Florida	2,258	9,270	310.5
Tulsa, Oklahoma	1,959	8,878	353.2
Detroit, Michigan	5,741	40,838	611.3
Akron, Ohio	657	5,580	749.3
Gary, Indiana	383	5,299	1,283.6

SOURCE: Hall, Negroes in the U.S., 1920–1932, 55.

TABLE I.3

Cities That Experienced a 60–100 Percent Increase in Their
Black Populations, 1920–1930*

	Number of Blacks in 1920	Number of Blacks in 1930	Percentage Increase
Dallas, Texas	24,023	38,742	61.3
Philadelphia, Pennsylvania	134,229	219,599	63.6
Tulsa, Oklahoma	8,878	15,203	71.2
Charlotte, North Carolina	14,641	25,163	71.9
Chattanooga, Tennessee	18,889	33,289	76.2
Oklahoma City, Oklahoma	8,241	14,662	77.9
Monroe, Louisiana	5,540	10,112	82.5
Tampa, Florida	11,531	21,172	83.6
Houston, Texas	33,960	63,337	86.5
Dayton, Ohio	9,025	17,077	89.2
Jackson, Mississippi	9,936	19,423	95.5
Akron, Ohio	5,580	11,080	98.6
Asheville, North Carolina	7,145	14,255	99.5

*Memphis; Cincinnati; Winston-Salem; Shreveport; Columbus, Georgia; Jersey City; and East St. Louis, Illinois, experienced at least a 50 percent growth of their black populations between 1920 and 1930.
SOURCE: Hall, Negroes in the U.S., 1920–1932, 55.

TABLE 1.4
Cities That Experienced More Than a 100 Percent Increase in Their
Black Populations, 1920–1930

	Number of Blacks in 1920	Number of Blacks in 1930	Percentage Increase
Cleveland, Ohio	34,451	71,899	108.7
Chicago, Illinois	109,458	233,903	113.7
New York, New York	152,467	327,706	114.9
Youngstown, Ohio	6,662	14,552	118.4
Newark, New Jersey	16,977	38,880	129.0
Toledo, Ohio	5,691	13,260	133.0
Greensboro, North Carolina	5,973	14,050	135.2
Durham, North Carolina	7,654	18,717	144.5
Los Angeles, California	15,579	38,894	149.7
Port Arthur, Texas	3,910	10,003	155.8
Miami, Florida	9,270	25,116	170.9
Detroit, Michigan	40,838	120,066	194.0
Buffalo, New York	4,511	13,563	200.7
Gary, Indiana	5,299	17,922	238.2

SOURCE: Hall, Negroes in the U.S., 1920–1932, 55.

TABLE 1.5
Population Growth of European Americans in Selected Cities, 1910–1930*

	1910	1920	1930
Akron, Ohio	68,404	202,718	249,744
Chicago, Illinois	2,139,057	2,589,169	3,117,731
Detroit, Michigan	459,952	952,065	1,440,141
Gary, Indiana	16,403	50,044	78,992
Los Angeles, California	305,307	546,864	1,073,584
Milwaukee, Wisconsin	372,809	454,824	568,807
New York, New York	4,669,162	5,459,463	6,587,225
Norfolk, Virginia	42,353	72,226	85,514
Pittsburgh, Pennsylvania	508,008	550,261	614,317

*The Census Bureau definition of European Americans included "Native" and "Foreign-born" whites.
SOURCE: Statistical Abstract of the United States, 1921, 55–57; Statistical Abstract of the United States, 1931, 22–27.

Increased African American urbanization during this period, among other things, resulted in an improvement in the income of both northern and southern black city dwellers. In 1910, before African Americans began to proliferate noticeably in U.S. urban areas, 76.4 percent of gainfully employed African Americans worked in either agriculture or domestic service.[20] The vast majority of these workers were at the absolute bottom of the U.S. wage hierarchy, alongside self-employed black farm owners. Consequently, when the domestic labor shortage that arose during World War I provided blacks an opportunity to enter the realm of better-paying industrial employment, the economic stature of both individual blacks and the collective African American community received a boost.

In Chicago, which attracted more than fifty thousand southern black migrants between January 1, 1916, and June 30, 1917,[21] African American newcomers found an environment conducive to economic improvement. As one observer noted:

> The most favorable aspect of their condition in their new home is the opportunity to earn money. Coming from the South, where they are accustomed to work for a few cents a day or a few dollars a week, to an industrial center where they can earn that much in an hour or a day, they have the feeling that this city is really the land overflowing with milk and honey. In the occupations in which they are now employed, many of them are engaged in skilled labor, receiving the same and, in some cases, greater compensation than was paid white men in such position prior to the outbreak of the war.[22]

Other cities known for the relatively high wages they offered to black migrants were Pittsburgh, Detroit, and Philadelphia, where some black workers were publicly condemned for misspending their new-found disposable income in "saloons and dens of vice."[23]

Ironically, in many locales, southern blacks who did not participate in the Great Migration also saw their standard of living improve during the war. The dispersal of black migrants reacting to a northern labor shortage quickly created a similar southern labor shortage. Thus, in the South, as in the North, prized black workers were able to command higher salaries. Even in the traditionally oppressive (for blacks) Mississippi, the wages of African American living in urban areas increased by from 10 to 100 percent.[24]

By 1920 a growing number of African American urbanites, in both the North and the South, had more money to spend than ever before. Among the first national companies to aggressively target this embryonic consumer market were record companies.

The music industry's keen interest in African American consumers sprang from black America's enthusiastic response to the blues singer Mamie Smith's August 1920 recording of "Crazy Blues" on the OKeh record label. "Crazy Blues" and its "B" side, "It's Right Here for You (If You Don't Get It, 'Taint No Fault of Mine)," represented the music industry's first conscious attempt to vigorously woo black consumers. Earlier in 1920, Smith had recorded two other songs for OKeh, "You Can't Keep a Good Man Down" and "This Thing Called Love." Yet, OKeh's employment of an all-white combo as a backdrop for Smith's February 14, 1920, recording session suggests OKeh's initial trepidation about marketing a clearly black-oriented product. Still, the sales generated from Mamie Smith's first recordings prompted OKeh Records' musical directors, Milo Rega and Fred Hager, to develop what came to be known as the "race records" genre.[25]

Although African American recording artists had appeared on records before Mamie Smith, their efforts had been aimed primarily at white audiences. Smith's "Crazy Blues" broke with this precedent by seeking to attract primarily African American music consumers. To accentuate its appeal to blacks, "Crazy Blues," besides featuring Mamie Smith's spirited vocal performance, showcased an all-black musical accompaniment group that came to be known as Smith's "Jazz Hounds." This strategy ultimately proved to be extremely profitable. Within weeks of its November 1920 release, "Crazy Blues" had sold more than seventy-five thousand copies.[26]

The OKeh record company, using the success of "Crazy Blues" as a springboard, launched its famous "race" series in 1921. After hiring the noted black musician Clarence Williams as the series' musical director, OKeh, whose advertising soon declared that it had "The World's Greatest Race Artists on the World's Greatest Race Records," employed the era's top blues and jazz artists. OKeh's "race" series, until its demise in 1935, also featured outstanding recording technology, and it remains a favorite of collectors.[27]

Predictably, other record companies, after witnessing OKeh's success with "race" music, sought to employ their own African American artists. Columbia featured perhaps the era's most noteworthy blues singer, Bessie Smith. Paramount's cadre of black performers included such luminaries as Alberta Hunter and "Blind" Lemon Jefferson.[28]

Black Swan records, the first black-owned recording company in the Unite States, represented another important player in the early 1920s music industry. Started in 1921 by a black entrepreneur, Harry H. Pace, its advertisements attempted to distinguish Black Swan from its competitors by stating that it was the:

[o]nly bonafide Racial company making talking machine records. All stock-holders are colored, all artists are colored, all employees are colored. Only company using Racial Artists in recording high class song records. This company made the only Grand Opera records ever made by Negroes.[29]

Black Swan records provided black consumers a wide variety of musical genres. Besides the blues, Black Swan recorded baritone and soprano solos, vaudeville duos, violin solos, vocal groups, dance orchestras, and jazz bands. Still, despite Pace's attempt to cultivate a genteel image for his company, blues recordings represented the cornerstone of Black Swan's popularity and profitability. In fact, Ethel Waters's 1921 recording of the blues singles "Down Home Blues" and "Oh, Daddy" was such a hit that Pace subsequently formed the traveling "Black Swan Troubadours," featuring Waters and the musical director Fletcher Henderson, to promote the company.[30]

Despite Black Swan's auspicious beginning, increased competition from OKeh, Columbia, and Paramount forced the company out of business in late 1923. During the spring of 1924, Paramount purchased the catalog of Black Swan recordings, and it later reissued the most popular ones.[31]

The major vehicle used by the 1920s recording industry to reach black consumers was the African American press. In fact, any business that sought black patronage viewed African American newspapers as a vital resource. Unfortunately, much of the of advertising in black newspapers during this period suggests that blacks were viewed as dupes, willing to try anything to change their skin color, hair texture, health, and luck.

First and foremost, there existed an overwhelming predominance of ads selling skin bleaches, hair straighteners, and other products to "assist" African Americans in assuming a more European look.[32] The following examples, taken from black newspapers of the period, exemplified this marketing genre:

LIGHTENS YOUR SKIN OR YOUR MONEY BACK—Safe—Sure—Quick—Bleacho. Be more popular. Earn more money. Safely and secretly you can now remove the greatest obstacle to your success. Bleacho is guaranteed to lighten your skin regardless of what it is now.

Wonderful Gland Discovery Goes Straight to Root and Grows BEAUTIFUL STRAIGHT HAIR. Full, Healthy, Abundant—Without Kinks . . . Ugly, kinky, scanty hair can be easily and quickly made to grow into lifeful, luxuriant abundance . . . Science has perfected a hair treatment that gives the Race beautiful, straight and glorious hair.

HOW TO OBTAIN BEAUTIFULLY SHAPED LIPS! Mr. T—'s new lip shaper, together with its thick lip astringent lotion, will now reduce protruding, prominent, thick unshapely lips to normal and thus improve your facial appearance 100 per cent.[33]

Advertisements for patent medicines also predominated in African American newspapers during this period. While similar ads also appeared in some white periodicals, there was a greater concentration of such ads in black papers. For example, the May 4, 1921, issue of the black New York *Amsterdam News* carried thirteen advertisements for patent cures and "so-called specialists" on one page![34]

"Clairvoyants" and religious charlatans also aggressively peddled their wares in black newspapers during the 1920s. One of the more absurd advertisements of this type involved a publication entitled *The Kingdom of God*. Readers were told that purchasing this material, for one dollar, would ensure their being among God's "elect" on "Judgement Day" (which would occur no later than June 30, 1921).[35]

Although advertisements for beauty preparations, patent medicines, and dubious religious publications predominated in African American newspapers during this period, more reputable businesses did advertise their goods and services in these periodicals. They included grocers, insurance companies, clothiers, real estate brokers, and educational institutions. Moreover, these periodicals featured advertisements from physicians and lawyers seeking clients within the black community.[36] Much of the "respectable" advertising found in African American newspapers in the 1920s was generated by black-owned businesses.

The 1920s, by most accounts, were a time of considerable interest in black business development. Black businessmen, both excited about African American urbanization associated with the Great Migration and cognizant of the white racism that restricted them to serving only black consumers, dreamed of establishing an independent economic structure within U.S. cities.[37]

The National Negro Business League (NNBL), composed of affiliated chapters across the United States, assumed an especially high profile during the mid- to late 1920s. Hoping to accentuate black consumer support of black-owned businesses, the National Negro Business League, through its local chapters, employed a variety of techniques that urged black shoppers to "Buy Something From a Negro Merchant!"[38]

One of the League's most important programs during this period was its "National Negro Trade Week." Typically, "Negro Trade Week" campaigns began on Sundays, when local ministers urged their congregations to support black-owned businesses. For their part, black-owned businesses made themselves more attractive to black consumers during "Negro Trade Week" by conducting special contests featuring cash and merchandise prizes. In sum,"Negro Trade Week," which also featured cooperative advertising campaigns by black-owned companies, benefited both business owners and consumers.[39]

Another noteworthy National Negro Business League undertaking during the mid- to late 1920s was its national survey of black business in the United States. Commencing in 1928, at the behest of League President Dr. Robert R. Moton, four investigators examined black-owned businesses in thirty-three cities, both northern and southern.[40]

Although this study generated important quantitative information about the status of black business in America, it also, to the chagrin of many African American businessmen, pointed out the growing number of white-owned businesses that employed black managers and salespersons to service black consumers. For instance, the survey cited a large, white-owned men's clothing store in Dallas that opened a branch store in the black community and staffed it entirely with blacks.[41]

The National Negro Business League's research also revealed that black-owned grocery stores in both the North and the South faced extremely stiff competition from large chain stores. In the North, companies like A & P, to make black consumers feel welcome and comfortable, readily hired black employees for stores located in black enclaves.[42] Moreover, in the South, national chain stores were associated with equal rights. As one observer noted:

> The Negro buying group in the South feels a sense of obligation to the chains for having solved one phase of the race problem. It was traditional in the South, particularly in small cities, for Negro customers, upon entering a store, to wait until all white people were served before advancing to the clerks to make known their wants. The chains came along with a standard service for all customers and changed this condition overnight.[43]

The plight of black-owned grocery stores ultimately resulted in the National Negro Business League's promotion of an organization known as the Colored Merchants Association (CMA).

The Colored Merchants' Association began in Montgomery, Alabama, in August 1928. Twelve local African American grocers, in a maneuver to counteract the national chains' growing influence among black consumers, decided to pool their merchandise and their advertising budgets. The dozen grocers, acting collectively, were able to buy commodities at bulk-rate prices and to share their savings with black shoppers in the form of lower prices. Moreover, by pooling their advertising budgets, members of the embryonic CMA were able to advertise both in local newspapers and through handbills that were distributed to African American homes in Montgomery.[44]

The success of the Montgomery Colored Merchants' Association quickly captured the attention of the National Negro Business League. In November 1928 Albon L. Holsey, the NNBL's secretary, visited Montgomery to confer with CMA members and to inspect their stores. His glowing report to the League president, Robert R. Moton, prompted Moton to decide that the National Negro Business League should spread the Colored Merchants' Association concept to other cities.[45]

By 1930, according to the 1931–1932 edition of the *Negro Year Book*, there were branches of the CMA in major cities across America.[46] However, economic strain associated with the Great Depression ultimately put an end to this ambitious collective black undertaking.

Another NNBL undertaking that, too, became an apparent casualty of the Depression was the League's proposed 1931 national survey of African American consumers. This undertaking, while conducted under the auspices of the National Negro Business League, had considerable input and support from both the U.S. government and certain major U.S. corporations. The planning committee, besides NNBL officials, included white government and business figures. Moreover, the survey was to be financed by a consortium of prominent companies including Montgomery Ward, Lever Brothers, and Anheuser-Busch.[47]

The National Association of Colored Women (NACW) played a vital role in this proposed study. State and local branches of the NACW were to coordinate the sending of fifteen thousand survey questionnaires to African American housewives across the country.[48]

The questionnaire itself, which consisted of nine sections, began with the following message to survey participants:

> The National Negro Business League is making a determined fight for the Negro to gain for him a more secure economic place in American life. The strongest argument we have is the power represented in the dollars we spend through stores of various kinds.[49]

The questionnaire went on to request such information as the number of persons in the respondent's family; the family's yearly income; the amount of money spent each month for various items; whether the family owned an automobile and/or various household appliances; factors that influenced purchasing decisions; advertising media consulted to make purchasing decisions, and the extent to which black consumers patronized black businesses (see appendix).[50]

The NNBL's plan to survey black consumers apparently never came to fruition. Still, during the late 1920s and early 1930s, other important studies appeared that discussed both the nuances of and the potential profits associated with an increasingly visible "Negro market."

H.A. Haring, a contributing editor for the advertising trade journal *Advertising & Selling*, emerged as one the notable researchers of black consumers during this period. Significantly, his two articles "Selling to Harlem" and "The Negro as Consumer," which appeared in the October 31, 1928, and September 3, 1930, issues of *Advertising & Selling*, respectively, were replete with condescending remarks about African Americans. Still, they represented pioneering attempts to provide American corporations with market research about black consumers.

In "Selling to Harlem," Haring offered the following introductory statement:

> The Harlem of the night clubs and cabarets is rather well known, but first-hand daytime information about the section is apt to be limited to the generalization that it is the home of a population of negroes. Harlem is that—and more. Occupying a territory of approximately a square mile, it is a buying ground for about 125,000 people who form a concentrated market which so far has been studied by only a few manufacturers.[51]

To Haring, the most striking aspect of Harlem's commercial life was a proliferation of drugstores that sold, almost exclusively, hair straighteners, skin whiteners, and laxatives. Other businesses that predominated in Harlem were beauty shops, which reflected, in Haring's eyes, the desire of Harlemites for "whiteness," and "pork shops," which both satisfied blacks' dietary desires and ensured a steady volume of laxative sales by druggists.[52]

H.A. Haring's survey of Harlem business, which necessarily focused on drugstores, also discovered that few of the various companies that sold hair straighteners, skin whiteners, and laxatives to African American consumers prepared special window displays to attract potential buyers. It was clear that most purveyors of these items believed they could sell their products with a minimum of advertising expense.[53] Moreover, Haring's examination of advertising and merchandising in Harlem drugstores elicited the following startling observation:

Speaking of displays brings to mind another peculiarity of drug store selling in Harlem. Everywhere there is a lack of the usual counter displays of candy, chewing gum, perfume, soaps, combs. Drug store counters, in Harlem, are bare![54]

In his September 3, 1930, *Advertising & Selling* article, "The Negro as Consumer," Haring, clearly influenced by the neglect of black consumers he observed in Harlem, began by asking corporate marketers the following:

What of the American Negro as a buyer and user of goods? Is he worth taking seriously? Is the traditional happy-go-lucky plantation life of the South still a measure of the race's standard of living? Or is it a marketing mistake to picture the Negro basking under genial skies, supremely happy if he has enough for the next meal; good-natured even when hungry, buying a pink shirt and a pair of No. 10 shoes for his wedding day, but never buying another new thing to wear until the undertaker does the buying for him?[55]

In the rest of "The Negro as Consumer" Haring provided evidence that certain corporations, especially the producers of musical instruments, phonograph records, and radio sets, could profit from taking black consumers seriously.

By 1930 African American interest in purchasing phonograph records was widely acknowledged. Yet, what was not so well known, according to Haring, was that there existed a huge demand among African Americans for musical instruments.[56] Moreover, he offered a strikingly prophetic observation about a potential market for radios among black consumers: "It would appear that a large market for radio sets might here be developed by someone who thinks out the proper appeal to the Negro mind."[57]

Significantly, 1930 census data, although unavailable at the time Haring wrote "The Negro as Consumer," corroborated his assertions about radio's important role in the lives of urban black consumers. Table 1.6 reveals the extent of radio ownership in black urban households during this period.

Although "The Negro as Consumer" began by questioning stereotypical notions about black people, it, ironically, concluded by reaffirming white racist notions about the mental capacities of blacks. After asking the rhetorical question "Is the Negro susceptible to advertising?," Haring answered with the following:

Those concerns that merchandise to the Negro learn that display is king. He is short on abstract thinking, so that a mere description falls flat. He can visualize only what he sees with the eye. Better yet, what he touches with the hand. Testimonial advertising has a great effect on his mind. He seems to be vulnerable to any fiction of wondrous results from anyone who has tried the article "and lived to tell the tale."[58]

TABLE I.6
Percentage of African American Families Who Owned Radios,
Selected Cities, 1930

	Percentage of African American Families Who Owned Radios	Percent of All Families Who Owned Radios
Boston, Massachusetts	34.7	56.2
Chicago, Illinois	42.6	63.2
Detroit, Michigan	29.6	58.0
Jersey City, New Jersey	39.5	63.2
Milwaukee, Wisconsin	32.8	62.8
Minneapolis, Minnesota	39.6	59.5
New York, New York	40.1	59.2
Philadelphia, Pennsylvania	23.3	56.3
Portland, Oregon	48.4	57.7
Seattle, Washington	33.8	52.3
Toledo, Ohio	29.7	61.3
Washington, D.C.	25.2	53.9

SOURCE: Hall, Negroes in the U.S., 1920–1932, 286.

Unlike H. A. Haring, whose conclusions regarding black consumers were based primarily on anecdotal evidence tinged with condescension toward blacks, Paul K. Edwards was a much more thorough and objective student of African American consumption. In fact, Edwards's 1932 book, *The Southern Urban Negro as a Consumer*, and his unpublished 1936 Harvard University dissertation, "Distinctive Characteristics of Urban Negro Consumption," represented the first truly systematic studies of African American consumers. Edwards, a white professor of economics at Fisk University in Nashville, Tennessee, received both encouragement and methodological insight from Charles S. Johnson, the famed black sociologist who chaired the social science department at Fisk during this period.[59]

Early on in *The Southern Urban Negro as a Consumer*, Edwards sought to establish the collective spending power of African Americans in the South's seventeen largest cities. A 1929 study of Nashville blacks determined that their aggregate annual income was approximately $14.6 million, or $347 per capita for the city's forty-two thousand blacks. Using Nashville's black per capita income figure, Edwards calculated that the aggregate annual income of the 890,000 blacks residing in the region's seventeen largest cities stood at $308 million in 1929.[60] Moreover, he noted, "this figure gives no evaluation to the income of more than a million rural Negroes living outside of these 17 cities, but within their trading areas."[61]

After using the Nashville data to generate aggregate black spending power figures for the entire region, Edwards returned to the Nashville survey to make informed assumptions about how urban southern blacks spent their $308 million in 1929. In Nashville, the average black family spent 27.2 percent of its income for food; 14.9 percent for clothing; 12.4 percent for rent; 4.7 percent for fuel and light; 1.4 percent for furniture and household furnishings; and 31.9 percent for miscellaneous items not accounted for; it also saved 7.5 percent of its income. Edwards noted that black savings included a significant investment in insurance.[62]

Generalizing from these Nashville data to the entire region, Edwards calculated that urban southern blacks spent their $308 million in the following fashion: $83,776,000 for food; $45,892,000 for clothing; $38,192,000 for rent; $14,476,000 for fuel and light; $4,476,000 for furniture and household furnishings; and $23,100,000 for savings and insurance.[63] It is significant that Edwards failed to calculate how much money, generalizing from the Nashville data, southern urban blacks spent on miscellaneous items. If he had (and it is safe to say that some contemporary southern businesspeople probably did), he would have discovered that urban southern blacks spent approximately $99 million on miscellaneous items in 1929.

In his examination of both how and where southern urban blacks spent their money, Edwards relied on data generated from extensive field research in Nashville, Birmingham, Atlanta, and Richmond. Overall, blacks, while clustered at the low end of the occupational and wage scales in these cities, tended to buy good-quality food and clothing. Moreover, black customers appeared to be welcome at most retail establishments in these cities. Among other things, African American shoppers were viewed as being easier to handle than white customers.[64] As one white store manager told Edwards: "I'd rather have Negro than white customers, they are so much easier satisfied. But if one of them ever gets fresh with me, I'll crack him over the head with a chair."[65]

Southern blacks, because of their overall subjugated position in the region, were not able to pursue their interests as consumers as aggressively as whites did. Still, black shoppers did not accept docilely whatever indignities came their way. A generation before the Civil Rights Movement, which, itself, represented a consumer justice campaign (see chapter 3), black consumers, when pushed too far, used their spending power to elicit respect. For example, Edwards cited a large department store that installed a drinking fountain and placed above it a "For White Patrons Only" sign. The resulting unofficial, yet effective, black boycott of the store led to the quick removal of the offensive sign.[66]

TABLE 1.7
Black Ownership of Insurance Policies, Nashville, Tennessee, 1929

Class Designation	Percentage with Policies from White Companies	Percentage with Policies from Black Companies
Common and semiskilled laborers	77.7	11.7
Skilled laborers	96.5	15.8
Businesspeople/Professionals	72.2	31.6

SOURCE: Paul K. Edwards, *The Urban Southern Negro As a Consumer* (New York: Prentice-Hall, 1932), 136–137.

TABLE 1.8
Black Readership of Black- and White-Owned Newspapers, Birmingham, Atlanta, Richmond, and Nashville, 1929–1930★

	Percentage of Black Respondents Who Regularly Read Black Newspapers	Percentage of Black Respondents Who Regularly Read White Newspapers
Birmingham	21.5	87.9
Atlanta	61.9	88.2
Richmond	48.1	87.1
Nashville	30.8	91.3

★In Edwards's Table 38, from which my Table 1.8 is derived, he distinguished among black common and semiskilled laborers, skilled workers, and business-men/professionals. I collapsed these three categories into one.
SOURCE: Edwards, *The Southern Urban Negro As a Consumer,* 172–173.

Considering the problems that some black consumers had with white-owned businesses, black-owned businesses, ironically, attracted relatively little of southern urban blacks' aggregate spending. The primary reason for this was the predominance of undercapitalized single proprietorships owned by blacks with little or no business background or training.[67] Data from Nashville, presented in Table 1.7, indicate that even black-owned insurance companies had a difficult time competing with their white counterparts. *The Southern Urban Negro as a Consumer* did, however, cite the success of several black-owned drugstores; these were owned primarily by college-trained pharmacists.[68]

Local black-owned weekly newspapers, according to Edwards's research, also had a difficult time competing for black readers with their white-owned counterparts. Table 1.8 provides an overview of black newspaper readership in Birmingham, Atlanta, Richmond, and Nashville in 1929 and 1930.

Because southern urban black consumers regularly read white newspapers, they were often exposed to advertising that caricatured and stereotyped

African Americans. One of the more interesting segments of *The Southern Urban Negro as a Consumer* dealt with black consumer attitudes about advertisements that featured blacks in subservient or demeaning situations. For instance, when blacks, of all classes, in Birmingham, Atlanta, Richmond, and Nashville were asked to react to ads for "Aunt Jemima Pancake Flour," their responses included:

> Appearance of Aunt Jemima and log cabin sufficient to keep me from buying flour.
>
> Wouldn't read it. Hate it.
>
> Not interested in picture of black mammy.
>
> Illustration of Aunt Jemima utterly disgusts me.
>
> Don't like exploitation of colored people. Whenever I see a picture such as this I am prejudiced against product.[69]

Edwards concluded *The Southern Urban Negro as a Consumer* by asserting that if white-owned businesses wanted to truly reach the increasingly important "Negro market," they would have to respect the feelings of black consumers. This meant, among other things, discarding advertisements that offended black consumers.[70] Edwards's advice, which attracted an increasing number of adherents in succeeding years, was based on the premise that white companies that disavowed overt racial prejudice to generate more profits from blacks were simply practicing "good business."

Edwards's 1936 Ph.D. dissertation, "Distinctive Characteristics of Urban Negro Consumption," not only elaborated on his earlier book but introduced comparative data related to northern urban black consumers. It also surveyed the impact of the Great Depression on black urban consumers in both the North and the South.

By 1935, a significant number of both northern and southern African American city dwellers were on general relief. Table 1.9, derived from Edwards's research, provides a barometer of the economic hardships faced by many urban blacks during this period. Still, Edwards found that "after six years of depression, from fair to good qualities of foods are still the rule and not the exception in the purchases of the urban Negro common and semi-skilled labor family."[71]

Edwards's discussion of the food-purchasing habits of urban blacks included those African Americans who cooked at the homes of wealthy whites. He noted that black cooks were generally given considerable leeway in selecting foods for preparation[72] and added this observation:

Certain alert manufacturers of branded food products have learned that in house-to-house canvassing in the better white residential communities the Negro cook is the proper person to see. She is often the only member of the household with whom contact is made. The large number of Negro cooks and chefs in white homes and institutions gives an added importance to the Negro in sales promotion plans.[73]

In addition to targeting African American cooks and chefs, some food companies sought to reach a broader constituency in the national black community. For example, the Kellogg Company's aggressive mid-1930s campaign to attract black consumers elicited special mention from Edwards. To promote Kellogg's Corn Flakes in the black community, the company advertised this product widely in the black press. Moreover, Edwards' comparative survey of grocery stores in Atlanta, Richmond, and Detroit revealed that Kellogg's ad campaign had, indeed, generated increased sales of Kellogg's Corn Flakes to blacks.[74] This episode, among other things, revealed the profit potential associated with a nonderogatory marketing campaign aimed at an attention-starved consumer market.

Although Kellogg's was one of the first major U.S. food companies to actively solicit African American consumer support, Edwards discovered a pronounced tendency among black female consumers, in both the North and the South, to buy major-brand food products, regardless of whether these companies devised special marketing campaigns for blacks:

> One explanation for this apparent importance of brand names to the Negro housewife may lie in her suspicion, often justified, of those with whom she has to do business. In purchasing foods in bulk she often not only suspects short weight, but has no way to assure herself as to quality. North and South the Negro all too often has been victimized by unscrupulous merchants. Brands have come to be relied on to provide protection in buying.[75]

Edwards's discussion of urban African Americans' clothing purchases, which critiqued popular stereotypical notions about black dress, has enduring relevance. To the many whites who viewed the clothing worn by some blacks as "loud" and flashy, Edwards offered the following insightful rebuttal:

> As a rule colors and styles are selected by the urban Negro which harmonize with the many varying shades of skin complexion of the group. Often certain colors of clothing worn, such as orange and purple, are condemned as loud when as a matter of fact they harmonize well with the color of the skin. Such shades might very well be condemned if worn by the average white man or woman because of skin color.[76]

TABLE 1.9
Estimated Number and Percentage of Blacks on "General Relief,"
Selected Cities, May 1935

City	Black Population 1930	On General Relief May 1935	Percentage
Dallas, Texas	38,742	10,000	25.7
Kansas City, Missouri	38,574	12,000	31.1
Chicago, Illinois	233,903	89,000	38.0
New York, New York	327,706	140,000	42.7
Atlanta, Georgia	90,075	42,000	46.6
St. Louis, Missouri	93,580	47,000	50.2
Los Angeles, California	38,894	20,000	51.4
Philadelphia, Pennsylvania	219,599	123,000	56.0
Newark, New Jersey	38,880	23,000	59.1
Cincinnati, Ohio	47,818	34,000	71.1
Camden, New Jersey	11,304	9,000	79.3

SOURCE: Paul K. Edwards, "Distinctive Characteristics of Urban Negro Consumption," unpublished Ph.D. Dissertation, Harvard University, 1936, 51–52.

Perhaps the most important aspect of Edwards's 1936 study was his placing of urban black consumption patterns within a broader social context. All consumers, black and white, have traditionally been motivated by such "needs" as the need for belonging and the need for status.[77] Yet, because of African Americans' unique historical experience, their consumption patterns took on a greater urgency and significance:

> Constant and humiliating subordination has done something to the Negro. It has had a profound psychological effect upon him. It has affected his consumption characteristics—in fact his whole mode of living. The tug of the Negro is to extricate himself from the caste system into which he has been placed.... The serious interest we have noted him giving to personal appearance bears evidence of this truth.[78]

Significantly, as later chapters demonstrate, African American consumption patterns continue to be based on an attempt to "buy" respect and dignity. Moreover, increasingly sophisticated market research and advertising campaigns have helped American corporations to continually profit from blacks' lingering social and psychological hangups.

Even before Paul K. Edwards's seminal research on urban black consumption, African Americans were becoming increasingly aware of their power and influence as consumers. The "Don't Buy Where You Can't Work" campaigns of the early 1930s graphically illustrated this phenomenon (see chapter 3). Moreover, various African American writers, during the 1930s, expounded on the various aspects of the "Negro market."

The October 1932 issue of *Opportunity*, the journal of the National Urban League, featured an article by T. Arnold Hill, the League's director of industrial relations, titled "The Negro Market." This essay provided a striking (and little appreciated) assessment of black consumer preferences. Hill declared:

> If whites object to being served by Negroes in hotels, department stores, and offices, have not Negroes the same right to object to whites serving them? If Negroes are objectionable as messengers to deliver electric lights and gas bills to homes of whites or to read their meters, why cannot Negroes deliver bills to their own homes and read gas meters in their own basements?[79]

This article noted that increased black consumer support of black-owned enterprises would better serve the interests of the larger African American community.[80]

Another National Urban League official with an interest in black consumers was Eugene Kinckle Jones, the organization's executive secretary. During the 1930s, Jones also headed the U.S. Department of Commerce's Division of Negro Affairs.[81] It was in this capacity that he published a brief report in the January 10, 1935 issue of *Domestic Commerce*, a publication of the U.S. Department of Commerce, entitled "Purchasing Power of Negroes in the U.S. Estimated at Two Billion Dollars."

Citing Paul K. Edwards's *The Southern Urban Negro as a Consumer*, Jones offered the following message to American corporations:

> Enterprising business along many lines might do well to explore the American Negro market for expansion. The annual purchasing power of approximately 890,000 Negroes in the South's 17 largest cities has been estimated at $308,000,000. This is most significant when compared with the nation's 1929 export trade of $224,619,486 with Mexico and all Central America, $208,969,847 with the West Indies and the Bermudas, and $374,851,619 with Argentina, Brazil, and Chile.[82]

Noting the growing body of research examining the consumption patterns of urban black consumers, Jones informed his readers that the consumption patterns of rural African Americans should not be totally dismissed:

> The Southern Negro farmer last year produced crops valued at $664,000,000, of which $119,000,000 represents value of crops produced by Negro farm owners whose farm implements and machinery were valued, in 1930, at

$19,784,411. Here is a market in itself for farm implements, seed and fertilizer larger than this figure suggests for there are 305,942 colored farmers other than croppers. These cash and share tenant farmers make their purchases direct, not depending upon their landlords for materials.[83]

In retrospect, Jones's essay appears to represent a significant turning point in African American writing about black consumers. Previously, as exemplified by T. Arnold Hill in his 1932 *Opportunity* essay, black writers had tended to discuss the "Negro market" in the context of using black dollars to enhance the black business community. Jones, however, ignored black business and instead focused on convincing white companies to recognize the potential profits associated with African American consumers. In succeeding decades, Jones's worldview would come to dominate published black writing about the black consumer market. Although this involves a very complex question of motivation, it appears plausible that Jones and his ideological descendants believed that if U.S. corporations could be made to view the African American consumer market as a proverbial "gold mine" of potential profits, it would enhance blacks' quest for full-fledged citizenship. Ironically, many African Americans have, in recent years, looked increasingly askance at the resulting overwhelming presence of U.S. corporations in their lives—especially since it has come at the expense of black-owned enterprises (see chapter 5 and Epilogue).

By the late 1930s, many white businesses, despite the efforts of Jones, Edwards, and Haring, remained relatively unaware of the potential benefits associated with courting black consumers. Still, the collective spending power or wages of urban blacks in the 1930s did receive extensive coverage in a two-volume U.S. government publication, *The Urban Negro Worker in the United States, 1925–1936*, released in 1938 and 1939. Although this study focused on skilled and white-collar black workers, rather than being all-inclusive, it provided a means to gauge, at least approximately, national black spending power during an important eleven-year period. The team of researchers responsible for this study included such African American luminaries as Robert C. Weaver, Charles S. Johnson, and Ira De A. Reid.[84]

In 1925 the collective wages of 171,644 black skilled and white-collar workers, in the seventy-four U.S. cities with African American populations of at least ten thousand, stood at $190,377,018. In 1930, 164,135 black skilled and white-collar workers collected $187,618,262 in wages. Six years later, as a result of the Depression, the earnings of 167,166 black skilled and white-collar urban workers dipped to $133,982,368. In each year studied, a significant proportion of African American workers in these categories did not supply earnings information to researchers. Thus, in 1925, the wages of 42,319 skilled or white-collar urban black workers were not included. For the years 1930 and 1936, these figures were 49,848 and 46,817, respectively.[85]

Although *The Urban Negro Worker in the United States, 1925–1936*, provided only partial information on skilled and white-collar urban black workers and totally excluded the wages earned by the unskilled black labor force, a majority of the black population, this report clearly revealed that urban African Americans were an economic force to be taken seriously. By the end of the 1930s, an increasingly urban African American population had established itself as an economic consumer force that merited increased scrutiny from both the U.S. government and mainstream American business. Still, while companies in some specific industries, such as record companies, actively sought black consumer support, other corporations continued to ignore the "Negro market." Events in succeeding decades, however, would dramatically disrupt lingering dismissive perceptions of black consumers.

2

New World A-Coming

Black Consumers, 1941–1960

In 1943 the African American journalist Roi Ottley wrote a well-received overview of African American life with the markedly upbeat and prophetic title, *New World A-Coming*. For African American consumers, the years 1941–1960, did, indeed, usher in a period of recognition and consideration that would have seemed unimaginable in previous decades. The urbanization of African Americans, which prompted initial business interest in black consumers, reached dizzying heights during the fifth and sixth decades of the twentieth century. As African Americans began to proliferate in even greater numbers in American cities, an increasing number of American businesses, from major league baseball teams to radio stations, decided it was in their best interest to actively seek the patronage of black consumers. As the disappearance of the Negro Baseball Leagues during this period suggested, however, black consumers' increased "recognition" by white companies would not come without cost.

The period from 1941 to 1960 witnessed what has been called "the relocation of black America."[1] The massive southern black migration associated with World War II and its aftermath possessed nearly the same "push" and "pull" characteristics as the World War I Great Migration. In both eras, southern agricultural conditions resulted in the displacement of numerous black sharecroppers. Also, the South's virulent white racism between 1941 and 1960 was as intense as it had been in 1915. Finally, the availability of relatively good-paying jobs in northern and western cities further predisposed southern blacks to change their places of residence.

An early stimulus for World War II–era black migration was President Franklin D. Roosevelt's issuance of Executive Order 8802 on June 25, 1941. This edict, delivered to avert a planned African American protest march in the nation's capital, stated: "There shall be no discrimination in the employment of workers in defense industries or government because of race, color, or national origin."[2] More important, Executive Order 8802 established a Fair Employment Practices Committee (F.E.P.C.) to coordinate the implementation of 8802. During World War I, the vast majority of transplanted southern black workers ended up in unskilled positions; in contrast, in World War II, the F.E.P.C., through its battles with unions, helped a significant number of black migrants gain entry into skilled industrial positions.[3]

Responding to the economic opportunity embodied in Executive Order 8802 and the Fair Employment Practices Committee, rural southern blacks streamed into northern, western, and southern cities. By 1942, there were nearly one million new African American urban residents across the country. Black population gains in such coastal shipbuilding centers as San Francisco, California; Portland, Oregon; Mobile, Alabama; Charleston, South Carolina; and Savannah, Georgia, were especially significant.[4]

As the number of blacks dramatically increased in U.S. cities during the war years, white businesses differed in their reaction. Some white businessmen, because of racism, refused to make special appeals to black consumers. Others, who sensed the growing practicality and profitability of wooing African American shoppers, sought insights into reaching this heretofore little-known segment of the American buying public. To assist those white businesses interested in courting blacks, business periodicals began to feature an increasing number of articles related to the "Negro market."

David J. Sullivan, an African American pioneer in the field of market research, emerged as the country's leading expert on black consumer activity during World War II. During this period he published several widely read articles and demographic/statistical profiles of black consumers.

One of Sullivan's most important essays, "Don't Do This—If You Want to Sell Your Products to Negroes!," which appeared in the March 1, 1943 issue of *Sales Management*, provided the following marketing advice to corporations seeking black consumer support:

1. Don't exaggerate Negro characters, with flat noses, thick lips, kinky hair, and owl eyes. They don't exist any more as a matter of fact.
2. Avoid Negro minstrels. Avoid even the use of white people with blackface and a kinky wig for hair to depict a Negro. We know, as well as you might, that they are phonies—minstrelsy is a dead issue.
3. Don't constantly name the Negro porter or waiter "George." He could be John, James, or Aloysius, for that matter. Nothing makes Negroes angrier than to be called "George."
4. Avoid incorrect English usage, grammar, and dialect. In other words, get away from "Yas suh, sho, dese, dem, dat, or dat 'ere, gwine, you all." (This

last white Southerners use more often than Negroes.) Avoid also, "I'se, dis yere, wif," and others in similar vein.

5. Don't picture colored women as buxom, broad-faced, grinning mammies and Aunt Jemimas. Negroes have no monopoly on size. Neither are they all laundresses, cooks, and domestic servants. By no means color them black. Use brown-skinned girls for illustrations; then you satisfy all. Don't refer to Negro women as "Negresses."

6. Don't overdo comedy situations, gag lines, or illustrations. Avoid, even by suggestion, "There's a nigger in the woodpile," or "coon," "shine," and "darky."

7. Don't illustrate an outdoor poster, car card, advertisement, or any other advertising piece showing a Negro eating watermelon, chasing chickens, or crap shooting. No race has a monopoly on these traits.

8. Don't picture the "Uncle Mose" type—the type whom Octavus Roy Cohen employs in his stories in *Collier's* and elsewhere. He is characterized by kinky hair and as a stooped, tall, lean and grayed sharecropper, always in rags. The U.S. Chamber of Commerce says, and facts prove, that Negroes spend more money for clothes per capita than do white people in New York City and other large cities.

9. Always avoid the word "Pickaninny," or lampooning illustrations of Negro children. They are as dear to their parents as are other children, irrespective of race.

10. Don't insult the clergy. The day of the itinerant Negro preacher has gone long since.[5]

Sullivan's advice to corporate marketers was important for two distinct reasons. First, it set the stage for the ongoing, continually modified "how to" genre in advertising trade journals related to reaching black consumers. Second, his observations, coupled with increased black consumer discontent with being caricatured by advertisers (see chapter 3), led to the eventual disappearance of "mammies," pickaninnies," "coons," and "niggers" from U.S. advertising.

Sullivan's July 21, 1944, article in *Printer's Ink*, titled "The American Negro—An 'Export' Market at Home," provided significant demographic information about the black consumer market. Besides providing figures related to blacks' rising aggregate national income in the years 1942–1944, Sullivan disclosed the buying patterns of African American shoppers for such items as over-the-counter drug remedies and cosmetics and toiletries.

To dispel the notion that the black consumer market was peripheral and irrelevant, Sullivan asserted:

Today's Negro market of over 13,000,000 consumers had a gross income in 1942 of $7,000,000,000 of which 62% was spent in consumer's goods and services. The effective buying income of the Negro market in 1942 exceeded nearly two and one-half times the total American exports to South America. . . . Its 1943 gross National income reached an all-time high of $10,290,000,000, far greater than Canada's 1943 total of $8,800,000,000.[6]

Sullivan went on to explain that black per capita expenditures for certain items exceeded those of whites. For instance, blacks tended to spend two to four times more money than whites for over-the counter remedies. Likewise, on a per capita basis, African Americans were the largest buyers of cosmetics and toiletries.[7]

To further convince U.S. corporations of the efficacy of wooing black consumers, Sullivan projected that aggregate African American income would rise to $10,500,000,000 in 1944. Moreover, he declared:

it is expected that Negroes will maintain substantially a large part of the gains they have made in employment, due to the war, and their increasing numbers in the labor unions . . . sales are waiting for the manufacturer who will investigate the Negro market, and plan sales and advertising campaigns to reach this expanding market of 13,000,000 Americans who yearly are increasing in both population and buying power.[8]

Besides writing articles, Sullivan produced important statistical tables related to the "Negro market." Perhaps his most detailed and useful creation appeared in the June 15, 1945, issue of *Sales Management* under the title of "How Negroes Spent Their Incomes, 1920–1943." Table 2.1 provides a sampling of this important research compilation.

TABLE 2.1

How African Americans Spent Their Incomes, Selected Characteristics, 1920, 1943

	1920	1943
TOTAL BLACK INCOME	$3,055,000,000	$10,290,000,000
Housing	647,744,800	1,718,430,000
Food	702,742,000	1,862,409,000
Clothing	336,094,000	1,121,610,000
Drugs, Proprietaries	119,160,600	318,990,000
Automobile	30,554,000	144,060,000
Tobacco	15,277,000	102,900,000
Education	3,055,000	154,350,000
Savings	128,326,800	812,910,000

SOURCE: David J. Sullivan, "How Negroes Spent Their Incomes, 1920–1943," *Sales Management* 54 (June 15, 1945): 106. Sullivan's original table examined the years 1920, 1929, 1935, 1941, and 1943. He also provided these additional categories of black spending: Household Furnishings, Fuel, Alcoholic Beverages, Medical, Transport, Personal Care, Recreation, Reading, Miscellaneous, Gifts/Contributions, and Taxes.

As more corporations, inspired by Sullivan's urging, began to take black consumers seriously, black newspapers, an effective means to reach these shoppers, likewise increased in stature.

Before the 1940s, white companies, excluding the purveyors of skin whiteners, hair straighteners, and patent medicines, all but ignored black newspapers as an advertising venue. In fact, the few large companies that did advertise in African American periodicals, such as Camel cigarettes, Lifebuoy soap, and Chevrolet automobiles, did so through a white intermediary, the W. B. Ziff Company of Chicago. In fact, W. B. Ziff carved out a special niche for itself by representing the "Negro market" and the "Negro press" to corporate America.[9]

Black newspapers were forced to rely on Ziff because their own efforts were often ignored and rebuffed. For instance, in 1933, Claude A. Barnett, the founder of the Associated Negro Press, the era's most influential black news service, sought corporate support for an extensive survey of Chicago's "Negro market." Barnett, who had been in contact with Paul K. Edwards, hoped to use Edwards' study of southern urban black consumers as a model for his (Barnett's) proposed study of black Chicago's consumption patterns. Nevertheless, lack of cooperation from corporations (who, ironically, stood to profit from the data generated from Barnett's proposed survey) ultimately forced him to abandon it.[10]

A milestone in the history of black newspapers' relationship with corporate America was the founding of Interstate United Newspapers, Inc., in 1940. Interstate, a consortium of African American newspapers, represented the brainchild of Robert Vann, editor of the Pittsburgh *Courier*. Significantly, it filled the void left by W. B. Ziff's recent withdrawal from its role as the intermediary between black newspapers and potential corporate advertisers.[11]

Ziff's abandonment of black newspapers, because of the difficulty of securing a significant number of corporate advertisers other than those promoting "beauty" products, turned out to be a bad business decision. As the African American population expanded in U.S. cities during the early 1940s, and as David J. Sullivan's research reached an ever widening audience, large companies became much more receptive to the idea of enhancing their presence in the black community. Consequently, Ziff's short-sightedness proved to be Interstate United Newspapers' gain.

The ascendancy of William G. Black to the position of Interstate's sales manager in 1942 represented another watershed event in the relationship between black newspapers and corporate America. Black, a master salesman who possessed an in-depth knowledge of the "Negro market," helped to dramatically increase the number of major U.S. corporations who advertised in African American newspapers. Within a couple years, Black and his staff had secured the patronage of such firms as Seagrams, Pabst, Coca Cola, Pepsi Cola, the Nehi Corporation, Ford, Buick, Chrysler, Best Foods, American Sugar Refineries, and Safeway.[12]

To maximize the effectiveness of corporate advertising in black newspapers, Black and Interstate utilized testimonial statements by noted black entertainers. For instance, black newspaper advertisements for the Nehi Corporation's Royal Crown Cola featured the endorsement of such celebrities as "Peg Leg" Bates and Erskine Hawkins.[13]

William Black's success in attracting more corporate advertising for black newspapers was based on his skill in convincing large companies that black newspapers were indispensable if the companies wished to reach the black consumer market. One of the tools that Black and his staff had at their disposal was a 1944 Interstate-produced pamphlet titled *America's Negroes Live as a "Country within a Country," in Many Places as a "City within a City."*

This booklet, whose target audience was potential corporate advertisers, began by presenting demographic information about black consumers derived from David A. Sullivan's research. It then went on to discuss the "invisibility" of African Americans in mainstream newspapers. To drive home this point, the Interstate publication asked its white readers if they had ever seen "a picture of a NEGRO WEDDING in your paper?"[14]

In closing, *America's Negroes Live As a "Country Within a Country"* left its readers with this powerful message:

> Where do YOU think your ad will win the Negro Market's Warmest Response? *ON HOSTILE GROUND:* the White Press, inadequate, indifferent, or worse! *OR AT "HOME"?* The Negro Press: Negro news, interests, welfare, achievements.[15]

Interstate United Newspapers' early success in increasing the number of national advertisers in African American newspapers prompted the company to take an historic step in 1946. In August, Interstate contracted with the New York–based Research Company of America to conduct a nationwide survey of African American purchases and brand preferences in which a total of five thousand families in twenty-seven cities from coast to coast would be asked to fill out a four-page questionnaire consisting of one hundred questions. Significantly, corporate sponsors, besides Interstate United Newspapers Inc., provided 75 percent of the funding for this project.[16]

The survey investigated black consumer preferences in such major markets as Atlanta; Birmingham; Chicago; Columbus, Ohio; Detroit; Indianapolis; Kansas City, Missouri; Los Angeles; Memphis; Nashville; New Orleans; New York City; Newark; and St. Louis. The results indicated definite preferences for certain items. For instance, Camel cigarettes, Gillette razor blades, and Maxwell House coffee were among black consumers' clear favorites.[17]

Besides revealing African American preferences for specific brand names, Interstate's national survey provided important insights about how blacks spent their estimated $10 billion aggregate income in 1946. Out of the $7 billion that could be described as African Americans' "disposable" income, more than $2.5 billion went for food purchases, and more than $2 billion went for clothing purchases. Other expenditures documented by the study included $750 million for housing; $350 million for home furnishings; $500 million for beverages (hard and soft); $350 million for toiletries and personal care products; $400 million for drugs and medical remedies; between $150 and $200 million for tobacco; and between $150 and $200 million for automobiles and related accessories.[18]

Although this study focused on the spending habits of black consumers, it also compiled other demographic data related to urban blacks. The survey's four-page questionnaire included questions about home ownership, family composition, employment status, and whether the responding family had a bank account.[19] Moreover, as William Black emphasized in a March 24, 1947, *Advertising Age* article about the survey's findings, none of the five thousand black families interviewed were paid for their time and cooperation. After the approximately one-hour interview, respondents were thanked and given cards that stated:

> You have answered questions which will help manufacturers to know more about the buying and shopping habits of the American Negro. American industry is recognizing more each day the necessity of first-hand knowledge of the American people. The study, when completed and tabulated, will do much to clarify manufacturers' thinking. . . . By answering these questions you have been most helpful and enlightening and have contributed in no small measure to a better inter-racial understanding.[20]

Interstate United Newspapers' successful sponsorship of the first national survey of African American consumer preferences, whose findings were subsequently summarized in a publication titled *The National Negro Market*,[21] further validated Interstate's stature as an invaluable ally to those companies seeking the patronage and goodwill of black consumers.

Because of Interstate's and William Black's dramatic success in securing more corporate advertisers for consortium newspapers, African American newspapers unaligned with Interstate formed their own group, Associated Publishers, Inc., in 1944. Between 1944 and 1948, the number of newspapers associated with Associated Publishers grew from ten to twenty-four. These figures paled in comparison to the 135 black newspapers aligned with Interstate United Newspapers by 1948. Nevertheless, Associated Publishers did carve out a comfortable niche for itself as a gateway to the increasingly important "Negro market." Moreover, Interstate apparently got its idea for a national survey of black consumer preferences from a earlier study sponsored by Associated Publishers (also coordinated by the Research Company of America) of black shoppers in Washington, D.C., Philadelphia, and Baltimore.[22]

Notwithstanding the increased appreciation during the 1940s of black consumers by the purveyors of food products, clothing, over-the-counter drugs, and cosmetics and toiletries, the decade's most spectacular recognition of African American consumers took place in major league baseball. The increased urbanization and the relative wealth of black workers during this period influenced the desegregation of the "national pastime."

By the mid-1940s, the national per capita income of African Americans stood at $779, compared to $1,140 for whites.[23] However, the per capita income of blacks residing in cities with major league baseball teams compared very favorably with national white per capita earnings. In fact, in some locales, urban blacks possessed a per capita income higher than the national white average. Consequently, in most major league cities at the time of Jackie Robinson's historic 1947 appearance with the Brooklyn Dodgers, there existed a significant black population with money to spend. Table 2.2 presents income data for selected cities.

One of the most debated questions in American sports history is what *really* motivated Brooklyn Dodger General Manager Branch Rickey to desegregate major league baseball? Some have argued that Rickey's propensity for racial fairness prompted his momentous decision. Advocates of this belief often refer to the "Charlie Thomas story," an incident that occurred on a road trip when Rickey served as Ohio Wesleyan University's baseball coach during the early twentieth century. Reacting to a South Bend, Indiana, hotel's refusal to provide Thomas the same accommodations as his white teammates, as well as to Thomas's emotional reaction to this racial insult, Rickey allegedly vowed to "always do whatever I could to see that other Americans did not face the bitter humiliation that was heaped upon Charlie Thomas."[24]

TABLE 2.2

*Black Population, Aggregate and Per Capita Income, in Cities
with Major League Baseball Teams, 1943**

City	Black Population	1943 Aggregate Buying Income	Per Capita
New York, New York	458,444	$448,363,000	$949
Philadelphia, Pennsylvania	280,986	210,248,000	758
Chicago, Illinois	349,941	378,286,000	1,081
Washington, D.C.	224,916	259,548,000	1,154
Detroit, Michigan	185,057	190,239,000	1,028
St. Louis, Missouri	108,765	119,642,000	1,100
Cleveland, Ohio	84,504	96,504,000	1,142
Pittsburgh, Pennsylvania	62,216	60,221,000	984
Cincinnati, Ohio	55,593	66,712,000	1,200

*Sullivan's list did not include Boston, which had two teams, the Red Sox and Braves. Also see Joseph L. Re-
ichler, ed., The Baseball Encyclopedia, 6th ed. (New York: Macmillan, 1985), 382–85.
SOURCE: David J. Sullivan, "Negro Incomes and How They Are Spent," Sales Management 54 (June 15, 1945): 106.

The Charlie Thomas incident, while an interesting anecdote, tells us little about Rickey's later feelings regarding racial justice. When he served in
the St. Louis Cardinal front office, before joining the Dodgers, he remained
silent about racial bias in the major leagues' then southernmost city.[25] Moreover, after joining the Dodgers, Rickey's plans to employ Robinson and
other black players had little to do with Charlie Thomas. As Rickey reportedly told his family:

> The greatest untapped reservoir of raw material in the history of the game is
> the black race! The Negroes will make us winners for years to come. . . . And
> for that I will happily bear being called a bleeding heart and a do-gooder and
> all that humanitarian rot.[26]

If Branch Rickey viewed black players as an "untapped reservoir," it appears plausible to assume that he viewed black consumers similarly. Since
baseball's (or any professional sports team's) profits are closely linked to fan
attendance at games, Rickey clearly hoped that African Americans fans,
coming out to see African American players, would make him a winner both
on the field and in the box office. In fact, as Ken Burns's magisterial documentary Baseball revealed, on April 15, 1947, Jackie Robinson's official entry
into the major leagues, blacks made up more than half of Ebbets Field's capacity crowd.[27] Robinson's presence also enhanced attendance at Brooklyn
Dodger road games. As one baseball historian has described the 1947 Brooklyn Dodgers' first major road trip:

> On Sunday, May 11, the Dodgers faced the Phillies in a doubleheader before
> the largest crowd in Philadelphia baseball history. Scalpers sold $2 tickets for
> $6, "just like the World Series." Two days later in Cincinnati 27,164 fans

turned out despite an all-day rain "to size up Jackie Robinson." Bad weather diminished the crowds for two games in Pittsburgh, but when the skies cleared, 34,814 fans appeared at Forbes Field for the May 18 series finale. The following day the Dodgers met the Cubs in Chicago. Two hours before game time Wrigley Field had almost filled. A total of 46,572 fans crammed into the ball park, the largest attendance in stadium history. The tour concluded in St. Louis where the Dodgers and Cardinals played before the biggest weekday crowd of the National League season.[28]

Besides Jackie Robinson, the great pitcher Satchel Paige, who joined the Cleveland Indians in 1948, was a box-office draw of major proportions. Although Paige was not the Indians' first black player—Larry Doby had joined in the team in July 1947—his presence immediately increased Indian attendance both at home and away.

Paige's first appearance for Cleveland, after he was signed in July 1948 to buttress the Indians' pitching staff for the remainder of the season, was a July 14, 1948 exhibition game against the Brooklyn Dodgers. Out of the nearly 65,000 fans who crowded into Cleveland's Municipal Stadium to see Paige's major league debut, an estimated 40 percent were black.[29]

Paige, whose age had been estimated from thirty-eight to forty-eight years when he joined the Indians, was a master showman who delighted in entertaining crowds with his unique pitching motion. When he joined the Indians' starting rotation in August 1948, his presence drew unprecedented audiences.

In an August 3, 1948, night game against the Washington Senators, 72,000 Cleveland fans watched Paige and the Indians beat the Senators. This represented the largest night crowd in baseball history. Ten days later, in Chicago, more than 51,000 fans, a new record for night baseball in that city, jammed into Comiskey Park to watch Paige shut out the White Sox, 5-0. On August 20, 1948, more than 78,000 fans crammed into Cleveland's Municipal Stadium, shattering the record for fans at a night game set only seventeen days earlier, to watch Paige and the Indians again beat the White Sox, 5-1.[30]

Although Paige's fortunes waned as the season progressed, fan support for Paige, both home and away, remained high.[31] Moreover, his presence, along with that of Jackie Robinson, Larry Doby, Roy Campanella, and other black pioneers in major league baseball, set the stage for an even greater proliferation of blacks on the field and in the stands.

Almost lost in the hoopla surrounding Robinson's and other black players' appearance in the major leagues was the simultaneous decline and disappearance of the Negro Baseball Leagues. For decades, when major league teams prohibited blacks from their rosters, Negro League teams had provided skilled African American baseball players an opportunity to make a living, and there existed a special bond between Negro League players and the cities they represented.[32] Yet, after 1947, not only the players but the fans quickly abandoned this important community institution. The dissolution of the Negro Baseball Leagues served as a precedent for the future (albeit slower) dissolution of other historic African American institutions, such as black-owned insurance companies (see chapter 5 and Epilogue).

At the same time that the Negro Baseball Leagues began to disappear from the American landscape, black-oriented radio stations began to proliferate across the United States. Yet, well before the late 1940s, radio had established an important presence in African American homes.

The origin of the black radio industry can be traced to "The All Negro Hour," which first aired in Chicago in November 1929. This program and a 1931 derivative, "The All Negro Children's Hour," were variety shows developed by the veteran black entertainer Jack Leroy Cooper to counteract mainstream radio's stereotypical depictions of African American life.[33]

Besides serving as a cultural oasis for black radio listeners, black-oriented radio programs, from the beginning, were used by companies seeking to reach black consumers. As one writer has asserted:

> Sponsors, starting in the 1930s, bought blocks of air time, day or night, to promote pork chops, chitlins, secondhand furniture, patent medicine, and anything else thought to appeal to blacks. A representative example is the "King Biscuit Time" broadcast in the early 1940s from the teeming little metropolis of Helena, Mississippi, deep in the heavily black Delta region. At noon, singer-harmonica player Rice (Sonny Boy Williamson) Miller and guitarist Robert Lockwood brought listeners fifteen minutes of blues and greetings from the makers of King Biscuit flour. At one point the broadcast became so popular that a line of Sonny Boy cornmeal was introduced.[34]

Still, as late as 1949, *Sponsor*, the advertising trade journal of the broadcasting industry, referred to black consumers as "The Forgotten 15,000,000."[35]

Although many corporations began to take black consumers more seriously during the 1940s, many others remained reluctant to actively court the "Negro market." Data from the 1950 census, however, helped to decrease this lingering reluctance.

Between 1940 and 1950, the number of African American city dwellers increased from 6,253,588 to 9,120,000, a 46 percent increase. At the same time, the black population grew from 12,53,588 to 14,894,000. This 15.8

percent increase compared to a 14.4 percent increase in the U.S. white population during the same decade.[36] Thus, by the early 1950s, the national African American community appeared to be increasing both in size and in urban concentration. This dramatic demographic phenomenon would have far-reaching consequences, especially for the radio industry.

Sponsor, in a July 28, 1952, follow-up to its 1949 articles relating to "the forgotten 15,000,000," featured an extensive section titled "The Forgotten 15,000,000 . . . Three Years Later." First and foremost, it seemed clear that black consumers were far less forgotten (or ignored). Whereas only a handful of U.S. radio stations featured "Negro-appeal" programming in 1949, by 1952 there were more than two hundred stations that featured this format on a full- or part-time basis. Moreover, these stations were attracting an increasing amount of corporate advertising.[37]

To assist corporate marketers contemplating using "Negro-appeal" radio, the July 28, 1952, *Sponsor* contained two articles that featured a question-and-answer format. "The Negro Market: $15,000,000,000 to Spend" and "Negro Radio: 200-Plus Specialist Stations—More Coming" provided white businesses with a crash course on both the "Negro market" and how it could be reached through radio advertising.

One especially illuminating aspect of this primer for prospective buyers of advertising on black-oriented radio was *Sponsor's* response to the question "Does the Negro have a standard of living (and a product consumption) that compares with the standard of living of U.S. whites?" The journal, quoting an "expert on Negro media," stated:

> Negroes are denied many recreations in many parts of the country that whites take for granted. I mean access to theaters, restaurants, night-clubs, beaches, vacation resorts, travel facilities and the like. . . . As a result, Southern Negroes can be considered largely as having as much money to spend on non-recreation items. Even in Northern, Midwestern, and Pacific areas where the discrimination is much less than in the South, this is true to quite an extent. . . . The Negro therefore will spend much more money on food, clothing, appliances, automobiles, and other items. . . . Negro standards of living, in many categories of goods, are a match for white standards.[38]

Another important insight provided to prospective advertisers on "Negro-appeal" radio was *Sponsor's* response to the question "From the standpoint of the spot advertiser who may thinking of building a series of Negro-appeal programs, either live or custom transcribed, what are the main Negro talent and program preferences?" Its multipart answer included these points:

1. Negro listeners tune to a particular station primarily for the entertainment they feel is slanted at them. For the most part, this will consist of a disk jockey with a strong sense of showmanship, and a loyal Negro following, who spins platters that feature Negro artists most of the time, and white artists some of the time. This may be 50% or more of the total Negro-appeal programming.
2. A deeply religious race, Negroes look to radio stations for broadcasts of a spiritual nature. Most often these consist of live pickups from churches or special programs (live or transcribed) of religious music.
3. Since few stations with a "general" program formula go out of their way to air news of special interest to Negroes, much of the success of Negro-appeal stations is their coverage of community events, sports events . . . and so forth that concern the Negro community.[39]

Sponsor relied on data generated by Memphis radio station WDIA to answer the question "How does the amount of radio listening done in a Negro family compare with the amount done on an over-all basis?" The broadcast advertising trade journal noted that Memphis blacks, because many avenues of entertainment were closed to them, tended to view their homes as primary recreational venues. Moreover, radio played a central role in black Memphians' at-home activities. Local African Americans spent twice as much time listening to radio as whites. In addition, 93 percent of black Memphis homes possessed at least one radio.[40]

Evidence from other cities further demonstrated radio's central role in the lives of blacks. The July 28, 1952, *Sponsor*, citing a survey of black radio ownership in New York City, Washington, D.C., Philadelphia, Charleston, Louisville, Atlanta, and New Orleans, noted that the vast majority (75–90 percent) of black homes in these areas owned at least one radio.[41]

Finally, to convince even the most skeptical potential advertiser of the efficacy of "Negro-appeal" radio, the July 28, 1952, *Sponsor* provided readers with case studies to graphically demonstrate this format's selling power. Among the "Negro-appeal" stations that shared their marketing success stories with *Sponsor* were:

- WERD, Atlanta, Georgia
  Margarine—Quickly noting that Nucoa margarine had started an announcement campaign over WERD, Danneman's Supermarket decided to tie in with an announcement of their own, offering the product at a bargain price. On the following day, after one announcement, the store reported sales of over three thousand pounds of margarine.

Auto tires—After Prior Tire Company started a saturation announcement schedule, one of its salesmen reported that his sales alone were up by $5,000 or more per week.

• WLOU, Louisville, Kentucky

Beer—Oertels beer started a campaign the day this station went on the air. They report that their sales have steadily increased until they now have 65% of the Negro market in the area despite competition from two other prominent local beers.

Men's clothing—Moskins Clothiers gives complete credit to the station for a 40% sales increase.

• WSOK, Nashville, Tennessee

Refrigerators—An appliance dealer reports selling 42 used electric refrigerators in one day as a result of nine half-minute announcements.

• WEDR, Birmingham, Alabama

Electrical appliances—A Birmingham dealer phoned the station to say he traced over $5,000 in appliance sales during one weekend to WEDR spot campaign.

Piano course—In spite of a four-week steel strike which had a telling effect on the community's buying power, a disk jockey on this station took orders for piano courses from 250 customers.

• WWCA, Gary, Indiana

Home equipment—Local concern reports 500 direct leads per week as aftermath of two quarter-hour sessions daily on this station.

• KOWL, Santa Monica, California

Beer—Maier Brew moved from seventh place in beer sales in the Los Angeles area to first with Negroes within a period of 18 months during which they used the Joe Adams show on KOWL.

Talent contest—Station received reassurance of high listenership during a recent talent contest. Over 7,000 telephone calls voting for talent contestants were registered in one afternoon.[42]

While *Sponsor's* July 27, 1952, special section on "Negro-appeal" radio provided an extensive overview of this growing business and entertainment industry, it gave limited coverage to disk jockeys, the central and most visible figures associated with this phenomenon. *Sponsor's* subsequent coverage of black-oriented radio remedied this deficiency.

By 1955, the number of "Negro-appeal" radio stations in the United States had grown to six hundred.[43] A major reason for this proliferation was the growing stature of disk jockeys. These individuals, who came to be known for their showmanship and salesmanship, represented the backbone of the black-oriented radio industry.

Before the boom in "Negro-appeal" radio that commenced in the early 1950s, few blacks earned a living as disk jockeys. As late as 1947, there were only sixteen black deejays in the United States. Moreover, this group, which included nine college graduates, tended to project a conservative, nonracial persona over the air waves.[44]

Of the sixteen black disk-jockeys employed in 1947, Al Benson of Chicago, whose style deviated from that of most of his peers, would become one of the most influential black radio personalities of all time. Benson, a mainstay at radio station WGES, was not a college graduate. In fact, many derided Benson for his "distressing grappling with words over two syllables."[45] Nevertheless, Benson's down-to-earth radio personality struck a responsive chord among his listeners and gained the attention of advertisers. As one of his admirers noted:

> Benson killed the King's English and I don't know if he did it on purpose or not. Everybody had to see Al if they wanted to sell to the black market in Chicago, whether it was beer or rugs or Nu Nile hair cream. . . . He wasn't pretending to be white. He sounded black.[46]

Moreover, as an authority on black disk jockeys has asserted:

> The lessons Benson taught about the appeal and profitability of his "black everyman" style were adopted all over the country, ushering in the era of the "personality deejays." . . . By 1955, there were over five hundred of Benson's children floating across the country on transistorized clouds, hawking records from faraway stores, along with the stuff to make your wife two or three shades lighter, even if she looked good to you already. The ads never distracted listeners from the music but could sound as wild and greasy, and cool as the platters played alongside.[47]

By the mid-1950s, it appeared clear that the increasing number of black "personality deejays," with their ability to flawlessly meld regular programming with advertisements, were becoming increasingly indispensable to station owners and advertisers. The research of Robert P. Leatherwood, an African American who emerged as an expert on black disk jockey selling techniques, provided additional insights on this important phenomenon. In *Sponsor's* September 28, 1957, special issue on "Negro-appeal" radio, Leatherwood responded to the question "How does the disk jockey sell?":

> Rhythm and excitement are the most important tools they use. . . . This enthusiasm is important because they perform for a highly critical group of listeners. . . . Negro disk jockeys are well aware that listeners demand feverish

excitement; they fulfill this through dynamic delivery and spirited record se-
lection. The fever is heightened by the rhythmic style in which they talk.
Commercials are read in a driving fashion that resembles an explosive drum
solo. The sponsor's written appeal is supplemented with convincing ad lib remarks delivered in unique and descriptive terms that honor the Negro gift of
creating unusual phrases with unusual meanings.[48]

Black deejays, during the 1950s (and afterward), were given considerable
leeway and visibility in terms of station operations, perhaps to deflect attention from the fact that "Negro-appeal" stations were primarily white
owned.[49] While black radio listeners were entertained by such characters as
New Orleans's "Okey Dokey," described by radio station WBOK's promotional material as "a frantic race showman that sells and sells,"[50] the whites
who owned these radio stations, along with the white businesses that sponsored "Negro-appeal" programming, profited handsomely from the antics of
"Okey Dokey" and others.

Station owners, hoping to maximize their advertising revenues, voluntar-
ily formed several "radio groups" within the growing 1950s "Negro-appeal"
radio industry. The largest grouping of "Negro-appeal" stations was within
the mainstream Keystone Broadcasting System, based in Chicago. In 1955,
278 of Keystone's 856 affiliated stations were "Negro-appeal." Two years
later, 347 of one thousand Keystone stations carried black-oriented programming. Most of the black Keystone stations were in the South. Prospective advertisers were encouraged to run ads simultaneously on all of Keystone's "Negro-appeal" stations.[51]

Rollins Broadcasting, Inc., of Wilmington, Delaware, coordinated a much
smaller but more geographically dispersed consortium of black-oriented
radio stations. Its members were WNJR (New York City area); WBEE
(Chicago area); KATZ (St. Louis); WGEE (Indianapolis); and WRAP (Norfolk).[52] To maximize its appeal to prospective corporate advertisers, Rollins
in 1958 conducted an extensive survey of black consumer preferences in the
cities where Rollins affiliates operated. Tables 2.3, 2.4, and 2.5 provide a
sample of the data generated by Rollins.

Another important "Negro-appeal" radio group was the Rounsaville
"Big 5," which consisted of WCIN (Cincinnati); WMBM (Miami); WLOU
(Louisville); WQOK (Greenville, South Carolina); and WWOK (Charlotte,
North Carolina).[53] After asserting that it owned "A Million Ears," a Roun-
saville advertisement that appeared in the September 19, 1955, issue of *Spon-
sor* informed prospective advertisers that "Individually or as a prize package,

TABLE 2.3
Product Brands Preferred by Urban Blacks, Selected Cities, 1958

	Aspirin	Beer	Toothpaste
New York	Bayer	Ballentine	Colgate
Chicago	Bayer	Budweiser	Colgate
St. Louis	Anacin/Bufferin	Stag	Colgate
Norfolk	Bayer	Budweiser	Colgate
Indianapolis	Bufferin	Wiedemann's	Colgate

SOURCE: *Sponsor* (Negro Issue) 12 (September 20, 1958): 29.

TABLE 2.4
Product Brands Preferred by Urban Blacks, Selected Cities, 1958

	Cigarettes (Men)	Cigarettes (Women)	Tea
New York	Camels	Viceroy/Winston	Lipton
Chicago	Pall Mall	Viceroy	Lipton
St. Louis	Pall Mall	Pall Mall	Lipton
Norfolk	Camels	Viceroy	Lipton
Indianapolis	Camels/Pall Mall	Pall Mall	Lipton

SOURCE: *Sponsor* (Negro Issue) 12 (September 20, 1958): 29.

TABLE 2.5
Product Brands Preferred by Urban Blacks, Selected Cities, 1958

	Soft Drinks	Tonics and Proprietaries	Laundry Soap
New York	Coca Cola	Black Draught	Tide
Chicago	Pepsi Cola	Scotts' Emulsion	Tide
St. Louis	Coca Cola	Black Draught	Tide
Norfolk	Coca Cola	Black Draught	Fab
Indianapolis	Coca Cola	Father John's	Tide

SOURCE: *Sponsor* (Negro Issue) 12 (September 20, 1958): 29.

these Rounsaville stations will deliver top audiences for your advertising dollar."[54]

Still, another significant "Negro-appeal" broadcast consortium was the "OK" group. Commencing in the mid-1950s, member stations, all located in the Gulf Coast region, shared "OK" in their call letters. They were WBOK (New Orleans); WXOK (Baton Rouge); KAOK (Lake Charles); and KYOK (Houston).[55]

Besides the ascendancy of "personality deejays" and the appearance of radio groups, the appearance of the National Negro Network, Inc., (NNN) in 1954 represented a milestone in the history of black-oriented radio. The NNN was a nationwide consortium of forty-two "Negro-appeal" radio stations formed to attract blue-chip corporate advertising. To assist this campaign, NNN members produced a daytime serial titled "Ruby Valentine" that aired on the network's affiliates.[56] In promoting "Ruby Valentine" to potential corporate advertisers, the NNN's promotional material declared:

> Now for the first time in advertising history . . . a single coordinated program can take you to the heart of the 16 billion dollar American Negro market. This new selling concept offers an advertiser a rich sales frontier virtually uncultivated by national advertising.[57]

"Ruby Valentine"'s subsequent success with both black radio listeners and corporate advertisers prompted the National Negro Network to expand its programming. Later NNN productions featured such noteworthy black performers as Cab Calloway and Ethel Waters. Moreover, by 1956, NNN's public affairs department fed live special-event broadcasts to member stations.[58]

Although rhythm and blues dominated the air-waves of "Negro-appeal" radio during the years following World War II, gospel music, another favorite of mid-twentieth century urban black consumers, also came into its own during this period. In fact, the years 1945–1955 have been called the first ten years of the "Golden Age of Gospel."[59]

While the overwhelmingly white owners of "Negro-appeal" stations derived profits from its gospel music programming,[60] black entrepreneurs within the gospel community, using alternative means to reach black consumers, also benefited.

Chicago's Thomas A. Dorsey, recognized as the "Father of African American Gospel Music," early on realized the merit of direct marketing to reach black consumers. In 1932, Dorsey established the first publishing house that exclusively sold gospel music created by African American composers (including himself). To ensure an immediate market for his publishing company's offerings, Dorsey, along with other gospel pioneers such as Sallie Martin, Magnolia Lewis Butts, Theodore R. Frye, and Beatrice Brown, started the National Convention of Gospel Choirs and Choruses (NCGCC) in 1933. This organization's membership, comprising black Baptist choirs from across America, eagerly bought the myriad songs that were available for purchase at the NCGCC's annual conventions.[61]

By the 1940s, other business-minded black gospel aficionados, seeking to emulate Thomas Dorsey, had established gospel publishing houses across the country. One of the most important was the Martin and Morris Publishing Company, established in Chicago in 1940.

Martin and Morris, named after Sallie Martin and Kenneth Morris, found a special niche in the evolving gospel music industry. Instead of limiting the number of composers they published, Martin and Morris sought to become a gospel music clearinghouse that featured both established and new talent.[62]

The business of Martin and Morris meshed the partners' talents perfectly. Sallie Martin, regarded as one of the most evocative gospel singers of all time, spent considerable time on the road with her "Sallie Martin Singers," advertising the songs published by Martin and Morris. Kenneth Morris, skilled in musical arrangement, composition, and notation, spent his time in Chicago working with the company's clients.[63]

Besides the sheet music sold at Martin and Morris's Chicago offices and at Sallie Martin Singers concerts, the company had a wide-ranging mail order business. Black consumers, nationwide, continually sent in money for Martin and Morris's wide range of gospel music. The company also employed agents across the country who received commissions for marketing Martin and Morris's gospel sheet music in their respective locales.[64]

Black gospel entrepreneurs, at mid-century, did not have the financial resources that white-owned businesses seeking to attract black consumers had at their disposal. Nevertheless, Thomas Dorsey, Sallie Martin, and Kenneth Morris possessed something that the advertising budgets of America's top corporations couldn't purchase. These African American artists/businesspeople were directly linked to black America's most potent social and economic network, the church.

One of the ways that white companies attempted to lessen their social distance from black consumers during this period was their employment of "Negro market" specialists to actively promote their corporations in the black community. Perhaps the most famous of the early African American pioneers in corporate America was James A. ("Billboard") Jackson.

Jackson, an extremely outgoing and congenial individual, joined Esso Standard Oil in 1937 as a special representative to the black community. Jackson quickly made his mark both within the company and within the national marketing community. By the mid-1940s, "Billboard" was the first and only black member of the American Marketing Society.[65] Also, as interest in the "Negro market" grew during this period, Jackson's work attracted much more attention. For instance, the March 7, 1947, issue of the marketing periodical *Tide* gave ample coverage to Jackson in an article titled "The Negro Market: An Appraisal." In a section that summarized Jackson's activities as "A Stand-out Job," *Tide* provided the following description of "Billboard"'s duties for Standard Oil:

Each year "the Esso man" swings around the circuit, cementing relations with the company's Negro dealers, their customers and Jackson's own 40,000-odd friends. Though it would be difficult to assess it in dollars and cents, the policy has paid off handsomely.[66]

The Pepsi Cola Company was another major corporation that, beginning in the 1940s, took an active interest in courting African American consumers. In fact, Pepsi, by the late 1940s, had established a Negro Sales Department, headed by an African American, Edward J. Boyd, to enhance the company's presence in the black community.[67]

Among Boyd's accomplishments was his 1949 "Leaders In His/Her Field" advertising campaign, which sought to link prominent African Americans with Pepsi Cola. The September 9, 1949, issue of *Printer's Ink* described this strategy as follows:

> What Pepsi-Cola did in these advertisements was to take some prominent members of the Negro race, compile concise summaries of their most important achievements, label them as leaders in their field and then explain that Pepsi-Cola also is the leader of its field. . . . The main illustration in these advertisements was intended to serve as an inspiration for the average reader. . . . Secondly, the physical proximity of the picture of the prominent Negro to the picture of the product suggested that he was a user of the product.[68]

Despite Boyd's creativity, Pepsi relieved him of his duties in 1952, replacing him with Harvey C. Russell. Russell, who joined Pepsi in 1950, went on to become Pepsi's vice president of special markets in 1961, making him the first African American to be named vice president of a multinational corporation.[69]

One of the highlights of Russell's ascension to upper-level management was his coordination of the company's extremely successful efforts to increase the number of black Pepsi drinkers in New Orleans during the early 1950s. Pepsi's subsequent entrenchment among New Orleans blacks revealed, among other things, how thorough market research can generate huge corporate profits.

Before Pepsi commenced its 1953 New Orleans campaign, Russell conducted a survey of the Crescent City's African American community. Among his findings, as reported in the September, 1954 issue of *The Pepsi Cola World*, were these observations:

> (1) Negroes, representing 35 percent of New Orleans' metropolitan population, were responsible for an estimated 50 percent of all soft drink consump-

tion; (2) motion pictures comprised the primary recreational facilities of the Negro population; (3) Negro schools were badly in need of various kinds of equipment; and (4) the attitude of local Negroes toward Pepsi-Cola bordered on apathy.[70]

After gathering this information, Russell developed a series of promotions designed to strengthen Pepsi's status among New Orleans black consumers, especially the young. To attract young potential Pepsi drinkers, local bottlers, on Russell's recommendation, sponsored Saturday children's matinees at local theaters patronized by blacks. The admission price to these shows was three Pepsi bottle tops; young moviegoers were also treated to free Pepsi.[71] Within a short period of time, as the September 1954 issue of *The Pepsi Cola World* proudly noted:

> The demand for Pepsi crowns became so great that the cap surplus which had once existed was almost immediately exhausted and the only way for children to get them was to buy the product, which they did in increasing quantities. Sales, in those areas where the promotion had taken place, rose 62 percent in four weeks and finally leveled off at a 40 percent permanent gain. One route increased its weekly sales by 600 in three months. Yet, the total cost of the matinee promotions was only $100 per week.[72]

Encouraged by the success of their Saturday matinee promotion, local Pepsi bottlers, again using Harvey Russell's research and recommendations, instituted a bottle-cap campaign for New Orleans's black schools. For accumulating from ten thousand to twenty thousand Pepsi crowns, schools were to receive a variety of prizes. Between February 1953 and February 1954, "128,000 Pepsi bottle caps were returned from the schools at a cost, in prizes, of only $400."[73]

Another profitable Pepsi campaign aimed at New Orleans's black youth was its summertime "Pepsi Day at the Beach" promotion. Pepsi arranged with a local amusement park for black New Orleans youth to be admitted and provided access to rides in exchange for Pepsi bottle caps. The 1954 "Pepsi Day at the Beach" attracted one thousand children who "paid" their way with 125,000 bottle caps.[74]

By the early 1950s, the number of companies seeking to emulate the success of companies like Pepsi-Cola and Esso Standard Oil in reaching black consumers increased dramatically, leading to an even greater prolif- eration of "Negro market" specialists throughout corporate America. These black trailblazers in U.S. corporations soon coalesced in a mutual support organization known as the National Association of Market Developers (NAMD).

The National Association of Market Developers grew out the needs of "Negro market" specialists for professional training and association. During the early 1950s, the black pioneers in corporate America tended to operate at the margins of their respective companies. As one early NAMD member has asserted:

> You weren't a part of anything real within the company marketing program or organization. You didn't participate in the meetings where they would discuss what's going on and what the new strategies were. . . . I don't think many of these company managers really gave a damn about anything more than the fact that they were going to have somebody out there identified with the Negro market.[75]

Besides being professionally isolated in the companies they represented, "Negro market" specialists were socially isolated from their white colleagues as well. Nevertheless, the African American trailblazers in corporate America circumvented this obstacle by establishing their own informal social network. For example, these individuals, while representing their companies at the annual meetings of such national African American organizations as the NAACP and the National Urban League, regularly shared ideas and offered encouragement to each other.[76]

When the National Association of Market Developers officially began in May 1953, it provided an institutional solution to the social and professional concerns of "Negro market" specialists. The organization's subsequent annual conventions provided a venue not only for socializing but, more important, for receiving additional professional training. In fact, until the late 1960s, when U.S. corporations began to substantively accord their black personnel the same respect and training as their white personnel, NAMD conventions represented perhaps the only place where African Americans could receive up-to-date information about sales and marketing.[77]

Because of NAMD's central role in the evolution of corporate America's interest in African American consumers, the organization's early membership represented a virtual "Who's Who" of blacks in U.S. business. Ironically, the first president of the organization, Moss H. Kendrix, was not an employee of a major corporation but headed his own firm, the Moss H. Kendrix Public Relations Company. His primary client during the 1950s was the Coca Cola Company.[78]

Samuel Whiteman was another independent entrepreneur associated with the early NAMD. Whiteman, one of the organization's founders, began his career with the white-owned Mars Contract Company, a distributor of hotel and motel furniture. However, in 1958, Whiteman formed his own company, Samuel Whiteman and Associates, which specialized in providing furniture to colleges and universities.[79]

Besides "Billboard" Jackson and Harvey Russell, other prominent NAMD members who began their careers as "Negro market" specialists for major companies included Herbert H. Wright, who worked for Phillip Morris; Wendell P. Alston and James Avery, who worked with "Billboard" at Esso Standard Oil; Chuck Smith, who worked for the Royal Crown Bottling Company; Joe Black, who worked for the Greyhound Corporation; Bill Porter, who worked for Anheuser-Busch; James "Bud" Ward, who worked for the Marriot Corporation; and Louise Prothro of Pet Milk.[80]

Another important figure associated with NAMD's formative years, one who was neither an independent entrepreneur nor an employee of a white-controlled corporation, was LeRoy Jeffries. Jeffries, who served as the organization's president from 1959 to 1960, was vice president and midwest advertising director of the black-owned Johnson Publications, publisher of *Ebony* and *Jet* magazines.[81] Jeffries's interest in the black consumer market mirrored that of his boss, John H. Johnson, who, during the 1960s, emerged as the major intermediary between corporate America and black consumers (see chapter 4).

Two other individuals who made invaluable contributions to the National Association of Market Developers' formation and development were Dr. Walter A. Davis, president of Tennessee A & I (now Tennessee State) University, where the National Association of Market Developers officially began in May 1953, and Dr. H. Naylor Fitzhugh, whose career included stints as a Howard University marketing professor, a vice president at Pepsi Cola, and president of NAMD.[82]

Another significant 1950s milestone related to the evolving "Negro market" was Clarence L. Holte's joining the major advertising firm BBD&O as a Negro market consultant in June 1952. Holte, described by the July 25, 1952, issue of *Tide* as "the Jackie Robinson of advertising's big leagues,"[83] served BBD&O clients who desired his special expertise. His success, soon led other major advertising agencies to employ their own in-house "Negro market" specialists.

Clarence L. Holte's ascension at BBD&O, the birth and growth of the National Association of Market Developers, and the rapid expansion of

"Negro-appeal" radio contributed to a dramatic increase in the number of publications about black consumers. One clear manifestation of the U.S. media's enhanced recognition of black consumers was the first appearance of the category "Negro Market" in volume 19 of the *Readers Guide to Periodical Literature* (April 1953–February 1955).[84]

A number of important book-length studies relating to African American consumers also appeared during the Eisenhower era. They included Joseph T. Johnson's *The Potential Negro Market* (1952); Henry A. Bullock's *Pathway to the Houston Negro Market* (1957); William K. Bell's *15 Million Negroes and 15 Billion Dollars* (1958); and Marcus Alexis's 1959 Ph.D. dissertation at the University of Minnesota, "Racial Differences in Consumption and Automobile Ownership." Like Paul K. Edwards's pioneering 1930s studies, the works by Johnson, Bullock, and Alexis provided useful information to white businesses seeking to get their share of the "Negro market." On the other hand, corporate marketers who perused Bell's *15 Million Negroes and 15 Billion Dollars* would have received a real eye-opener.

Bell, writing for an African American audience, decried white businesses' increased prominence in the economic lives of black consumers. After surveying the increasing white business interest in gaining the patronage of African American consumers, he declared:

> Why should not 15 MILLION NEGROES become more conscious of their condition by developing their own market for the advancement of their own lives? There is no record in history to show that any race on the face of this earth has ever become great that did not develop itself economically. . . . 15 MILLION NEGROES cannot be kept from gaining economic power if they determine to keep within the race a certain portion of that 15 BILLION DOLLARS that is running daily through their fingers, as water does over a dam. . . . There is GREAT POWER in 15 BILLION DOLLARS![85]

Bell's assertions about the potential power associated with black consumer spending were dramatically legitimized by the period's evolving Civil Rights Movement. In fact, the Montgomery Bus Boycott of 1955–1956 clearly demonstrated the power of disciplined black consumer activism (see chapter 3).

By the late 1950s, the "Negro market" had become an increasingly important part of the U.S. economy. Yet, in many parts of the country, especially in the South, African American consumers still were not treated with the respect that their collective dollars merited. This unacceptable situation sparked the civil rights protests of the mid-twentieth century. Moreover, the subsequent campaigns of black consumer economic retribution were not isolated, spontaneous occurrences. Events such as the Montgomery Bus Boycott and the "sit-in" phenomenon were part of a historic African American protest tradition.

3

African American Consumer Activism before and during the Civil Rights Era

The Civil Rights Movement, in the minds of many, is synony-mous with the public career of Dr. Martin Luther King Jr. His eloquent or-atory, coupled with the media's near constant coverage of his activities from Montgomery to Memphis, has made him an American icon. Yet, while King's place in history has been deservedly illuminated, consumer activism, the most potent nonviolent strategy employed by African Americans during this period of civil rights activity, has not been similarly spotlighted. Mini-mizing the central role of African American economic retribution erro-neously suggests that civil rights legislation resulted from white "moral transformation," rather than from the skillful use of African Americans' growing economic clout. Moreover, the sentiment of Civil Rights Move-ment—era black consumers to "hit 'em where it hurts" had clear historical precedents.

Decades before the commencement of the modern-day Civil Rights Movement, African Americans sought to use their collective spending power to affect positive social change. For example, Ida B. Wells, best known for her efforts to eradicate the bestial crime of lynching, stood as a pioneer advocate of African American economic retribution. Wells, after the brutal 1892 lynching of three African American businessmen in Memphis, used her po-sition as editor of the Memphis *Free Speech* to urge fellow blacks to either leave the city or boycott Memphis's newly opened streetcar line. Signifi-cantly, her plea resulted in approximately two thousand blacks leaving Mem-phis and the near bankruptcy of the city's streetcar line.[1]

A few years later, at the turn of twentieth century, African Americans in more than twenty-five southern cities conducted systematic consumer boy-cotts to protest "Jim Crow" streetcars.[2] A June 9, 1906, editorial in the black-owned Lynchburg (Virginia) *News* summed up the goal of this movement when it stated:"Let us touch to the quick the white man's pocket. 'Tis there his conscience often lies."[3]

Although the forces of southern white racism ultimately crushed the 1900–1906 boycott movement against "Jim Crow" streetcars,[4] this early manifestation of African American economic self-determination planted the seeds for later, more successful demonstrations of enlightened consumer activity.

Long before the celebrated Montgomery Bus Boycott of 1955–1956, the various "Don't Buy Where You Can't Work" campaigns of the 1930s fired the imagination and the initiative of the national African American community. After beginning in Chicago, at the behest of Joseph D. Bibb and A. C. MacNeal, editors of the militant Chicago *Whip*, this movement quickly spread to other cities. African Americans, whether they resided in Chicago, New York City, Cleveland, or Richmond, suffered the same overt economic exploitation; white-owned business establishments, which all but monopolized the commercial life of black enclaves, often refused to hire neighborhood residents.[5]

While the "Don't Buy Where You Can't Work" campaigns primarily sought to increase the number of jobs available to blacks, they also educated the African American community as to the power and the potential of its collective economic strength. For example, in a July, 1931, *Crisis* editorial that supported the growing consumer boycott movement, W. E. B. Du Bois asserted:

> If we once make a religion of our determination to spend our meagre income so far as possible only in such ways as will bring us employment consideration and opportunity, the possibilities before us are enormous . . . a nation twice as large as Portugal, Holland, or Sweden is not powerless—is not merely a supplicant beggar for crumbs—it is a mighty economic power when it gets vision enough to use its strength.[6]

Predictably, white ghetto merchants attempted to counteract organized black consumer retribution. In New York City, Cleveland, Baltimore, Newark, and Washington, D.C., these businesses obtained court injunctions that prohibited African American protestors from picketing establishments that practiced racial discrimination. Then, on March 28, 1938, the U.S. Supreme Court, reversing a lower court decision, guaranteed the right to picket establishments that practiced such discrimination.[7]

Besides merely seeking to increase African American employment opportunities at white-owned businesses, some black consumers, during the Great

Depression, used their dollars to enhance African American business development. The Housewives' League of Detroit epitomized this phenomenon.

Convened in June 1930 by Fannie B. Peck, by 1935 the organization had grown from fifty to ten thousand members. To join the League, African American women pledged to support black businesses, buy black-produced products, and patronize black professionals. Realizing that African American women generally coordinated their families' spending patterns, the League sought to mobilize this power in support of community development. The Housewives' League of Detroit, along with similar organizations in Chicago, Baltimore, Washington, D.C., Cleveland, and New York City, were indeed powerful forces in their respective communities.[8]

Besides the various "Don't Buy Where You Can't Work" campaigns and the activities of local African American Housewives' Leagues, the 1930s featured growing interest in consumer cooperatives within the black community. Cooperative enterprises, characterized by a communal distribution of profits, had a special appeal to African American consumers during this period.

Traditionally, individual black entrepreneurs have tried to convince black consumers that supporting black-owned businesses allowed their dollars to do "double duty" (simultaneously purchasing a product and building African Americans' collective strength). Still, a significant number of black consumers have viewed—and continue to view—black businessmen's promotion of the "double-duty dollar" as self-serving. In response, an increasing number of blacks came to believe that the best way for black businessmen to gain more black consumer support was for them to transform their enterprises into consumer cooperatives. As St. Clair Drake, a well-known contemporary proponent of cooperative ventures, asserted:

> While the plea to make the dollar do "Double Duty" often falls on deaf ears, a dollar that will do "Triple Duty" might awaken some response, and a dollar spent with a co-operative (1) secures the desired goods, (2) helps to support a fellow Negro, and (3) brings a dividend on purchase at the end of the fiscal year.[9]

Supporters of consumer cooperatives also contended that their widespread implementation and coordination within the black community would substantially enhance the group's collective economic and political bargaining power.[10]

Perhaps the decade's most noteworthy black consumer cooperative was the Consumers' Cooperative Trading Company (CCTC), organized in

Gary, Indiana in 1932. The CCTC, the brainchild of Jacob L. Reddix, a local black teacher, sought to ameliorate the adverse effects of the Great Depression on Gary's black community.

In 1932, a reported 50 percent of Gary's twenty thousand African Americans were on public relief. In this setting of despair and frustration, Reddix, after familiarizing himself with the principles of organized cooperation and with initial working capital of $24, started the Consumers' Cooperative Trading Company as a buying club for fifteen families.[11]

A major milestone in the evolution of the CCTC occurred in fall 1933, when Reddix began teaching night classes on cooperative economics at Gary's Roosevelt High School. A contemporary article, describing what the author called the "Miracle in Gary," elaborated on the significance of these classes:

> With this move the negroes of Gary really launched their co-operative venture. The women members of the class, beginning to understand the true meaning of co-operation, formed a guild and began to organize buying power and co-operative sentiment. The class continued through the winter of 1934–35 with the largest attendance of any academic class at the evening schools, adding new and intelligent members to Gary's co-operative movement.[12]

By 1935, mainly through the efforts of Reddix and his disciples, the Consumers' Cooperative Trading Company had grown to four hundred member families. Moreover, the organization now coordinated myriad enterprises, including a cooperative grocery store with annual sales of $35,000, a community credit union, and a cooperative ice cream and candy shop run entirely by children. Although the CCTC met an untimely demise in 1940 for undetermined reasons, its earlier success inspired similar projects across the country.[13]

At the same time the Consumers' Cooperative Trading Company, albeit on a small scale, was demonstrating the potential of black economic cooperation, the venerable W. E. B. Du Bois sought to focus the national black community's attention on a collective economic project of massive proportions. Significantly, Du Bois's controversial June 1935 *Current History* article, "A Negro Nation within the Nation," all but repudiated his previous association with the integrationist-oriented National Association for the Advancement of Colored People (NAACP).

After citing various manifestations of ongoing white racial bias and invoking the political, consumer, and intellectual potential of the African American community, Du Bois concluded:

There exists today a chance for the Negroes to organize a cooperative State within their own group. By letting Negro farmers feed Negro artisans, and Negro technician guide Negro home industries, and Negro thinkers plan this integration of cooperation, while Negro artists dramatize and beautify the struggle, economic independence can be achieved. To doubt that this is possible is to doubt the essential humanity and the quality of brains of the American Negro.[14]

Ironically, Du Bois's proposed blueprint for the future of black America appeared markedly reminiscent of the agenda of his former ideological adversary, Marcus Garvey.

Although African Americans did not subsequently embrace Du Bois's panoramic vision of racial self-sufficiency, his proposal, along with other consumer empowerment efforts of the 1930s, contributed to African Americans' growing assertiveness regarding their role as consumers. Moreover, black consumers' enhanced sense of self-determination increased during World War II.

The consumer militancy of African Americans during the World War II years was linked to the era's "Double V" concept. Popularized by the Pittsburgh *Courier*, blacks sought victory in their fight against fascism both abroad and at home.[15] Consequently, black consumers were disinclined to passively ignore cultural assaults by U.S. advertisers.

During the early 1940s, several corporations incurred the wrath of American blacks. African American smokers boycotted American Tobacco Company products for its marketing of "Nigger Hair" tobacco. Black consumers also punished the Whitman Candy Company for its "Pickaninny Chocolate" product line. Similarly, African American automobile owners eschewed Shell Oil Company products because of the company's advertisements featuring a black man eating watermelon. These companies' subsequent public apologies to black consumers and their removal of offensive ads and products graphically demonstrated the potential power of black consumer activism.[16]

This overview of enlightened African American consumer activity before the modern civil rights era reveals the most prominent historical reasons for black economic retribution. First and foremost, African Americans have staged consumer boycotts to respond to extreme acts of white racist violence. Similarly, blacks have constrained their spending with European American enterprises to protest against humiliating treatment based on race; white-owned businesses solely interested in blacks as consumers (rather than as employees); and white companies that used demeaning images of blacks in their advertising. Moreover, African Americans have proactively withheld economic support of European American businesses in order to more fully support African American economic development.

These characteristics of African American consumer activism were, and remain, the primary motivations for black economic retribution and self-determination. An examination of the years 1955–1964 further clarifies this assertion.

The Montgomery Bus Boycott of 1955–1956 remains the model instance of organized black consumer retribution and self-determination. Although the actions of certain individuals have, over time, been magnified to almost mythical proportions, one cannot overemphasize the resolve demonstrated by Montgomery's black community during this action.

The internal unity associated with the Montgomery Bus Boycott appears all the more significant when Montgomery's preboycott African American community is examined. In *Stride toward Freedom*, a firsthand account of the Montgomery Bus Boycott, Martin Luther King Jr. described a sorry state of affairs in preboycott Montgomery. Factionalism had retarded the effectiveness of the leadership class. The middle class appeared self-absorbed and apathetic; the working class seemed passive and resigned to second-class citizenship.[17]

In attempting to explain how a previously disorganized community could achieve the unity necessary to undertake a successful boycott of city buses, King mulled over a number of possibilities. He noted how the Supreme Court's May 17, 1954, *Brown vs. Board of Education* decision seemed to inspire blacks throughout the country. He also observed how the Rosa Parks incident touched a nerve that even a fractured, apathetic, and passive community could feel. Yet, King, the theologian, concluded that "God had decided to use Montgomery as the proving ground for the struggle and triumph of freedom and justice in America."[18]

Notwithstanding King's assertions regarding divine intervention, the Montgomery Bus Boycott was motivated by several of the historical reasons for African American economic retribution against white-controlled enterprises. While there were no extreme acts of white racist violence perpetuated against Montgomery blacks immediately prior to the boycott, African Americans suffered from humiliating differential treatment on city buses. Moreover, while black bus riders accounted for nearly 70 percent of Montgomery Bus Lines' receipts, the company employed no African American drivers. Finally, as the boycott evolved, Montgomery's African American community sought to use its decreased spending with white enterprises to stimulate black economic development.

Historians, as well as participants in the Montgomery Bus Boycott, have focused considerable attention on the deplorable situation faced by African American bus riders before the boycott.[19] Moreover, the Montgomery Bus Boycott has been placed in the context of the Civil Rights Movement's quest for racial integration. Under these circumstances, it is not surprising that relatively little coverage has been given to the ways Montgomery blacks attempted to use the boycott to enhance community economic development.

For example, by the spring of 1956, King repeatedly told his listeners at public meetings that the Montgomery Improvement Association (MIA) had to move beyond simply fighting bus segregation. At one MIA gathering, King declared to his audience, "Until we as a race learn to develop our power, we will get nowhere. We've got to get political and economic power for our race." He followed up his public exhortations by recommending to the MIA executive board that "a strong emphasis . . . be placed on increasing our political power through voting and increasing our economic power through the establishment of a bank." Shortly thereafter, the MIA board, among other things, established a banking committee to seek a federal charter for a building and loan association.[20]

King's increasing focus on economic empowerment, especially a community-based bank, reflected a growing interest in business development among Montgomery blacks. A contemporary examination of the Montgomery Bus Boycott that appeared in the October and November 1956 issues of *Negro History Bulletin* clearly indicated a strengthening of Montgomery's black business community in the wake of the boycott:

> It was common knowledge that many Negroes found it difficult to get downtown and found it easier to shop at neighborhood stores, particularly if they were owned by Negroes. . . . Thus the neighborhood business, be it a gas station or grocery store, got a new front or was able to buy fresher vegetables and meats because of the quick turnover. Moreover, the thousands of dollars per week that left the Negroes' hands and perhaps went to the bus company was now being spent among Negroes. The clubs, the stores, the cleaners and almost every Negro business shared directly or indirectly in the new income.[21]

Ironically, the unity that sustained Montgomery's black community during the bus boycott slowly evaporated after its successful conclusion. Among other things, the petty jealousies and factionalism that existed before the boycott resurfaced. Some MIA members became increasingly upset with the widespread attention and praise that King received for his role in the movement; at the same time, some of King's supporters sought to downplay the role of other blacks associated with the boycott. One King partisan even publicly referred to Rosa Parks as simply "an adornment to the movement."[22] Still, while the spirit of Montgomery Bus Boycott dissipated in Montgomery, it spread, through the Southern Christian Leadership Conference (founded in January 1957), to such places as Atlanta, Birmingham, and Tallahassee.[23]

While blacks in Montgomery were conducting an organized, systematic bus boycott to protest racial discrimination, their brethren in the Mississippi Delta were engaged in a less structured, but equally successful, campaign of economic retribution. The brutal 1955 lynching of Emmett Louis Till represented the spark for this boycott.

After Till's accused murderers, the half-brothers Roy Bryant and J. W. Milam, were acquitted by an all-white Mississippi jury, they openly admitted their guilt in a January 24, 1956, article in *Look* magazine.[24] However, in a follow-up report that appeared in the January 22, 1957, issue of *Look*, both men appeared down on their luck. Before Roy and J.W.'s slaying of Till, their family, the Milam-Bryant clan, had operated a number of small country stores in the Mississippi Delta that largely depended on African American patronage. In the wake of the brothers' public "confession" to murdering Emmett Till, local blacks, without the benefit and direction of a charismatic leader such as King, quietly yet resolutely stopped doing business with the Milam-Bryant stores. Consequently, by early 1957, the family's lucrative business had been all but destroyed.[25] Thus, while the legal system permitted Roy Bryant and J.W. Milam to literally get away with murder, black Mississippians ultimately meted out punishment in the "court" of consumer choices.

Traditionally, when the evolution of the modern-day Civil Rights Movement is presented, the scene jumps from the Montgomery Bus Boycott to the 1960 Greensboro, North Carolina, sit-ins. Although new evidence suggests that the sit-in movement actually began in Wichita, Kansas, in 1958,[26] its birthplace is, perhaps, less important than its overall impact on the African American community. Regardless of where the sit-in movement actually started, this disruption of white business operations quickly captured the imagination of the black community, especially the youth.

Whether an African American resided in Wichita, Oklahoma City (site of another pre-1960 sit-in campaign), Greensboro, Nashville, or Atlanta, local custom provided blacks with only take-out service at downtown lunch counters. This disrespect was more marked given the fact that black consumers, although prohibited from eating at lunch counters, were encouraged to freely spend their money in other sections of white-owned businesses. An examination of *Business Week* for the years 1960–1962 provides special insight into the campaign to force southern retailers to treat black consumers respectfully.

An article titled "Negro Groups Put the Economic Pressure On," which appeared in the February 27, 1960, issue of *Business Week*, declared: "More directly than earlier legalistic efforts at Negro equality, this movement affects businessmen. It hits straight at the pocketbook."[27] *Business Week's* bluntness appeared ironic in that many in the white business community initially dismissed the black-student-instigated sit-ins as "college hi-jinks."[28] Yet, as this strategy for black consumer empowerment rapidly spread throughout the South, the "hi-jinks" theory seemed to reflect more wishful thinking than reality.

Predictably, as southern whites began to realize that the "sit-in" movement represented the first stage of a concerted African American campaign for human dignity, they sought to suppress the movement. Throughout the South, tough enforcement of trespassing laws came to be seen as a means to dissipate the embryonic sit-in movement. Yet, strict enforcement of trespassing laws could have had dire consequences for stores that relied heavily on African American patronage. As an anonymous southern retailer told *Business Week*, "It's difficult to sell a Negro a ribbon at the notions counter, while you're having his friend arrested at the lunch counter."[29] In fact, in most southern cities by 1960, African American consumer support determined whether a particular product reached the top spot in sales.[30]

These economic realities, and their implications, received more coverage in an article titled "Negro Business Pressure Grows," which appeared in the April 23, 1960, issue of *Business Week*. Among other things, the business periodical informed its readers that the relatively spontaneous sit-in movement appeared to be evolving into a well-organized boycott of discriminatory stores throughout the South.[31]

Nashville, Tennessee, according to *Business Week*, seemed especially affected by blacks' growing recognition of their economic clout. As one of Nashville's leading white retail executives described this phenomenon: "This thing has frightening ramifications. It is more serious than many people realize. It has now become an economic situation affecting the entire community, the whole city, the whole country."[32]

A study conducted by Vivian Henderson, a professor of economics at Fisk University in Nashville, verified these observations. Henderson discovered that African American expenditures in shops in downtown Nashville accounted for approximately 20 percent of these stores' sales. Moreover, during a recent black boycott of downtown Nashville, these stores had witnessed a 90 percent decline in revenue from African American customers.[33]

In Nashville, as in other southern cities, black consumer boycotts spawned a similar, retaliatory movement by whites. Whereas African Americans boycotted stores that discriminated against them as consumers, whites threatened to boycott those stores that ceased to treat blacks as second-class customers. As one exasperated merchant told *Business Week*, "We're damned if we do integrate our eating facilities and damned if we don't."[34]

Some Nashville whites, citing an increase in local racial tension, questioned the wisdom of black economic retribution.[35] In response, Vivian Henderson, speaking for the African American community, forthrightly asserted: "I believe the withdrawals are the most effective weapon the Negro has. . . . It is simple—stores with the best service get the Negro dollar."[36]

As it became increasingly clear that black consumers in the South were prepared to employ economic retribution, regardless of the short-term consequences, the region's business community became increasingly concerned. As the president-elect of Atlanta's Chamber of Commerce declared in a December 17, 1960, *Business Week* interview, "Business just doesn't like chaos and confusion."[37]

Although southern white businessmen found themselves in an increasingly uncomfortable situation, economic imperatives necessitated their finding a solution. The August 5, 1961, issue of *Business Week*, which featured an article titled "New Business Ways in the South," revealed that many southern merchants were solving their predicament by fully desegregating their eating facilities (and taking their chances with white consumers). This gamble, for the most part, proved successful.[38]

Despite a conscious decision to placate their black customers, southern white retailers, in the wake of the sit-ins, realized that African Americans would intensify, rather than diminish, their demand for respect.[39] As one southern department store manager told *Business Week* in 1961: "After this eating thing has settled down, we're going to have more upheaval. It's a social revolution, and we can't have it painlessly."[40]

No southern city experienced more pain and upheaval during the early 1960s than Birmingham, Alabama. The African American population of Birmingham, like that of other cities, was determined to be respected as consumers. The May 12, 1962, issue of *Business Week* included coverage of black Birmingham residents' boycott of discriminatory retailers during the

1962 Easter season. As a result, some downtown Birmingham stores witnessed a 90 percent decline in African American patronage.[41]

Besides a resolute black consumer community, Birmingham also featured a white business community that, out of self-interest, sought to mitigate racial tension. Determined to emulate the partially successful efforts of their counterparts in other southern cities, Birmingham businessmen attempted to establish biracial meetings among themselves, representatives of the African American community, and political officials. Yet, as the president of a large local corporation told *Business Week:* "With a belligerently antagonistic governing body, little can be done."[42]

The most "belligerently antagonistic" public official in Birmingham during this period was the infamous Eugene ("Bull") Connor, who left an indelible mark on history during the celebrated Birmingham campaign of 1963. Connor's reaction to 1962 African American consumer boycotts signaled his sadistic nature.

Besides the Easter boycott of 1962, black students from local Miles College coordinated a protracted boycott against discriminatory downtown Birmingham stores. Among other things, this campaign of economic retribution demanded the desegregation of lunch counters and the removal of racial designation signs on drinking fountains and restrooms.[43]

Birmingham's three-man City Commission, dominated by Public Safety Commissioner Connor, ignored pleas for moderation from the white business community and struck back hard. It suspended the city's significant subsidy of the county surplus food program. Since 90 percent of this fund went to needy African Americans, this action had an immediate negative impact upon Birmingham's black community. Yet, as Mayor Arthur J. Haynes rationalized this decision to *Business Week*, "We've got to do something to nip this boycott in the bud."[44]

Despite the City Commission's perverse use of economic retribution to quell black consumer discontent, Birmingham's African American community remained steadfast in its quest for self-respect. In fact, the Reverend Fred Shuttlesworth, a prominent Birmingham minister and activist and one of the founders of the Southern Christian Leadership Conference, arranged for SCLC's 1962 annual convention to be held in Birmingham and announced that the September convention would feature well-publicized demonstrations against local merchants who discriminated against African Americans. Mass demonstrations during the SCLC meeting were averted only after downtown stores agreed to remove racial designation signs from restrooms and water fountains.[45]

This victory, however, proved to be short-lived. Soon after the SCLC convention ended, the segregationist restroom and water fountain signs reappeared. An understandably irate Fred Shuttlesworth had little difficulty in persuading SCLC leadership to return to Birmingham for a protracted battle against local racial discrimination.

Significantly, Martin Luther King Jr. and the SCLC used their recent unsuccessful experiences in Albany, Georgia, to devise a winning strategy in Birmingham. In Albany, black activists focused on pressuring politicians through mass marches to city hall. Yet, because African American political strength was then nonexistent, the Albany movement fizzled. On the other hand, during the 1963 Birmingham campaign, white businessmen felt the heat from mass demonstrations of disgruntled African American consumers. While southern blacks may not have wielded political power, they did possess noteworthy spending power. In fact, King himself, after Birmingham, concluded that organized black economic retribution represented the best strategy for achieving civil and human rights.[46]

Although black consumers achieved a stunning victory in Birmingham during the spring of 1963, the national spotlight tragically returned to that city a few months later. On September 15, a powerful dynamite blast damaged the Sixteenth Street Baptist Church, killing four young black girls who were attending Sunday School. In addition, two black men were killed during disturbances following the bombing.[47] These incidents, among other things, led to a call for a national black boycott during the Christmas season in late 1963.

The proposed Christmas boycott was the brainchild of an ad hoc organization known as "Actors and Writers for Justice." The members of this group included the author James Baldwin, the journalist Louis Lomax, and the husband-and-wife acting team of Ossie Davis and Ruby Dee.[48] Baldwin, the apparent organizer of Actors and Writers for Justice, told one public rally that what occurred in Birmingham "cost this nation the right to be called Christian." Moreover, he declared: "We have got to bring the cat out of hiding, and where he is hiding is in the bank."[49]

From the standpoint of American businesses, the call by the Actors and Writers for Justice for a national black boycott during Christmas could not have come at a worse time. Ten days after the Birmingham murders, the Center for Research in Marketing released the findings of a study that, among other things, examined African American attitudes concerning consumer boycotts. When asked the question "If a prominent Negro were to tell you to boycott against a store or brand, what would you likely do?," 89 percent of the blacks interviewed replied that they would follow the suggestion.[50]

Armed with the data from the Center for Research in Marketing, along with a fervent belief in the righteousness of their proposal, Actors and Writers for Justice sought the support of other black leaders for a national boycott during the Christmas shopping season. To their disappointment, they received a lukewarm response. Of the six major civil rights organizations, only SCLC endorsed the proposed boycott. The other groups, most notably the NAACP, expressed doubt as to whether blacks could indeed carry out such a dramatic demonstration of economic retribution.[51]

The October 17, 1963, edition of *Jet* magazine provided insight into the intracommunity debate concerning the feasibility of the Christmas boycott. An article that asked the question "Should Negroes boycott Santa Claus?" started by acknowledging the concerns of Roy Wilkins of the NAACP and other critics.[52] Yet, after surveying recent developments regarding the behavior and growing power of black consumers, the essay's author asserted:

> Bluntly put, available research, even that from white sources, scream loudly that Negroes, just like Congressman Adam Clayton Powell urges, are ready at a moment's notice to "withhold the dollar to make the white man holler."[53]

Ironically, while the October 17, 1963, issue of *Jet* appeared to subtly support the proposed Christmas boycott, the magazine's publisher, John H. Johnson, staunchly opposed such an action. In an October 16, 1963, interview with *Advertising Age*, Johnson blasted the proposed boycott as a senseless endeavor proposed by a minuscule segment of the Civil Rights Movement. Moreover, he stated, children should not be denied the right to enjoy Christmas.[54]

Johnson's aversion to the Christmas boycott may have been based on more than a concern about children. By 1963 corporate marketers increasingly viewed advertising in *Ebony* and *Jet* as an ideal means to reach the black consumer market. Thus, Johnson, pleased with rising advertising revenues, had a vested interest in promoting African American consumption (see chapter 4).[55]

Because of the strength and influence of its opponents, the 1963 black consumer boycott of Christmas shopping never came about. Still, just the *threat* of this action had a profound effect on white American business. As study after study revealed the growing importance of African American consumers to the U.S. economy, U.S. companies actively sought to befriend, rather than antagonize, black shoppers.[56] In fact, as the June 20, 1964, issue of *Business Week* noted, businessmen played an important role in smoothing the passage and the acceptance by whites of the monumental Civil Rights Act of 1964.[57] Still, white business support of this watershed legislation appeared to have much more to do with potential profits than with altruism.

Title II, Section 201, of the Civil Rights Act of 1964 focused on issues related to black consumerism:

> All persons shall be entitled to the full and equal enjoyment of the goods, services, facilities, privileges, advantages, and accommodations of any place of public accommodation, as defined in this section, without discrimination or segregation on the ground of race, color, religion, or national origin.[58]

It went on to enumerate the establishments that would be covered by the new law. These included:

1. any inn, hotel, motel, or other establishment which provides lodging to transient guests
2. any restaurant, cafeteria, lunchroom, lunch counter, soda fountain, or other facility principally engaged in selling food for consumption on the premises
3. any motion picture house, theater, concert hall, sports arena, stadium, or other place of exhibition or entertainment.[59]

On the surface, the Civil Rights Act of 1964, in large part, appeared to be the culmination of years of sustained black consumer economic retribution. African Americans consumers, by legislative mandate, now had to be treated with respect wherever they spent their money. Nevertheless, succeeding decades would clearly suggest that white-owned businesses, rather than unfettered black consumers, were the primary beneficiaries of the Civil Rights Act of 1964.

4

The Revolution Will Be Marketed

American Corporations and Black Consumers during the 1960s

The 1960s are generally viewed as a decade in which African American activism, supported by the liberalism of the Kennedy and Johnson administrations, resulted in both social and economic gains for many blacks. Yet, when we consider the impact of black consumerism on white business, we see that any changes in business practices among white-owned companies resulted from pragmatic white conservatism, rather than from altruistic white liberalism. White-owned corporations, in response to the accelerated urbanization of African Americans, accelerated their quest to reach these increasingly important consumers; aided by black consultants, most notably John H. Johnson, they were able to maximize their profits and appear "socially responsible" at the same time. In addition, the 1960s graphically demonstrated the elasticity of American capitalism. Corporate marketers began the decade by developing advertisements that catered to African Americans' perceived interest in racial desegregation. By decade's end, as African Americans moved politically from a more passive to a more confrontational stance, U.S. corporations promoted the "soul" market, which extolled black culture and customs, to retain the allegiance of black consumers.

Although the African American experience in the 1960s often conjures up images of sit-ins, freedom rides, massive protest marches, clenched fists, and huge Afros, perhaps, the most striking characteristic of the national black community during this period was its overwhelmingly urban character. Between 1940 and 1960, the percentage of African Americans who lived in cities had grown from 48.6 to 73.2.[1] By 1960, for the first time in U.S. history, the percentage of blacks who lived in cities exceeded that of whites (65.5). Table 4.1 provides a more detailed examination of the extent of African American migration and urbanization by 1960.

TABLE 4.1
Percent of Urban Population by Region and Race,
1940–1960

	1940	1950	1960
United States			
Black	48.6	62.4	73.2
White	57.4	64.3	65.5
Northeast			
Black	90.1	94.0	95.6
White	76.1	78.7	79.1
North Central			
Black	88.8	93.8	95.7
White	57.3	62.6	66.8
West			
Black	83.1	90.3	92.7
White	58.8	69.7	77.6
South			
Black	36.5	47.7	58.5
White	36.8	48.9	58.6

SOURCE: Daniel M. Johnson and Rex R. Campbell, *Black Migration in America* (Durham, N.C.: Duke University Press, 1981), 132.

TABLE 4.2
Percentage of African Americans Involved in Southern Agriculture, 1940–1960
(Male/Female)

	1940	1950	1960
Farmers and farm managers	25.9/3.8	19.3/2.5	7.1/1.0
Farm laborers and foremen	23.8/16.6	14.5/11.4	11.7/4.8
TOTAL	49.7/20.4	33.8/13.9	18.5/5.8

SOURCE: Daniel O. Price, *Changing Characteristics of the Negro Population: A 1960 Census Monograph* (Washington, D.C.: U.S. Bureau of the Census, 1969), 119.

Massive African American migration to cities across the country resulted not only in a change of address for the migrants but also in a distinct improvement in their occupational status. As Table 4.2 reveals, the percentage of African Americans in relatively low-paying southern agriculture work declined dramatically between 1940 and 1960. Moreover, as Tables 4.3, 4.4, and 4.5 demonstrate, both African American men and women, by 1960, were moving into more prestigious and better paying occupations. These significant demographic developments contributed mightily to increasing the notice taken by U.S. corporations in the 1960s of the lucrative black consumer market.

To accommodate companies that had been slow to appreciate the importance of African American consumers, the 1960s witnessed a virtual ex-

TABLE 4.3
Percentage of Black Men in Selected Occupations, 1940–1960

	1940	1950	1960
Professional, technical workers	1.7	2.2	3.9
Proprietors, managers	1.4	2.1	2.3
Clerks, sales workers	2.6	4.3	6.5
Skilled workers, foremen	4.4	7.7	10.2
Semiskilled operatives	11.7	21.0	23.5
Unskilled laborers	22.9	23.3	19.4
Service workers	13.7	14.4	14.4

SOURCE: Marion Hayes,"A Century of Change: Negroes in the U.S. Economy, 1860–1960," *Monthly Labor Review* (December 1962), 1364.

TABLE 4.4
Percentage of Black Women in Selected Occupations,
1940–1960

	1940	1950	1960
Professional, technical workers	4.2	5.4	7.5
Proprietors, managers	.7	1.1	1.2
Clerks, sales workers	1.4	5.4	10.2
Skilled workers, foremen	.1	.6	.7
Semiskilled operatives	13.5	14.6	12.8
Unskilled laborers	.8	1.5	1.0
Service workers	63.4	60.7	55.0

SOURCE: Hayes,"A Century of Change," 1364.

TABLE 4.5
Comparative Annual Median Income of Blacks and Whites, 1939, 1947, 1957, 1960

	1939	1947	1957	1960	Percentage Increase 1939–1960
Males					
Black	$460	$1,279	$2,436	$3,075	568.5
White	$1,112	$2,347	$4,396	$5,137	362.0
Females					
Black	$246	$432	$1,019	$1,276	418.7
White	$676	$1,269	$2,240	$2,537	275.3

SOURCE: Hayes,"A Century of Change," 1364.

plosion of"how-to" articles in various advertising trade journals offering advice on selling to African Americans.[2] An October 9, 1961, article in *Sponsor* titled "Know-How Is Key to Selling Negro Today," epitomized this trend.

Sponsor advised its readers that the key to success in marketing to African Americans could be summed up in three words: recognition, identification, and invitation:

The Negro needs to be recognized as a person. The very fact that an advertiser will undertake a special campaign [for] the Negro is interpreted as a form of recognition to the Negro. And that advertiser immediately stands to gain an important competitive edge over the advertisers who have not taken this step . . . identification is equally important. Can the Negro identify with your product? Can the Negro identify with the ad that promises "lovelier, whiter hands with ABC soap"? Because of the Negro's history of suppression his need to be "invited" to try the product appears to be a strong one indeed. True, he may use it without invitation, but this power of a special invitation to him, alone, can be considerable.[3]

Some corporations, besides relying on trade journal articles for insights about black consumers, employed African American consultants to obtain additional information about the African American consumer market. Perhaps the two most influential black consultants to corporate America during the 1960s were John H. Johnson, the publisher of *Ebony* magazine, and D. Parke Gibson, the president of D. Parke Gibson Associates, Inc.

Johnson had long been interested in making U.S. corporations aware of the potential profits associated with black consumers. As early as 1947, *Ebony* asserted that major corporations were missing lucrative opportunities by ignoring the African American market. Johnson's observations appear to have been based upon self-interest; in the years immediately following its 1945 founding, *Ebony* had experienced difficulty in attracting advertising from large corporations.[4]

Nevertheless, by the early 1960s, *Ebony* had established itself as a major American magazine, and John H. Johnson stood as one of the country's top executives. Johnson's success as a publisher appeared to have been based on his ability to gauge the mood and the interests of his readers.[5] Therefore, to white corporate leaders seeking insights about black consumers, Johnson appeared to be an ideal ally. In his autobiography, *Succeeding Against the Odds*, Johnson described his consulting role to corporate America:

In the decade of the long hot summers, I held the unofficial position of special ambassador to American Whites. . . . Enlightened self-interest: that was my theme. I asked corporate leaders to act not for Blacks, not for civil rights, but for their corporations and themselves. For it was true then and it's true now that if you increase the income of Blacks and Hispanics and poor Whites, you increase the profits of corporate America. And if you decrease the income of the disadvantaged, you decrease income and potential income of American corporations. . . . What it all boiled down to was that equal opportunity was good business.[6]

Johnson's advice to major U.S. corporations deserves closer examination. His theme of "enlightened self-interest" suggests a major reinterpretation of the 1960s. If corporate leaders took Johnson's message to heart, it can plausibly be argued that some of the gains associated with the Civil Rights Movement were based on "conservative," rather than "liberal," impulses. For example, during the 1960s, the Congress of Racial Equality (CORE) stood in the forefront of the movement to force U.S. corporations to use African American models in their print and television advertising. To CORE and other civil rights organizations, this was a "civil rights" issue. However, when U.S. businesses realized that using black models increased black purchases of their products without alienating white consumers, corporations gladly utilized black models in print media and television.[7]

John H. Johnson's concern about the "enlightened self-interest" (i.e., profits) of large white corporations appeared intimately connected with his concern about *Ebony's* financial well-being. Once he convinced corporate leaders that it was good business to reach more black consumers in a tasteful manner, these same corporations had to find a vehicle to do just that. Although Johnson's autobiography asserts that he did not directly approach white corporate leaders about advertising in *Ebony* during the 1960s, the magazine's advertising revenue nearly tripled between 1962 and 1969 (see Table 4.6).[8]

Another manifestation of Johnson's service to American corporations during the 1960s was the Johnson Publishing Company's 1966 publication, *The Negro Handbook.* This book, on the surface, appeared to be a reference book aimed at a general audience. Considering Johnson's interest in assisting corporate America, however, as well as U.S. companies' growing desire for any and all information about blacks, *The Negro Handbook* may, in actuality, have represented a guide to black America for white corporations. Regardless of the motivation behind the production of *The Negro Handbook*, this book conveyed a distinct bias against black-owned businesses:

> As the barriers of race are hurdled, the Negro consumer who was once the *private property* of the Negro owner and operator of hotels, restaurants, night clubs, and beauty and barber shops has turned with increasing *alacrity* to white establishments which offer, in many cases, extra services, luxury atmosphere, and a degree of glamour for the same dollar. Even the long held monopoly of burying the dead is no longer an exclusive function of the Negro mortician, increasingly white undertakers have learned that Negroes spend vast sums of money annually in "putting their people away right," and are wisely seeking this lucrative market.[9] (emphasis added)

TABLE 4.6
Advertising Revenue, Ebony *Magazine, 1962–1969*

1962	$3,630,804
1963	5,129,921
1964	5,641,895
1965	5,495,537
1966	7,020,279
1967	6,895,379
1968	8,551,463
1969	9,965,898

SOURCE: "Records of *Ebony* magazine," Publishers Information Bureau/Magazine Publishers of America, New York, New York.

This excerpt suggests that African American consumers have historically been ill treated by African American businesspeople. Moreover, it implies that this situation existed because black businesses did not have to compete with white businesses for black customer support.

Besides denigrating the historical relationship between black consumers and businesses, *The Negro Handbook* implied that white businesses who sought black customers were not only increasing their profits but were freeing thankful blacks from the stranglehold of unscrupulous black-owned enterprises. Thus, *The Negro Handbook* subtly assured U.S. corporations that seeking more black customers was both profitable and socially responsible. Considering this publication and Johnson's other activities, it seems clear why he was the leading black consultant to corporate America during the 1960s.

While Johnson urged large, white-owned businesses to take a greater interest in selling to African American consumers, D. Parke Gibson advised corporate America on how to most effectively reach this increasingly important market. D. Parke Gibson Associates, Inc., established in 1960, specialized in market research and public relations consulting. The company provided its services to myriad companies, including Avon Products, Coca Cola USA, Columbia Pictures, Greyhound, and the R. J. Reynolds Tobacco Company.[10] Gibson also wrote two books about the African American consumer market, *The $30 Billion Dollar Negro* (1969) and *$70 Billion in the Black* (1978).

An example of the advice Gibson's company gave its corporate clients appeared in the July 25, 1966, issue of *Sponsor*. Elsie Archer, director of the company's Women's Interest Bureau, published a brief article titled "How to Sell Today's Negro Woman." Archer offered the following insights about the black female consumer:

She wants advertising and marketing people to understand that her needs and desires are often different. For example, she does not want a blue-eyed suburban housewife telling her to use a particular product when she is faced with urban living. Particularly in the area of personal care products, advertisers should use extreme caution to avoid pricking the high sensitivity of the Negro woman. . . . One last word—never, never, under any circumstances refer to the Negro woman as "Negress" or "Negresses," a phrase guaranteed to produce an unfavorable reaction.[11]

About the same time Archer was instructing corporate America on how to best reach African American female consumers, the black community was in the throes of a dramatic shift in political orientation. Despite corporate America's increasing recognition of black consumers, as well as the passage of the Civil Rights Act of 1964 and the Voting Rights Act of 1965, a significant proportion of African Americans remained frustrated and angry about continuing racial injustice in the United States. The Watts rebellion of 1965, along with the immediate popularity of the term "Black Power" in 1966, reflected a growing militancy toward, and distrust of, white society.

The appearance of overt black nationalist sentiment during the mid-1960s initially confused corporate executives. Earlier in the decade, they had been led to believe that African Americans were preoccupied with trying to assimilate into mainstream U.S. society. For example, the October 4, 1963, issue of *Sales Management* featured an article titled "The Negro Market: Growing, Changing, Challenging," which not only surveyed basic characteristics of black consumers but projected their activities into the immediate future. Considering what *actually* happened, the prediction it contained turned out to be way off the mark: "Negroes will de-emphasize race consciousness and differences, and focus attention on social and cultural similarities compatible with the concept and practice of an integrated society."[12]

Despite their initial confusion, corporate marketers quickly adjusted their marketing campaigns aimed at African American consumers. Ad campaigns in the early 1960s that sought to promote the image of a racially desegregated society[13] were replaced with attempts to exploit blacks' growing sense of racial pride. The development of the "soul market" exemplified corporate America's attempt to adapt to African American consumers' political and cultural reorientation. Corporate marketers co-opted growing black pride by extolling the virtues of African American life and culture. Moreover, such things as "soul music" and "soul food" were promoted for both black and white consumption.[14]

From a business point of view, the "soul market" appeared to be especially profitable. U.S. corporations would reach not only African Americans but also faddish whites wanting to be viewed as "hip." Nonetheless, as this excerpt from a June 1969 article in *Sales Management* suggests, corporations seeking to exploit the "soul market" had to demonstrate some knowledge of African American consumers and their cultural world:

> A few weeks ago, 800 people sat down to a $100-a-plate "authentic Soul Food" supper in the Grand Ballroom of New York City's stately Waldorf-Astoria Hotel. After sampling the fried chicken, corn bread, collard greens, and sweet potato pie, TV star Bill Cosby, the charity affair's co-chairman, announced over the public address system that his meal had left an authentic grease ring around his mouth all right, but, he complained, "this is not how real Soul Food tastes." The Waldorf's flop with Soul is par for the course in the long, sad history of white encounters with virtually everything Negro. . . . Now unless they are plugging into today's Soul scene, many a marketer risks yet another blunder with the nation's 23 million blacks—and a sizable number of whites too.[15]

To help themselves "plug" into the "soul" scene, U.S. corporations once again relied on the expertise of black consultants. The black-owned Vince Cullers Advertising Agency of Chicago surfaced as the leading consultant to companies seeking to make their advertisements convey "soul." Perhaps Cullers's most noteworthy creation was a print advertisement used by the Lorillard Corporation to promote its Newport cigarette brand. A young bearded black man, wearing a dashiki, stood next to a huge pack of Newport cigarettes. The copy read" "Bold Cold Newport . . . a whole new bag of menthol smoking."[16]

For white-owned companies that desired to construct their own campaigns to reach "soul brothers and sisters," the June 1, 1969, issue of *Sales Management* offered a "primer," titled "Communicating Soul Style." Readers were assured that the following definitions were part of "the vocabulary Soul Brothers cherish":

Boss—The ultimate in compliments.

Burn—To improvise superlatively, in music or in life. "Burn baby" was shouted at singers years before the first ghetto riot.

Dap—impeccably dressed.

Down—If something is so good it's out of sight, or is the best ever, it's "down."

Fox—A beautiful woman.

Gig—A job. Synonyms are "slave" and "hustle."

Hog—A very large automobile.

Jive—A persuasive talker but one prone to lies or excuses.

Pig—A sadistic, sometimes also corrupt person, usually a policeman. Blacks rarely qualify.

Whale—To run very fast, think very clearly, or be the top man in your field.[17]

Despite such ludicrous discourse, which caricatured African American consumers of the late 1960s, some advertising professionals did indeed take black shoppers—and their concerns—seriously. Zebra Associates, a racially integrated advertising agency headed by an African American, Raymond A. League, represented one such instance.

The New York City-based Zebra Associates, established in 1969, viewed African American consumers as part of a larger inner-city consumer market. In a promotional document titled *Zebra Associates: Why We Are . . . What We Are . . . Who We Are*, the firm portrayed itself as the only advertising firm with both the sociological knowledge and the marketing expertise necessary to reach inner-city consumers.[18]

To build on its self-stated strengths regarding the inner-city consumer market, Zebra Associates early on established a training program to bring more African Americans into the advertising industry.[19] To further accentuate its standing as a community-minded enterprise, Zebra Associates instituted a program to have its professional staff assist small African American and Latino businesses, especially those operating in "hard-core" inner-city areas. As a June 19, 1969, Zebra press release, quoting League, described the program:

> Our first such account is Le Mans, a men's clothing store located at 715 Amsterdam Avenue, New York City. We recently completed a Father's Day promotion for the store and the results were highly successful. Frankly, we expected it. Our key people in publicity, promotion, and advertising worked on the promotion. Right now these same people are putting together a complete advertising campaign for Le Mans. Not only do we feel this is part of our responsibility to the community, but we believe that our staff benefits greatly from continuous first-hand experience in the heart of minority markets.[20]

As Zebra Associates sought to become a truly socially responsible company; urban black consumers, Zebra's primary interest, had become even more of an economic force in America's major markets. As Table 4.7 reveals,

TABLE 4.7
African American Population, Selected Cities, 1960, 1970

	1960	1970	Percentage of Total Population 1970
New York, New York	1,087,931	1,666,636	21.2
Chicago, Illinois	812,637	1,102,620	32.7
Detroit, Michigan	482,223	660,428	43.7
Philadelphia, Pennsylvania	529,240	653,791	33.6
Washington, D.C.	411,737	537,712	71.1
Baltimore, Maryland	325,589	420,210	46.4
Cleveland, Ohio	250,818	287,841	38.3
New Orleans, Louisiana	233,514	267,308	45.0
Atlanta, Georgia	186,464	255,051	51.3
St. Louis, Missouri	214,377	254,191	40.9
Memphis, Tennessee	184,320	242,513	38.9
Newark, New Jersey	138,035	207,458	54.2
Oakland, California	83,618	124,710	34.5

SOURCE: Harry A. Ploski and Warren Marr II, eds., *The Negro Almanac: A Reference Work on the Afro-American* (New York: Bellwether Company, 1976), 379.

the increasing number of African Americans living in U.S. cities by 1970 removed all doubts about the worth of courting black shoppers. Consequently, the next decade would witness even more aggressive attempts to influence the consumption patterns of African American urbanites. Moreover, it would become increasingly clear that, while many in the 1960s associated African Americans with the word "revolution," it was corporate marketers who had actually conducted a successful coup.

5

Blaxploitation and Big Business
American Corporations and Black
Consumers during the 1970s

It's something kind of funny,
How the man take your money,
He's shrewd as he can be,
In such a way you'll never see[1]

These lyrics, taken from the soundtrack to the enormously popular 1971 "blaxploitation" film *Superfly*, exemplify the relationship between
U.S. corporations and black consumers during the 1970s. This chapter fo-
cuses on three major marketing trends involving African Americans during
this period: Hollywood's successful attempt to reach the African American
consumer market through the blaxploitation film genre; the increased interest within white-owned companies in producing African American personal
care products (especially for black women); and the move by white-owned
insurance companies to secure black policyholders. In addition, we examine
the debate that went on throughout the 1970s over whether black-owned
magazines, newspapers, and advertising agencies were the most cost-effec-
tive means for corporate America to reach the African American consumer
market.

By 1970 African Americans were an overwhelmingly urban population.
The 1970 census revealed that 81 percent of the national African American
community resided in urban areas, compared to 72 percent of whites.[2] This
represented a continuation of post–World War II urbanization trends. So-
called white flight to the suburbs, during the 1950s and 1960s, contributed
to this demographic disparity.[3]

At the same time central cities across America were becoming increasingly black, Hollywood producers were desperate for ways to resuscitate an
ailing motion picture industry. Television's birth and growth had contributed

to a dramatic decline in U.S. movie attendance. For example, between 1946 and 1970 the average weekly attendance at U.S. theaters dropped from 90 to 17.7 million moviegoers.[4] Moreover, white flight to the suburbs included the abandonment of large downtown movie theaters.[5] Consequently, in what one contemporary observer called "one of the greatest ironies of our time,"[6] Hollywood turned to urban black consumers to help it avert financial ruin.

Although the African American consumer market became a prime target of Hollywood moguls during the early 1970s, the film industry, similar to other sectors of the American economy, had begun to take black consumers more seriously in the 1960s. The socioeconomic ramifications of the Civil Rights Movement, along with increasing African American urbanization, contributed to this reassessment.[7]

American movies at any given time tend to reflect contemporary social realities. During the early to mid-1960s, as the United States grappled with the implications of the Civil Rights Movement, Sidney Poitier emerged as a superstar black actor. Poitier's carefully crafted "respectable Negro" image had enormous economic implications. Both white and black moviegoers flocked to his movies, but for different reasons. For whites, Poitier's nonthreatening screen persona reassured them about the implications of racial desegregation. For blacks, Poitier's roles, while contrived, represented a welcome relief from earlier, overtly offensive, African American screen depictions.[8]

Just as existing social realities contributed to Poitier's preeminence during the early 1960s, a changed social reality contributed to his decline later in the decade. An increasingly militant and black nationalist–oriented African American population had grown tired of what one critic described as the "Sidney Poitier syndrome," which consisted of "a good boy in a totally white world, with no wife, no sweetheart, no woman to love or kiss, helping the white man solve the white man's problem."[9]

The former football star Jim Brown's rise in box office appeal during the late 1960s reflected a change in the taste of African American moviegoers. Brown, described as the "Black Buck Hero of a Separatist Age," seemed the antithesis of Poitier's screen persona. Unlike the nonthreatening, neutered Poitier, Brown virtually radiated unabashed physical prowess, including sexuality.[10] When market research in the late 1960s indicated that blacks, although approximately 15 percent of the U.S. population, represented nearly 30 percent of the moviegoing audience in American cities (where the largest theaters were located), Hollywood featured Brown in eleven films between 1967 and 1970.[11]

Jim Brown's popularity in urban black America set the stage for Melvin Van Peebles's pivotal 1971 film, *Sweet Sweetback's Baadasssss Song*. Shot in nineteen days, with a budget of $500,000, *Sweet Sweetback*, which chronicled the radicalization of a black stud, grossed more than $10 million within a couple months. This feat appeared all the more remarkable in that no major distributor would touch Van Peebles's film. Because of *Sweet Sweetback*'s overt sexual content, Van Peebles had to rely on Cinemation Industries, a small distribution house that handled only pornographic films, to distribute *Sweetback*. Although this film debuted in only two theaters, one in Detroit and one in Atlanta, it quickly broke box office records in both locales. Moreover, through word of mouth, *Sweet Sweetback* soon became a nationwide box office smash.[12]

Sweet Sweetback's financial success quickly captured the attention and the imagination of Hollywood studios. By 1971 most studios were reeling from a variety of financial woes. Besides facing a shrinking moviegoing audience (because of television) and the failure of most expensive "blockbuster" films to turn a profit, the American movie industry had to share the U.S. domestic market with an increasing number of foreign films. Studios, attempting to cover their losses, increased the amount of money they charged the television networks (Hollywood's most important secondary market) to lease motion pictures for re-exhibition. Yet, by the late 1960s, as the cost of the average film lease increased from $150,000 to $800,000, television executives, in apparent revolt, dramatically reduced the number of films they leased from Hollywood. Consequently, Hollywood was tottering on the edge of bankruptcy.[13]

If some film moguls, despite their problems and *Sweet Sweetback*'s overwhelming financial success, remained apprehensive about actively courting the black consumer market, Metro-Goldwyn-Mayer's success with another 1971 film, *Shaft*, removed all doubts about the potential profits associated with black-oriented films. *Shaft*, described as a black James Bond movie, proved to be an economic godsend to MGM (which had posted losses of $43 million for the previous two years). Costing only $1.8 million to produce, within a year *Shaft* had reportedly grossed more than $17 million.[14] Predictably, MGM's success with *Shaft* reverberated throughout the motion picture industry. In fact, by late 1972, nearly 25 percent of Hollywood's total planned production were black-oriented movies. By contrast, only 3 percent of Hollywood's 1970 releases were films primarily intended for African American audiences.[15]

Although Hollywood by 1972 had committed itself to actively woo the African American filmgoing public, the emphasis appeared to be on quantity, not quality. In fact, the overwhelming commercial success of the low-budgeted *Sweet Sweetback* and *Shaft* apparently convinced Hollywood producers that movies made for African American consumers did not need large budgets to be successful. Moreover, in the majority of the black-oriented movies of the 1970s, African American audiences were given extra heavy doses of the film industry's unholy trinity of sex, violence, and crime.[16] Thus, the term "blaxploitation," while not grammatically correct, does accurately convey the fleecing of African American moviegoers during this period.

Historical and psychological insight helps explain why black consumers were so easily manipulated by the film industry during the early 1970s. As one contemporary pundit noted:

> Right now, there is no question that the black audience, starved for years for films that see the world from a black point of view, is eating up just about anything that is slickly served. It is no accident that the most successful of the black films—both good and bad—invariably serve up heroes who "stick it to the Man." The intent of the new black films is not art but the commercial exploitation of the repressed anger of a relatively powerless community.[17]

In fact, many of the advertisements for blaxploitation films, with their stress on "getting Whitey," conveyed the message that African Americans, in film if not in reality, were "winning" in their efforts for full equality.[18]

Perhaps, the most profitable subgenre of blaxploitation films was the exaltation of the black male, or "Buckmania." Between 1972 and 1974, Hollywood, seeking to mimic the earlier success of the Jim Brown movies, *Sweet Sweetback*, and *Shaft*, churned out a number of black male "superhero" movies including *Trouble Man* (1972), *Black Gunn* (1972), *Slaughter* (1972), *Black Caesar* (1973), and *Hit Man* (1974). In these films, the African American male screen image underwent a dramatic transformation. The servile Stepin Fetchit and the polite Sidney Poitier were replaced by brash, super-studs who "put Whitey in his place." These films had special appeal to black audiences in that other well-recognized former athletes, notably Fred Williamson and Bernie Casey, joined Jim Brown in starring in many of these films.[19]

Although most of the films associated with "Buckmania" were relatively harmless fantasies, two films within this subgenre, *Superfly* (1972) and *The Mack* (1973), projected truly troubling images of black male achievement. *Superfly* sympathetically surveyed the activities of a Harlem cocaine dealer; *The Mack* sympathetically surveyed the activities of a Los Angeles pimp.

Significantly, *Superfly*, which featured a pernicious glorification of cocaine use, represented the brainchild of a consortium of black New York professionals, including the screenwriter Phillip Fenty and the director Gordon Parks Jr. Having produced *Superfly* independently on a shoestring budget of $350,000, the film's African American investors subsequently entered into a mutually lucrative distribution agreement with Warner Brothers. By 1974 *Superfly* had grossed more than $12 million. Moreover, the stylish fashions worn by the main character, Priest, were reproduced and marketed to urban black males seeking to emulate the character's on-screen persona.[20]

The Mack, which featured a gaudily dressed pimp named Goldie, also became a financial success. Grossing a reported $2.5 million in its first few weeks,[21] *The Mack* exploited the fantasies of some young black males about pimping more skillfully than Goldie handled his female charges in the movie.

Although all of the "Buckmania" films tended to characterize women (black and white) as little more than sexual playthings, *The Mack* appeared to be especially demeaning to women. In a paper read at the 1974 annual meeting of the National Medical Association, a black psychiatrist, discussing the black film boom, asserted that African American women in *The Mack* "came across as being so stupid and naive that the question of retardation has to be raised."[22]

Ironically, while African American women were devalued in "Buckmania" films, they were simultaneously exalted in the "Superbadd Supermama" movies. Films such as *Cleopatra Jones* (1973), *Coffy* (1973), and *Foxy Brown* (1974) featured black women who were the match of "Buckmania" stars in terms of wreaking violence and mayhem. In fact, Pam Grier, featured in *Coffy* and *Foxy Brown*, emerged as a major box office draw. Yet, in keeping with the "bottom line" mentality of blaxploitation movie producers, Grier's ample cleavage and athletic body, rather than her acting ability, were spotlighted.[23]

Despite Hollywood's apparent preoccupation with African American superstuds and Amazons in the 1970s, there were some black-oriented films that were both "respectable" and profitable. *Sounder* (1972), *Lady Sings the Blues* (1972), and *Uptown Saturday Night* (1974) epitomized such movies.

Sounder, which examined the plight of a family of African American sharecroppers during the 1930s, represented a welcome deviation from *Superfly*, *The Mack*, and other grossly sensationalist depictions of African American life. Unlike most blaxploitation films' fixation with "street life," where family relations were peripheral or nonexistent, *Sounder* squarely focused on the African American family and its resiliency. Moreover, *Sounder's* over-whelming financial success ($700,000 production cost; $13 million box of-fice gross in the first year) clearly indicated that there was, indeed, a market for quality, family-oriented black films.[24]

Motown's *Lady Sings the Blues*, like *Sounder*, provided African American consumers with a quality alternative to standard blaxploitation fare. The film, an inaccurate yet entertaining biography of the singer Billie Holliday, cost a then unheard of (for black-oriented films) $3 to $4 million. Moreover, unlike most blaxploitation films, which provided heavy doses of loveless sex-ual activity, *Lady Sings the Blues* offered African American filmgoers a gen-uine romantic melodrama. In addition, the gross box office receipts ($8.3 million in the first year) earned by *Lady Sings the Blues* were another demon-stration of the profit potential of meaningful black-oriented films.[25]

The Sidney Poitier–produced *Uptown Saturday Night*, which featured Poitier and an all-star cast including Bill Cosby, Harry Belafonte, Flip Wil-son, and Richard Pryor, represented a conscious attempt to counteract the negative images foisted on African American moviegoers by the blaxploita-tion genre. Trumpeted as a family film with "no foul language whatsoever,"[26] it emerged as the top grossing black-oriented film during the summer of 1974, earning $5.3 million between June and October.[27]

Despite the appeal of films such as *Sounder, Lady Sings the Blues*, and *Up-town Saturday Night*, most nonblaxploitation African American films were box office disasters during this period. To many African Americans, espe-cially the young, "Buckmania" and "Superbadd Supermama" films provided a communal cathartic release from everyday problems associated with racism.[28]

Although a significant number of African American consumers eagerly paid to view fictional racial retribution, an increasing number of blacks began to criticize what one scholar called the emotional and economic ex-ploitation of African American moviegoers.[29] The Beverly Hills/Hollywood branch of the NAACP, appropriately, emerged as a focal point of African American discontent with blaxploitation films. At its August 9, 1972, meet-ing, which included representatives from the Congress of Racial Equality (CORE), People United to Save Humanity (PUSH), the Urban League, the Southern Christian Leadership Conference (SCLC), and the Black Panther Party, the branch president, Junius Griffin, vociferously lashed out against the genre. Griffin described blaxploitation movies as a cancer that ate away at the moral fiber of the black community. Moreover, he told a standing-room-only audience:

These films continue taking our money, while feeding black people a forced diet of violence, murder, drugs, and rape. Yet, we go on paying millions of dollars for our own cultural genocide at the box offices of white folks' movie houses.[30]

Griffin closed his comments by calling for a coalition of the various groups present to challenge Hollywood. He added that the ensuing confrontation "should not exclude street demonstrations or any other means necessary."[31]

Griffin's appeal resulted in the establishment of the Committee Against Blaxploitation (CAB). This group primarily sought to raise the consciousness of both black consumers and the motion picture industry regarding film depictions of African Americans. CAB, among other things, demanded the right to preview scripts of future black films and urged Hollywood to hire more African Americans throughout the film industry.[32]

Hollywood producers, predictably, balked at approving CAB's proposed "watchdog" role. Unfortunately for CAB, two internal problems kept the coalition from formulating an effective reactive strategy. First, because there were diverse groups within CAB, disagreements arose as to what tactics the group should use to make its point to the movie industry. Some individuals within CAB, perhaps reacting to Griffin's strident rhetoric, espoused physical retribution against Hollywood moguls. This segment of the Committee Against Blaxploitation reportedly bombed the automobiles of several studio heads.[33]

Another philosophical and tactical disagreement within the organization dealt with whether CAB should give top priority to promoting affirmative action in Hollywood or to pressuring producers to immediately change film depictions of blacks. The fact that some CAB members were employed within the motion picture industry intensified this dilemma. This bloc within CAB apparently feared that Hollywood moguls would negatively react to pressure regarding African American film depictions by ceasing to make black-oriented movies altogether and eliminating African Americans from the film industry.[34]

Besides internal problems, the Committee Against Blaxploitation came under attack from white studio executives and some of the black actors and actresses associated with the blaxploitation genre. Samuel Z. Arkoff, head of American International Pictures, reacted to CAB by asserting, "I rather resent and I think blacks resent the implication of this organization that black audiences are somehow not able to recognize something that is degrading to themselves."[35] Similarly, Ron O'Neal, the star of the controversial film *Superfly*, declared:

> They're saying that they know better than the black people themselves what they should look at, that they're going to be the moral interpreters for the destiny of black people. I'm so tired of handkerchief-headed Negroes moralizing on the poor black man.[36]

Many African American actors, actresses, and screenwriters, Ron O'Neal notwithstanding, were sensitive to issues related to black screen depictions. On July 23, 1972, Lonnie Elder III, the screenwriter of the acclaimed film *Sounder*, organized a panel discussion in Los Angeles centered around the theme, "The Current Rash of New Black Films: A Blessing or a Curse?" The audience at the well-attended meeting, made up primarily of blacks in the motion picture industry, resulted in a public repudiation of the films that many on the panel and in the audience had been involved in. Shortly thereafter, these individuals, among them such notables as Ossie Davis, Cicely Tyson, and Denise Nichols, established an organization known as the Black Artists Alliance (BAA).[37] In an open letter that appeared in the August 18, 1972, issue of *Variety*, the group declared:

> We will no longer tolerate the cheap movies about us. Cheap in terms of the range of human emotions expressed, and cheap in their one-dimensional investigations of human problems. We will no longer tolerate the visual images of Black people that are paraded across the screen as little more than reincarnations of racist stereotypes which demean our women and make ludicrous caricatures of our men.[38]

Along with such organizations as the Committee Against Blaxploitation and the Black Artists Alliance, the black psychologist Dr. Alvin J. Poussaint emerged as a leading critic of the blaxploitation movie genre. In his widely discussed February 1974 *Psychology Today* article titled "Blaxploitation Movies: Cheap Thrills That Degrade Blacks," Poussaint assessed the psychological impact of blaxploitation films on the African American community. He sadly noted:

> Black youth in Brooklyn dramatically increased their use of cocaine after the movie Superfly glamorized the narcotic. . . . On the other side of the continent, practically the entire student body of a high school in Los Angeles is wearing the gold "coke" spoon necklace after a showing of the same movie. . . . The fluffed natural hairdo has undergone a dramatic change into the slick,

conk, style, as urban youth copy the hair styles of film characters. They mimic the stars' hip, violent personalities that suggest that success comes with a cool "rap," flashy clothes, big expensive cars, and a gun.[39]

Poussaint concluded his essay by calling for a nationwide African American boycott of movies to force Hollywood to "produce more positive forms of entertainment."[40]

In addition to objecting to blaxploitation movies' psychological manipulation of African American consumers, critics of this genre also decried the profits these films generated, primarily for white businessmen. White theater owners, especially, benefited from the black films of the early 1970s. Out of the approximately fourteen thousand motion picture theaters in the United States during this period, fewer than twenty were owned and operated by African Americans.[41]

A 1974 study of theaters in Chicago's Loop clearly revealed the profits associated with appealing to black consumers. The eight theaters in downtown Chicago featured black-oriented films (by themselves) fifty-five times. These engagements of a week or longer generated box office receipts of $7,716,534, or an average of $140,300 per engagement. By contrast, the eight Loop theaters featured white-oriented films (by themselves) ninety-four times. These movies generated box office receipts of $8,667,900, or an average of $92,212 per engagement. The same downtown Chicago movie houses featured Oriental martial arts films (by themselves) thirty-one times. This genre, also very popular among urban black moviegoers, generated box office receipts of $2,778,329, or an average of $89,624 per engagement. Combined, black-oriented and Oriental martial arts movies clearly generated the majority of box office receipts for Chicago Loop theater owners.[42] Furthermore, this scenario was repeated across America.[43]

The mostly white producers of blaxploitation movies also received significant returns for minimal investment. A widespread technique used to minimize "above-the-line" costs (such as salary for cast and directors) was the utilization of unknown talent for low wages.[44] The case of Richard Roundtree, the star of MGM's megahit *Shaft*, epitomized this phenomenon.

Although *Shaft* reportedly grossed more than $17 million from a $1.8 million investment, Roundtree received compensation of only $12,500. Had it not been for the vehement protestation of *Shaft*'s black director, Gordon Parks Sr., MGM would have paid Roundtree a salary of only $25,000 for *Shaft*'s 1972 sequel, *Shaft's Big Score*.[45] Roundtree did, after intense negotiations, ultimately receive $50,000 for this reprise role. Yet, his experiences demonstrated that the term "blaxploitation" referred to the exploitation of black actors and actresses as well as black consumers.

A survey of the film credits of fifty-three black-oriented films made between January 1973 and August 1974 further documents white control of the production (and profits) of blaxploitation films. Only six, or 11 percent, of these films were produced by African Americans.[46]

While whites apparently received a lion's share of the profits associated with the black-oriented movies of the 1970s, some African Americans did materially benefit from this phenomenon. Besides Melvin Van Peebles's stunning success with *Sweet Sweetback's Baadasssss Song*, two African American musician-songwriters, Isaac Hayes and Curtis Mayfield, achieved far-reaching success during this period.

Part of the formula associated with attracting black consumers to blaxploitation movies was the utilization of popular African American recording artists to develop film scores. Isaac Hayes's soundtrack album to the 1971 film *Shaft* both earned him an Academy Award and generated several million dollars in sales. Likewise, Curtis Mayfield's 1972 soundtrack album for *Superfly* went to platinum, with more than a million sold.[47] Other notable blaxploitation soundtracks that successfully encouraged African American consumers to make two purchases (movie ticket and album) included Marvin Gaye's *Trouble Man* (1972), Willie Hutch's *The Mack* (1973), and James Brown's *Black Caesar* (1973).

Despite the profits associated with the blaxploitation film genre, by the mid-1970s a number of factors had contributed to its demise. First, as the sheer novelty of black-oriented films began to wear off, African American consumers became more discerning. This was crucial in terms of profits, because few whites patronized these films. In fact, the relatively disappointing box office receipts of two 1973 sequels, *Shaft in Africa* and *Superfly T.N.T.*, alerted Hollywood producers that blaxploitation films' most profitable days were probably behind them.[48]

Another factor that contributed to the decline of the blaxploitation film genre was Hollywood's discovery that it could reach the African American consumer market through quality "mainstream" movies. For instance, market surveys revealed that black moviegoers represented nearly 35 percent of the audience for such megahits as *The Godfather* (1972) and *The Exorcist* (1973).[49]

Perhaps the final deathblow to the blaxploitation film genre was Hollywood's realization that African American consumers would enthusiastically support "mainstream" films with blacks in prominent supporting roles. Two

1976 films, *Rocky* (which featured Carl Weathers) and *Silver Streak* (which featured the inimitable Richard Pryor), attracted large numbers of both black and white filmgoers. In fact, in the late 1970s Hollywood, sensing yet another profitable trend, subsequently created a number of "crossover" films to spotlight the multitalented Pryor.[50]

On the surface, the blaxploitation film genre appeared to have been just another Hollywood craze. Yet, black-oriented movies, made between 1971 and 1974 seem to have had a profound subliminal effect on the African American psyche. First, the sense of racial unity generated by the Civil Rights Movement gave way to the "rugged individualism" of such movie characters as Priest, Goldie, and Shaft. Furthermore, the films stimulated conspicuous consumption as young black males sought to emulate the lifestyles of these dubious film icons.

In sum, the 1970s blaxploitation film genre represented an extremely effective means to more fully incorporate blacks as American consumers. Hindsight suggests that the millions of dollars blacks spent visiting a fantasy world of African American triumph and achievement might have been better spent trying to effect changes in the real world.

Although Hollywood may have denigrated the role of African American women during the 1970s, other sectors of the U.S. economy, especially the personal care products industry, took black female consumers very seriously. This interest in African American women had its basis in census data that revealed their unique and vital economic role.

At the beginning of the decade, 29 percent of black families were female-headed, compared to 9 percent of white families. Moreover, 54 percent of married black women worked, compared to 38 percent of white wives. Even more startling, from the standpoint of corporate marketers, was 1970 census data that indicated that married working black women below the age of 35 and living in the North or West actually earned more than their white counterparts.[51]

Black women's economic status during the early 1970s could be directly linked to enhanced African American socioeconomic mobility associated with the Civil Rights Movement. Moreover, because 55 percent of black women in the labor force had at least a high school diploma (compared to 45 percent of black men), African American women were especially well situated to take advantage of new employment opportunities. In addition, commencing in the late 1960s, there existed an increased demand for clerical workers, teachers, and nurses—occupations that traditionally attracted women.[52]

Corporate marketers of women's beauty and personal care products subsequently sought to link African American women's enhanced sense of self-worth with increased spending on beauty and personal care products. This association, while focused on black females, was not unique. American women, regardless of race, had long been socialized to equate self-worth with personal appearance. Still, the 1970s campaign by the beauty and personal care products industry to woo African American women was especially significant in that it sought to sell black women both "beauty" and "status." One important consequence of this accelerated campaign was the decline of black-owned companies, which had historically served the needs of black women.

A June 11, 1973, article in the trade industry publication *Chemical Marketing Reporter* titled "Beauty Chemicals: The Ethnic Market" provided a cogent survey of the evolving black beauty products market. Quoting Alfred Forney, a prominent black makeup artist, it cited black women's need for race-specific beauty products:

> Our history is that we were always getting scrubbed down and greased down . . . we have the same problems with dryness and oiliness as do whites, except that our skin is sensitive in maintaining a proper oil and moisture balance and thus we especially need a mild astringent. Many astringents offered by regular lines are found too harsh for black women, producing an undesirable "ashy" look to the skin.[53]

Forney went on to predict (correctly) that beauty products for black women would be most effectively marketed in department stores rather than in self-service drug stores. Such a marketing strategy would provide interaction between the consumer and a knowledgeable salesperson. Moreover, black women were becoming increasingly amenable to premium quality and higher-priced cosmetics.[54]

The Flori Roberts Company, established in 1965, was one of the first companies to take advantage of black women's increased interest in higher-priced beauty products. Roberts, a white woman with an extensive background in the fashion industry, started her company because of her knowledge of the problems faced by black models seeking facial makeup that was compatible with their skin tones and texture. With both financial and technical assistance from her physician husband, Roberts began her product line, which, from the beginning, was sold only in department stores. By the mid-1970s, Flori Roberts Products had satisfied customers throughout the United States and in Africa.[55]

Another important player in the premium black beauty products market in the 1970s was the Fashion Fair Cosmetics Company. This company was an outgrowth of *Ebony* magazine and its popular *Ebony* Fashion Fair Show. The models with this traveling fashion show, along with their fashion coordinators, regularly mixed and blended various cosmetics to devise a look that satisfied them. After each show, women in the audience inquired as to how they could duplicate the "look" of the models.[56]

Because of this interest, the *Ebony* Fashion Fair Show, using *Ebony* magazine as a test-marketing venue, offered black women a relatively high-priced kit containing samples of the exact cosmetics used by its models. Black women's overwhelmingly positive response to this campaign convinced the *Ebony* Fashion Fair Show to accentuate its new Fashion Fair Cosmetics division. Along with an ongoing ad campaign in *Ebony*, Fashion Fair Cosmetics, by the mid-1970s, were being marketed in such upscale department stores as Bloomingdale's in New York City, Marshall Field in Chicago, and Neiman-Marcus in Dallas.[57]

Although there existed a sizable market for high-priced black cosmetics during the 1970s, the beauty and personal care products industry did not ignore the needs of less affluent African American women. The August 1977 issue of *American Druggist* featured an article titled "Selling Black Cosmetics Proves a Tricky Business," which provided advice to drugstores on how best to reach black women seeking more economical products. The article advised its readers that if African Americans made up at least 30 percent of the population surrounding their business locations, they should carry black cosmetics . The trade journal, however, was far less definitive in advising how black cosmetics should be displayed. On the one hand, some retailers believed that black cosmetics should be featured in a separate department. Others felt that black cosmetics should be included within the regular cosmetic department. Moreover, there existed the question whether black beauty products produced by black companies or similar products produced by white companies yielded the greatest profits for store owners.[58] Despite leaving this question unanswered, *American Druggist* assured its readers that stores with a significant African American consumer base would profit by carrying *some* black beauty products.[59]

Another visible force in the moderately priced black cosmetics market was the venerable Avon Products Company. Avon, like other companies in the beauty and personal care products industry, came to view African American women as a lucrative market to be tapped. The company believed that black consumer support would compensate for the declining

TABLE 5.1
Advertising Revenue, Essence Magazine, 1974–1980*

Year	Advertising Revenue
1974	$1,868,788
1975	2,389,360
1976	4,065,712
1977	4,607,807
1978	6,183,934
1979	6,471,982
1980	7,957,772

*Advertising revenue figures for the years 1970–1973 are unavailable.
SOURCE:"Records of Essence Magazine," Publishers Information Bureau, Inc./Magazine Publishers of America, New York, New York.

profits associated with its traditional, white-oriented "Avon calling" campaign.[60]

An examination of African American expenditures on personal care products during the 1970s helps explain corporate interest in this phenomenon. In 1972 blacks spent a reported $350,000,000 on beauty and personal care items. Five years later, this figure had skyrocketed to approximately $750,000,000.[61]

Even before the 1970s, market research had revealed that African Americans spent proportionately more on beauty and personal care products than whites. Yet, as the disposable income of blacks, especially women, rose in the 1970s, the disparity between black and white spending on personal care items dramatically increased. In fact, some surveys estimated that African Americans, by the mid- to late 1970s, spent approximately 40 percent more of their disposable income on beauty and luxury items than did whites.[62] As one corporate marketer told *Chemical Week* for a June 8, 1977, article related to the burgeoning black cosmetics industry: "Blacks have always spent a lot on their looks. It's a cheap way to show opulence. If you look great, who's to know you haven't a dime in your pocket?"[63]

Essence, established as a magazine for black women in 1970, also profited from the enhanced presence of black women in the U.S. marketplace during this decade. *Essence*'s rising advertising revenues between 1974 and 1980 (see Table 5.1) suggests that corporate marketers came to view the magazine as an ideal mechanism to reach black female consumers.

To reinforce *Essence*'s strategic role as an important intermediary between corporate America and black female consumers, the magazine's first publisher, Clarence Smith, and its beauty and fashion editor, Susan Taylor, regularly urged American corporations to take black female consumers more seriously. An interview with Smith and Taylor that appeared in the December 1977 issue of *Product Marketing*, a national newsletter surveying the cosmetics, toiletries, fragrances, and drug industries, focused on their efforts.

In an article titled "*Essence* Urges R & D for Blacks," Taylor forcefully urged cosmetic marketers to commit more resources toward developing additional hair care and facial makeup products for black women.[64] Smith, for his part, suggested that U.S. corporations were hurting their profitability by not conducting substantive market research related to black female consumers:

> In not studying the purchasing habits of Black women, marketers are overlooking an important aspect of the Black women's psyche. They don't see how much Black women are competing with White women to prove they are as good or better. Since childhood they have been inundated with media images of beauty as the White woman. They want to be as attractive as possible and show the Black man that her beauty is fine. Marketers should see that she is overcompensating in buying products to dispel negative stereotypes.[65]

By the late 1970s, U.S. corporations began to fully heed Taylor and Smith's advice. While this move resulted in more consumer choices for African American women, black-owned producers of African American personal care products found themselves losing ground in an increasingly crowded and competitive marketplace.

The experiences of the Chicago-based Johnson Products Company epitomized the problems faced by black beauty entrepreneurs during this period. Ironically, before the late 1970s, Johnson Products Company represented one of the more spectacular instances of African American business success. The originator of the popular "Ultra Sheen" and "Afro Sheen" product lines, in 1973 the company became the first black business to be listed on a major stock exchange.[66]

Johnson Products' fortunes began to change for the worse in 1975 after it was forced to sign a Federal Trade Commission consent decree acknowledging safety problems with its popular "Ultra Sheen Permanent Creme Relaxer." According to the FTC, this product contained sodium hydroxide, which could cause both hair loss and eye and skin damage. The Federal Trade Commission mandated that Johnson Products place a special warning on all its hair-straightening products warning consumers that improper use could result in eye and skin damage.[67]

George Johnson, the president of Johnson Products, agreed to the consent decree with the distinct impression that his competitors, including the white-owned Revlon Company, would quickly be forced to follow suit. To his surprise and disappointment, Revlon was not required to place a similar warning in its advertising or on its comparable products until nearly two years later. In the meantime, black women consumers were given the impression that Revlon's "French Perm" and "Realistic Protein Creme Relaxer," which also contained sodium hydroxide, were safer products than Johnson Products' "Ultra Sheen Permanent Creme Relaxer."[68]

An understandably bitter Johnson later asserted that the FTC's actions represented a conscious attempt to inhibit black business development. In a 1978 speech to black beauticians, he alluded to an even broader attempt to diminish the influence of black entrepreneurs in the black hair care industry:

> White people, for the most part, ignored this industry as long as they thought it was a nickel and dime business. We were overlooked or else looked down upon as just "nigger business." It was too little to be involved with or concerned about. Today, they are making strong efforts to take over every level of the kinky hair business. They want the manufacturing business. They want the beauty shop business. And they want the beauty jobber business.[69]

Like black-owned companies in the black personal care products industry, black-owned insurance companies faced increased white competition during the 1970s. For most of the twentieth century, white-owned companies had disdained the black consumer market. Yet, as the collective African American standard of living began to rise at mid-century, large insurers began to actively seek black clients. A technique widely used by white-owned insurance companies to make inroads among black consumers was to recruit the top agents from black insurance companies by offering them higher pay.[70]

Perhaps, the major problem facing African American insurance companies during the 1970s was the need to adjust to a new social reality. The Black Power Movement of the late 1960s, with its emphasis on "buying black," had provided black insurers a temporary respite from increased white competition. Still, many African American consumers welcomed the wider range of buying choices associated with increased racial desegregation. As a contemporary analysis of the black insurance industry noted:

> There is another side to the "buy black" coin. It is "buy white." Many blacks evidently feel that whites and white companies give superior products and superior services. There exists, moreover, among some blacks the feeling that dealing with white companies constitutes a status symbol, a badge of "arrival" for upwardly mobile blacks.[71]

African American insurance companies' heavy reliance on industrial insurance further hindered their efforts to impress black consumers. Industrial insurance, a form of coverage characterized by the weekly collection of premiums in policyholders' homes and by low policy face values, had long been deemphasized by mainstream insurance companies. By 1970, only 2.9 percent of all U.S. companies provided industrial coverage. On the other hand, industrial insurance represented 43.9 percent of black companies' total insurance in force.[72]

Despite the disadvantages of industrial insurance, which included high administrative costs that were passed on to consumers, some African American insurance company executives reminded their critics that this form of coverage represented the cornerstone of the historical personal relationship between black insurers and their policyholders. Still, as the 1970s unfolded, it seemed increasingly clear that African American consumers were becoming less interested in nostalgia and more concerned about contemporary money saving.[73]

Along with their seemingly unwise focus on industrial insurance, the relatively small size of black insurers hampered their attempts to compete for prospective black policyholders. By 1978, the combined assets of the top thirty-nine African American insurance companies stood at $635 million.[74] By contrast, in the same year, the assets of Prudential and Metropolitan Life were $50 billion and $42 billion, respectively.[75] Because of economies of scale, large mainstream insurers were able to offer cost-conscious African American consumers more economical coverage than their black competitors.

The mounting problems of black insurance companies were graphically illustrated in the influential *Best's Review*'s yearly ranking of the premium income of the top five hundred U.S. and Canadian insurance companies. Between 1970 and 1980, the ranking of the top six African American insurers steadily declined (see Table 5.2). Moreover, the downward spiral of black insurance companies continued during the 1980s.

The 1970s also challenged African American entrepreneurs in the realms of mass media and advertising. This appeared especially ironic because black media outlets, both radio and print, along with black advertising agencies, had previously been viewed as ideal vehicles to better reach African American consumers.

During the early 1970s, black-owned media outlets, along with black-owned advertising agencies, were generally acknowledged by corporate America to be the most effective means to reach potential African American customers. For example, the New York-based black-owned UniWorld

TABLE 5.2

Ranking of the Top Six African American Insurance Companies
within Best's Listing of the 500 Leading Insurance Companies in Total Premium Income,
1970, 1972, 1974, 1976, 1978, 1980*

	1970	1972 1980	1974	1976	1978	
North Carolina Mutual	160	167	166	188	195	211
Golden State Mutual	292	264	271	296	306	336
Atlanta Life	248	284	306	339	338	387
Universal Life	296	315	339	360	389	424
Supreme Life	395	409	401	395	421	454
Chicago Metropolitan	430	443	453	472	492	—

*North Carolina Mutual is based in Durham, North Carolina; Golden State Mutual is based in Los Angeles, California; Atlanta Life is based in Atlanta, Georgia; Universal Life is based in Memphis, Tennessee; Supreme Life, once based in Chicago, Illinois, no longer exists; Chicago Metropolitan, once based in Chicago, Illinois, merged with Atlanta Life in 1990.
SOURCE: *Best's Review: Life/Health Insurance Edition* 72 (July 1971): 41–42; 74 (July 1973): 40–41; 76 (August 1975): 36–37; 78 (August 1977): 36–37; 80 (August, 1979): 37–38; 82 (September, 1981): 71–74.

Group advertising agency received widespread positive recognition for co-ordinating the nationwide publicity campaign associated with MGM's 1971 megahit *Shaft*. Working closely with black newspapers, magazines, and radio stations, UniWorld Group's efforts contributed mightily to *Shaft*'s overwhelming popularity (and profitability).[76]

Considering widely held beliefs regarding the efficacy of using black-owned media outlets and advertising agencies to reach African American consumers, an April 4, 1972, *Advertising Age* article with the provocative title "Black Media Less Efficient, Y & R Says" sent severe shock waves throughout the corporate advertising community. A report prepared early in 1972 for General Foods by the Young & Rubicam advertising agency questioned the efficiency of using black magazines and newspapers to reach African American consumers. Young & Rubicam told General Foods that black (specialized market) magazines such as *Ebony*:

> are all more expensive on a cost-per-thousand total readers basis than books like *Family Circle, Reader's Digest, TV Guide, Life, Parade,* and others. . . . *Ebony* cannot match the black readership of *TV Guide* and is almost equaled by *Life* and *Parade*. The vast reach of these publications makes them a vehicle of broad appeal cutting across all demographic lines.[77]

Referring to black-owned newspapers, Young & Rubicam informed General Foods that:

> in many instances, the black newspaper cannot deliver the coverage of the market that is available through the major city daily. For example, in New

York, the New York *Daily News* attracts over 1,000,000 black adult readers every day, certainly many more than the *Amsterdam News* with its 80,000 weekly circulation.[78]

Predictably, the black-owned media industry quickly responded to the concerns raised in the controversial Young & Rubicam report. Not surprisingly, John H. Johnson, the "Godfather" of African American media entrepreneurs, emerged as this group's primary (and most visible) advocate.

After quickly denigrating Young & Rubicam's assessment of African American media resources,[79] Johnson spent the rest of the decade trying to reconvince corporate marketers of black media's unique and indispensable role in reaching African American consumers. His April 16, 1979, *Advertising Age* article titled "Black Media Fills Needs Not Recognized Elsewhere" declared:

> New markets are constantly being formed and new media are constantly being created to reach them. Black media already exist. The advertiser does not have to reinvent them. . . . To the advertiser in search of an all-purpose medium, in the interest of media efficiency, I say that the quest will remain elusive. . . . At present, I see no prospect of an all-purpose medium that works to the exclusion of black media. We are a nation of special markets![80]

Although Johnson and others were apparently able to confirm the usefulness of black-owned media to corporate marketers, the fortunes of black-owned advertising agencies diminished as the 1970s progressed. Early on, such notable African American firms as New York's UniWorld Group, Zebra Associates, Howard Sanders Advertising and Public Relations; Chicago's Vince Cullers Advertising; and Washington, D.C.'s New Wave Communications, had carved out a comfortable niche within the advertising industry.[81] Yet, by the late 1970s, the world of black-owned advertising agencies had been turned topsy turvy.

First and foremost, while black-owned agencies were thought to possess special insights regarding African American consumers, a significant number of the accounts they received could be characterized as "corporate reparations." Unfortunately for black-owned advertising agencies, by the mid- to late 1970s, when American business was grappling with a recession, many companies economized by severing their ties with black-owned advertising agencies. As one black advertising agency executive observed: "Whatever is left of the guilt market is very low now. On a long-range basis, you can't build a business on the white man's guilt."[82]

In addition to facing declining revenues from white corporations seeking to assist black business development, black advertising agencies, like their cohorts in the insurance industry, helplessly watched their best employees defect to larger mainstream companies for better pay. A trend, led by Young & Rubicam, was established in which large advertising agencies established in-house ethnic marketing divisions to compete with the black-owned agencies.[83]

To make matters worse for black-owned advertising agencies (and black advertising professionals), doubt arose as to whether these companies (and individuals) actually possessed the special expertise they claimed regarding black consumers. A May 16, 1977, *Advertising Age* article examining African American ad agencies noted: "Sociologists who explain race in America today as a class rather than a skin color phenomenon might wonder to what extent a black executive living in, say, Scarsdale, is in touch with the black masses."[84]

Despite black-owned advertising agencies' overall problems, some African American firms, most notably UniWorld of New York, Proctor & Gardner and Burrell Advertising of Chicago, and Vanguard Advertising of Minneapolis, remained solid operations that were holding their own in a volatile environment.[85] Still, as the 1970s drew to a close, the situation of black advertising agencies, like that of black insurance and personal care products companies, appeared tenuous. Ironically, African Americans' increasing importance as consumers resulted in limited rewards for most African American businesses.

Just as the 1970s clearly revealed that some black-owned businesses (such as *Essence*) fared much better than others in a changing economic environment, it also became increasing clear that some African American individuals were more prosperous than others. Although most blacks continued to reside in financially unstable inner-city enclaves, there also existed a numerically significant African American middle class whose taste in consumer goods differed, sometimes dramatically, from that of their less affluent cohorts. This distinct segmentation within the black consumer market did not escape the notice of corporate marketers. Consequently, during the next decade, an even wider spectrum of American businesses sought to attract black shoppers and clients.

6

A Tale of Two Markets

African American Consumers during the 1980s

It was the best of times, it was the worst of times.[1]

This quotation from Charles Dickens's classic work *A Tale of Two Cities* accurately reflects the situation of African American consumers during the 1980s. While aggregate black income increased from $183 billion to $242 billion between 1978 and 1988, other census data, along with the introduction of the words "underclass" and "buppie" to the national vocabulary, demonstrated growing class distinctions within the black community. This "market segmentation" prompted corporate marketers to develop class-specific advertising aimed at African Americans. The 1980s also witnessed the accelerated marketing of liquor and tobacco in the black community. The overt (and sometimes outrageous) manipulation of black consumers by tobacco and liquor companies had, by the end of the decade, generated an angry, national response among African Americans of all classes. In addition, revelations in the late 1980s concerning the lack of substantive black economic progress, despite increased consumerism, had a sobering effect on thoughtful African Americans.

One of the illusions to grow out of the Civil Rights Movement was that all African Americans had gained from remedial changes in U.S. society. Yet, by the 1980s, it became increasingly clear that not all blacks were benefitting equally from the partial desegregation of America. The national African American community during the 1980s consisted of readily observable "haves" and "have-nots." Moreover, the socioeconomic distance between the two groups appeared to be increasing. Predictably, this significant development attracted the attention of journalists, scholars, and corporate marketers.[2]

During the early 1980s, African Americans, especially those without college training, were hard hit in a recession-riddled economy. In 1980 the black unemployment rate hovered around 13 percent, compared to a nationwide peak rate of 7.8 percent. By October 1982 the official black unemployment rate stood at 20 percent, but the National Urban League's "Hidden Unemployment Index," which factored in discouraged blacks who had ceased looking for work, placed the actual African American unemployment rate at nearly twice the U.S. Labor Department's figures.[3]

Although the U.S. economy began to rebound in 1983, economic improvement, to use the parlance of the times, barely "trickled down" to the African American community. According to government statistics, the unemployment rate among African American men, in the significant age cadre of 18–34 dropped from 33.0 percent in 1982 to 29.3 percent in 1983. Yet, among African American women in the same age group, the unemployment rate increased from 27.0 percent in 1982 to 35.7 percent in 1983.[4] The black economist Denys Vaughn-Cooke, in a widely read essay published in 1984, responded to these and other similar data by charging the Reagan administration with adherence to a public policy agenda that consciously worked to the detriment of the black working class:

> The administration, obviously in its concern about inflation and its acceptance of an overall unemployment rate of 6 or 7% as the point at which inflation accelerates, has accepted high rates of black unemployment as the price for this inflation control. (Historically, black unemployment has been just over twice as high as white unemployment) ... it now seems to be accepted in formulation of public policy that blacks will continue to have an unemployment rate of 14% or more.[5]

Despite Vaughn-Cooke's prediction, the official black unemployment rate did not remain at 14 percent or above for the rest of the 1980s. In fact, the official 1989 African American unemployment rate stood at 11.3 percent. Nevertheless, the economic position of African Americans during the decade of the 1980s appeared disproportionately bleak. For example, although aggregate black unemployment declined between 1983 and 1989, the gap between black and white unemployment rates actually increased during this period. In fact, the ratio of black to white unemployment in 1989 (11.3 percent versus 4.5 percent) stood at a decade-high 2.5 to 1.[6]

Perhaps the most significant consequence of the high black unemployment rates of the 1980s was the extremely large percentage of African Americans possessing incomes below the poverty level. At the peak of the 1982 recession, a mind-boggling 35.6 percent of blacks, compared to 12 percent of whites, were officially categorized as poor (a ratio of 2.85 to 1). In 1988 comparative black/white poverty figures stood at 31.6 to 10.1 percent (a ratio of 3.13 to 1). These figures, along with comparative unemployment statistics, indicate that the economic recovery of the late 1980s all but passed a significant number of African American consumers by.[7]

The widespread economic deprivation in the African American community puts into better perspective the actions of certain cigarette and liquor companies during the 1980s. The consumption of cigarettes and especially alcohol have historically been viewed as effective short-term escapes from the sometimes harsh realities of everyday living. For a significant number of African Americans during the 1980s, "reality" consisted of protracted, demoralizing unemployment. In this context, the accelerated marketing of cigarettes and alcohol in urban black enclaves could be construed as an attempt to profit from human misery. But, before we examine this phenomenon in depth, let's look at the proverbial "other side of the street" in black America during these years.

Except for the dramatic urbanization of African Americans, perhaps the most significant demographic change among blacks in mid- to late-twentieth-century America was the increase in the number of individuals categorized as middle or upper class. In 1960 only 13 percent of black workers had middle-class earnings. By the late 1980s one third of all black households had solidly middle-class incomes, and one in ten African American families could be characterized as upper class.[8]

The intensification of class differences among African Americans during the 1980s, while significant, merely reflected long-standing segmentation in the black community. During slavery, free blacks, along with house slaves and slave artisans, represented an elite segment of the African American population. Moreover, these individuals and their descendants tended to maintain their status in post-Emancipation black America.[9]

The growth of the mid- to late-twentieth-century black middle and upper classes could be directly linked to the Civil Rights Movement. Although ongoing, widespread black poverty demonstrated that African American gains were far from universal, a significant number of blacks did, indeed, benefit from the campaign to desegregate America. For instance, the years 1960–1980 witnessed a dramatic increase in the number of African Americans with a college education. During this period, the proportion of blacks 25 years and older with some college education nearly tripled from 7 to 20 percent.[10] These educational gains manifested themselves in occupational advances for African Americans.

During the 1970s, the number of African Americans in the professions and the skilled trades increased at a rate higher than that for whites. For example, the number of black professional and technical workers increased by 55 percent, compared to 34 percent for whites. Even more dramatic, the number of African American managers and administrators grew by 69 percent, compared to 34 percent for whites. Yet, despite these gains, blacks continued to hold a relatively small proportion of upper-echelon jobs. In 1980, 53 percent of all white men held such positions, whereas 31 percent of black men and 19 percent of black women were in professional, managerial, or skilled trade positions.[11]

Besides education attainment and occupational mobility, the majority of 1980s black middle-class families during this period featured married couples. While 57 percent of all African American families in 1979 were headed by married couples, 82 percent of middle-class black families included a husband and a wife. Moreover, in the vast majority of African American middle- and upper-income families, both spouses were in the labor force (either working or looking for work). For example, data for 1979 revealed that 78 percent of black wives in middle-class families were in the labor force, compared to 58 percent of their white counterparts.[12]

In recent decades the "American Dream" has become associated with getting a college education, a solid job, and a house in the suburbs. Although middle-class blacks in the 1980s attained the first two elements of the "holy trinity" of success, they continued, for the most part, to reside in central cities. In 1983, only 29 percent of middle- and upper-income African Americans resided in suburban areas, conversely, 22 percent of middle- and upper-income whites resided in American central cities. Ongoing white racism undoubtedly accounted for some of this discrepancy. Still, a significant number of middle- and upper-income blacks, despite their enhanced educational and occupational status, were not culturally or politically predisposed to reside in predominantly white suburban areas.[13]

One of the decade's most illuminating profiles of African American economic achievement was a November 1989 *American Demographics* article titled "In the Black." This essay, which focused on affluent blacks, began by asserting:

> Affluence means different things to different people, but most would agree that a yearly income of $50,000 or more puts a family in a reasonably affluent position. A growing number of blacks are in this position. The number of affluent black households grew from 212,000 in 1967 to 764,000 in 1987—a 360 percent increase.[14]

The bulk of "In the Black" consisted of an analysis of a statistical composite created by the Claritas Corporation of Alexandria, Virginia, titled "Cluster 31" or "Black Enterprise." Claritas used a sophisticated computer program to identify "Cluster 31" (and other clusters) by grouping all U.S. zip codes and census tracts into forty clusters on the basis of their demographics. The company then ranked the clusters by size and affluence and gave each a catchy name. "Cluster 31" or "Black Enterprise" ranked eleventh in affluence.[15]

Moving beyond just quantitative analysis, *American Demographics* provided the following qualitative assessment of "Cluster 31":

> They live in unpretentious middle-class neighborhoods like Washington's Capital Heights, Chicago's Auburn Park, Atlanta's South Dekalb, or Los Angeles' Crenshaw. But their tastes run to convertibles, expensive stereos, and sailing. If you're in cluster 31, you pursue the good life with the enthusiasm of someone who's just discovered it.[16]

Besides identifying general characteristics of "Cluster 31" inhabitants, *American Demographics* provided specific information that could be used by corporate marketers:

> Overall, just 0.9 percent of all households bought a new convertible last year, according to Simmons Market Research Bureau. In cluster 31, 2.5 percent did. This group is also more likely than average to sail, drink scotch, to buy classical music, to smoke menthol cigarettes, to own a satellite dish, to belong to a book club, and to travel by rail. . . . Cluster 31 adults spend heavily on dress shirts, overcoats, slacks, and sweaters, and they are more likely than average to remodel their bathrooms, and to have two or more telephone lines in their homes. . . . Affluent blacks will respond to marketers who affirm both their social status and their heritage.[17]

In addition to *American Demographics*, which is not generally known for giving advice on how to reach African American consumers, conventional marketing publications sought to provide their readers with profitable insights about black America's middle and upper classes. A survey of these periodicals revealed a wide range of opinion, sometimes contradictory, on how to best reach black middle- and upper-class consumers.

An example of the varied opinions on this subject is the May 18, 1981, *Advertising Age* article titled "Product Appeal: No Class Barrier." The essay begins by suggesting that income disparities within the African American community do not necessarily reflect class differences among blacks. To support this assertion, the author offers the following:

As president of the country's largest black advertising agency, with $20,000,000 annual billings, Tom Burrell lives in one of the most exclusive condominiums on Chicago's posh Gold Coast. And though he can afford to dine nightly on all manner of *haute cuisine*, he often opts for such "soul foods" as collard greens, cornbread and cabbage smothered with onions. . . .[18] [original emphasis]

While it's debatable whether "soul food" is the great leveler of African American society, this assertion provides an important window into the psyches of some middle- and upper-income blacks (who came of age during the 1960s Civil Rights and Black Power Movements) in the 1980s. Most had long abandoned dashikis and big Afros for a more conservative appearance. Yet, many still, if more subtly, adhered to notions of racial consciousness. Moreover, it is plausible to assume that persons associated in the 1960s with black activism, which often charged the black middle class with being "window-dressing Negroes" or "Uncle Toms," may have felt uneasy about their own movement into the American economic mainstream. Consequently, in the 1980s some middle- and upper-class African Americans sought to minimize the existence of class differences among blacks. In the advertising industry this sentiment, whose chief proponent was Burrell Advertising, came to be known as "cross-class" marketing.[19]

Perhaps the best-known Burrell creation in this genre was the "Misting" campaign for Canadian Mist whiskey. These ads featured an attractive and well-dressed African American couple in an isolated setting. Burrell Advertising purposely employed a nondescript background in these ads to allow consumers' imaginations to fill in the rest of the situation. Moreover, as Thomas Burrell told *Advertising Age*, "people view those ads from their personal reference as dictated by their lifestyles."[20]

For the millions of African Americans who lived below the poverty level during the 1980s, their imaginations would have to have been exceptionally strong to see themselves in the stylishly dressed "Misting" couple. Ironically, this type of ad may have accentuated the desire of some poor blacks to use alcohol consumption as an escape mechanism.

While some African American marketers were reluctant to acknowledge class segmentation within the African American community, white advertising executives exhibited no such trepidation. For example, Robert Baxter, then marketing research manager for Mercedes Benz, acknowledged in a 1981 interview:

We are aware of the increasing number of blacks who drive our cars. They are upscale blacks who conform to the general profile of our users, meaning col-

lege educated, professional-managerial types with median incomes of
$62,000 or so.[21]

Similarly, Fred Heckel, vice president of advertising and promotion for
United Airlines, told *Advertising Age* in 1981:

> Of course we are aware of the fact that there is a black middle class. It's man-
> ifest among our own employees. . . . But our efforts are aimed at that black
> consumer market segment which is capable of travel, whether you want to call
> that segment middle class or not.[22]

Despite Heckel's vague disclaimer, it is clear that United's 1980s black-
oriented advertising campaigns were not aimed at the black poor.

Notwithstanding the early confusion about class distinctions among
blacks in the 1980s, most marketing professionals, including many blacks,
subsequently conceded the inadequacy of viewing black Americans as a
monolithic consumer market. The rise in prominence of such African
American publications as *Black Enterprise, Dollars and Sense, Black Family,* and
Black Collegian, which were aimed at an affluent and educated audience, further vouched for the existence of upscale black consumers.[23]

Once it became clear that distinct black middle- and upper-class markets
existed and that there were direct advertising venues available to reach these
individuals, the major task facing corporate marketers was to devise campaigns aimed at these groups. This task was especially daunting because
many marketers had long operated from a "one size fits all" approach to
wooing black consumers.

A 1989 article in *Psychology and Marketing* titled "Middle-Class Black
Consumers and Intensity of Ethnic Identification" is an example of the information available to corporate marketers seeking potentially profitable insights about the black middle class. The authors noted that:

> advertisers often vary the degree of black English dialect incorporated into
> copy. Some have adopted what has been referred to as the "right on" school
> of advertising, often injecting black slang in their ads. Some even go to the
> extreme of asking actors to adopt a street style of speaking, even when it may
> be unnatural for them, for commercials targeted to blacks. *On the other hand,
> advertisers have been cautioned that while a particular segment may respond more fa-
> vorably to slang, it is important for advertisers to understand which segment is most re-
> sponsive to that approach. By using "slanguage" and stereotypical presentations of
> blacks, they run the risk of turning off another segment of black consumers, particularly
> middle-class blacks.*[24] [emphasis added]

Although many industries agonized whether to use "slanguage" to reach African American consumers, financial services companies did not face this dilemma. These companies, during the 1980s, made considerable inroads among the black well-to-do.

For banks that marketed credit cards, insurance companies, and investment brokerage firms, it seemed clear that the African American constituency they were seeking would feel insulted by overtly "ethnic" marketing campaigns. Consequently, many of these companies used general media advertising that included a requisite number of African Americans.[25] Although financial services companies tended not to employ special advertising to reach black clients, they used other techniques to "invite" African Americans to use their products. One especially innovative strategy was a joint venture between *Black Enterprise* magazine and the investment brokerage Dean Witter Reynolds.

In 1986 *Black Enterprise*, the premier gateway to the African American well-to-do, and Dean Witter Reynolds teamed up to cosponsor one-day, four-hour seminars for black professionals in Chicago, Dallas, Philadelphia, Los Angeles, San Francisco, Washington, D.C., Greensboro, and Atlanta. The large crowds that attended these meetings heard Dean Witter professionals talk about personal finance and career planning. This project proved so successful that *Black Enterprise* and Dean Witter Reynolds held similar seminars in six additional cities in 1987, and other financial service companies sought their own partnerships with *Black Enterprise*.[26]

The 1980s generated a growing amount of market research related to the specific spending patterns of the African American middle class. Table 6.1, extracted from data contained in a marketing publication titled *Facts about Blacks*, illustrates the type of information about middle-class blacks that corporate marketers had at their disposal. For example, purveyors of beer, wine, and liquor used the kind of information presented in the table to enhance the consumption of their products by all African Americans, regardless of class.

Historically, African Americans, notwithstanding popular perceptions, have tended to use alcoholic beverages less frequently than whites. In fact, as late as 1980, market research indicated that total black expenditures for alcoholic beverages, despite the group's statistically significant penchant for certain products, did not exceed their proportion of the population (approximately 12 percent).[27] Nevertheless, a 1981 report on liquor consumption by urban blacks had a dramatic effect on both corporate marketers and African American city dwellers.

TABLE 6.1
*Consumption Patterns of Middle-Class Blacks
in the 1980s, Selected Items*

Item Bought	Middle-Class Blacks	U.S. Total
Pork sausage	72.4 %	59.8 %
Butter	52.8	45.1
Table syrup	70.3	65.9
Grapefruit juice	32.3	20.4
Nondiet cola drinks	72.3	60.6
Bleach	88.1	81.4
Nail polish	70.0	62.6
Breath fresheners	61.5	45.1
Deodorant	96.2	91.3
Cigarettes	50.5	36.9
Malt liquor	19.9	4.5
Cognac	17.7	4.6
Rum	20.9	13.4
Scotch whiskey	14.2	10.0
Brandy	12.9	7.3
Pop wines	10.2	4.4

SOURCE: *Facts about Blacks* #8 (Los Angeles: Leroy W. Jeffries & Associates, 1986), 30–35.

In 1981, Viewpoint, Inc., a Chicago market research firm, published a widely read report that refuted existing statistical data relating to African American drinking. As Viewpoint's president, Felix A. Burrows, told *Advertising Age*:

> traditional data tend to underestimate black consumer buying power by using Areas of Dominant Influence or Standard Metropolitan Statistical Areas as population bases. If the focus were placed on city population, where blacks are concentrated, figures would show the fuller impact of black consumption.[28]

Table 6.2, taken from Viewpoint's "corrected" data, which appeared in the July 27, 1981, *Advertising Age*, suggests the importance of urban black consumers to the alcoholic beverage industry. This type of information undoubtedly contributed to the accelerated marketing of alcohol to African Americans during the 1980s.

While statistics related to African American alcohol consumption helped purveyors of beer, wine, and liquor to refine their enticements to black consumers, another study reveals the ramifications of black drinking patterns. In its influential 1987 publication *Marketing Booze to Blacks*, the Center for Science in the Public Interest highlighted alcohol's profoundly negative impact on the health of African Americans. Citing studies that documented disproportionately high black death rates from cirrhosis of the liver and esophageal cancer, both associated with alcohol and cigarette consumption,[29] *Marketing Booze to Blacks* apportioned the blame for this appalling situation. Besides offering a predictable critique of beer, wine, and liquor companies, the study criticized the government for not providing the funds necessary to counteract alcohol's growing presence in the black community. It also blasted those African American businessmen and politicians who, for personal gain, encouraged the growing relationship between the marketers of alcoholic beverages and black consumers.

The marketing of malt liquor in the African American community in the 1980s is a good example of what the authors of *Marketing Booze to Blacks* and others would describe as corporate "misconduct." Market surveys clearly revealed African Americans' (especially black men's) preference for these "power brews" (which generally contain as much as 20 percent more alcohol than regular beer). For many undereducated and unemployed young black men, these beverages provide both a potent and a relatively inexpensive means to escape a depressing reality.[30]

Besides the "cheap high" produced by the product itself, the producers of malt liquor devised advertising campaigns to accentuate their product's desirability among black male consumers. For example, Anheuser-Busch employed the actor Fred Williamson to enhance the "macho" image of its King Cobra brand. Likewise, Schlitz featured such popular entertainers as Kool and the Gang, the Chi-Lites, and the Four Tops to sing the praises of the Schlitz Malt Liquor Bull.[31]

TABLE 6.2

African American Alcohol Consumption, Selected Cities, 1981

	Black residents of legal drinking age (percentage)	Black consumption (percentage) of		
		Liquor	Wine	Beer
New York	17.4	21.3	17.9	18.8
Chicago	24.7	30.2	25.4	26.7
Los Angeles	10.9	13.3	11.2	11.8
Houston	17.2	21.0	17.7	18.6
Detroit	40.4	49.4	41.6	43.6
Washington, D.C.	47.5	58.1	48.9	51.3
Cleveland	28.3	34.6	29.1	30.5
Boston	14.0	17.1	14.4	15.1
St. Louis	28.8	35.2	29.6	31.1
Pittsburgh	15.9	19.4	16.5	17.2

*Some of Viewpoint, Inc.'s recalculations appear sloppy. For example, in Miami, although blacks represented 16.2 percent of the population at or above the legal drinking age, Viewpoint listed blacks as consuming 77.5 percent of the beer in that city. SOURCE: *Advertising Age* 52 (July 27, 1981): S-12.

The Heileman Brewing Company, the makers of Colt 45 malt liquor, devised the most talked-about advertising campaign to sell malt liquor to African American men. Utilizing the suave image of the black movie star Billy Dee Williams, Heileman, through Williams, implicitly told black men that Colt 45 would assist them in getting sexual favors from women. As Williams stated in a controversial television commercial that featured him and an attractive woman, "the power of Colt 45, it works every time."[32]

While the makers of malt liquor sought to reach its primarily young black male constituency with allusions to sexual conquest and the alcoholic "kick" of its products, purveyors of other alcoholic beverages sought to reach African American consumers by linking drinking to wealth and glamour. This strategy, which exploited historical black anxiety related to "status," proved successful. As one contemporary black advertising executive observed, "the average black consumer can't talk about his stock portfolio or second home in the country, but he can certainly demonstrate that he has good taste by ordering premium liquor."[33] Prominent examples of the "drink-to-success message" included Martell Cognac's ad featuring an attractive, well-dressed black woman pouring a glass of cognac, with the banner "I assume you drink Martell"; a Canadian Club whiskey ad, featuring a well-dressed African American couple, that proclaimed, "The C.C. man is a winner. . . . He drinks the best because he is the best"; and various ads for Johnny Walker scotch that included vignettes illustrating the social habits of affluent blacks.[34]

Even lower-priced products sought to glamorize their image to attract black consumers. For instance, Riunite wine, which *Marketing Booze to Blacks* described as a "cheap Italian import," featured ads "showing a tuxedo-clad gentleman and his attractive, bejeweled, female companion."[35]

Black consumers in the 1980s were bombarded with such sales pitches from the purveyors of alcoholic beverages. A content analysis of popular African American periodicals revealed a preponderance of such ads in these magazines. For example, 40 percent of the ads that appeared in the December 1985 issue of *Black Enterprise* were for alcoholic beverages.[36]

Although the marketing of alcoholic beverages on television during the 1980s was aimed at a general audience (malt liquor notwithstanding), African Americans received proportionately more exposure to the blandishments associated with beer and wine companies' $700 million annual television advertising budget. A contemporary research study by the Arbitron Rating Company documented that blacks viewed considerably more television than their nonblack counterparts.[37]

African American television viewers, besides being exposed to Heileman's tasteless Colt 45 commercials, witnessed a well-researched ad campaign aimed at them by Anheuser-Busch. Anheuser-Busch, the maker of Budweiser and Michelob beer, developed television advertising that reflected its awareness of the growing market segmentation within the black community. Budweiser's black television spots regularly featured scenes of drinking camaraderie among working-class men. On the other hand, black Michelob commercials featured actors who appeared to be professionals or entrepreneurs.[38]

The Miller Brewing Company's black celebrity spokesmen campaign for Miller Lite also struck a responsive chord among black viewers. Featuring a number of former African American athletes, including Deacon Jones, Roosevelt Grier, K. C. Jones, Wilt Chamberlain, Frank Robinson, and Joe Frazier, these ads emphasized "that *real* men drink Lite beer."[39]

To buttress television and magazine advertisements for alcoholic beverages aimed at African Americans, the purveyors of these products utilized outdoor advertising in urban black enclaves. In fact, during the 1980s, the number of eight-sheet billboards (three hundred square feet or less) that extolled the benefits of drinking alcohol or smoking cigarettes proliferated at an alarming rate in African American neighborhoods across America.[40] For example, in 1986 the Los Angeles metro area, with a population of nearly eight million people, contained 1373 eight-sheet billboards. Of these, 663, or 48 percent, were placed in predominately black neighborhoods. This was especially significant considering that African Americans represented just 15 percent of the Los Angeles metropolitan area population at 1.2 million. Similar data for St. Louis appeared even more striking. Although African Americans represented only 28 percent of that city's population, 95 percent of the eight-sheet billboards in that city were located in the black community.[41] A similar proliferation of cigarette and liquor billboard advertising in black Atlanta neighborhoods prompted U.S. Representative John Lewis to declare that such ads were:

> an insult and an affront to the black community. This form of advertising is really targeted toward the most vulnerable segment of our population. When little kids are on their way to school they can see over and over again a message to smoke or drink wine or beer . . . this is the way to get ahead or to be happy.[42]

While the producers of alcoholic beverages spent tens of millions of dollars annually on outdoor, television, and magazine advertising to entice the African American consumer market, government agencies spent far less to examine the negative effects of alcohol consumption among African Americans. In 1986 the National Institute on Alcohol Abuse and Alcoholism (NIAAA) allocated only $512,193 for programs related to African American problems with alcohol, despite the fact that during the same year, the NIAAA declared that alcohol abuse represented the number one health problem in the black community.[43]

Another obstacle to reducing consumption of alcoholic beverages among African Americans was the fact that businessmen and politicians welcomed the alcohol industry's growing presence in African American life, because manufacturers of alcoholic beverages, unlike other industries, were regularly involved in black community affairs.[44]

Perhaps the alcoholic beverage industry's most prominent public relations campaign related to blacks was, and still is, Anheuser-Busch's underwriting of the annual "Lou Rawls Parade of Stars Telethon" (in support of the United Negro College Fund). In addition to supporting the United Negro College Fund, which it began assisting in 1979, Anheuser-Busch, during the 1980s, made substantial contributions to the National Urban League.[45]

The Joseph Coors Company was another brewery interested in cultivating a favorable image in the black community. Ironically, during the early 1980s blacks and organized labor coordinated a national boycott of Coors because of the company's apparent racist and antiunion policies. In 1984, to stifle this criticism, Coors entered into a "national covenant" with such organizations as the NAACP, Operation PUSH, and the National Newspaper Publishers Association in which Coors agreed to invest approximately $625 million in African American and Hispanic communities during the next five years.[46]

To keep the African American community informed of its various community service activities, Coors established a widely circulated newsletter titled *New Horizons*. In 1986, for example, readers learned that Coors sponsored such black-focused events as:

> black rodeo events, broadcasts of black collegiate football games, tennis tournaments, rock concerts, boxing matches, college interview fairs, film workshops, and even a gala concert at the October 1986 meeting of the Congressional Black Caucus Foundation.[47]

Although Coors's enhanced presence in the African American community represented its sense of social responsibility, "bottom-line" considerations remained the company's primary motive for sponsoring African American events. A joint report from Coors's national program manager and the director of its community relations department that appeared in the November/December 1986 issue of *New Horizons* declared:

> the Community Relations Department together with the Sales and Marketing Department has worked diligently to enhance Coors' relationship with the minority market. . . . As a result, sales of our product have increased and our markets have expanded.[48] [emphasis added]

Despite the funds distributed in the black community by Coors and other alcohol and tobacco companies,* a growing number of African Americans began to question the excessive influence of these corporations in African American enclaves. An important organization associated with this phenomenon was the National Black Alcoholism Council (NBAC). A June 7, 1986, NBAC position paper that opposed the linkage of liquor companies' community relations and sales departments asserted:

> This credo of the more you drink, the more you get, shows a callous disregard for the well-being of the black community. . . . This community does not need more alcohol abuse to help break the long chain of oppression. There should not be such a price attached to its economic development.[49]

During the 1980s, the relationship between cigarette companies and the black community also underwent close examination. Like the purveyors of alcoholic beverages, tobacco companies had a long history of activity in the African American community. Moreover, cigarette companies, like their liquor-producing counterparts, spiced up their blandishments to black consumers during the decade. Just as market research revealed the special popularity of certain alcoholic beverages in the African American community, cigarette companies during the 1980s were aware of the special preference of black smokers for menthol cigarettes, which were preferred by an estimated 70 percent. Consequently, such mentholated brands as the Brown and Williamson Corporation's Kool cigarettes were acknowledged favorites in the black community.[50]

Another popular mentholated brand among African American smokers was Lorillard's Newport. In fact, commencing in the mid-1980s, Newport

---

*Besides Coors and Anheuser-Busch, other liquor and tobacco companies that featured black community relations programs were the Miller Brewing Company, Joseph E. Seagram & Sons, Inc., Stroh Brewing Company, Phillip Morris Companies, Inc., R. J. Reynolds Tobacco Company, and the Brown & Williamson Corp. (makers of Kool cigarettes). See "Who Donates What to Minority Groups," Miami *Herald*, August 13, 1989, p. 3G.

began to seriously threaten the market share of Salem, the nation's number one menthol cigarette, produced by the R. J. Reynolds Tobacco Company. Because proportionately more African Americans smoked during the late 1980s than whites (34 versus 28 percent), R. J. Reynolds felt compelled to buttress its apparently fading support among African American consumers. This sentiment ultimately resulted in R. J. Reynolds's ill-fated Uptown cigarette campaign.[51]

According to R. J. Reynolds's marketing strategy, Uptown was to be test-marketed in Philadelphia in September 1989, with national distribution to follow. Employing extensive market research, which focused on the subliminal impact of the word "uptown" on African Americans, R. J. Reynolds felt confident that it had devised a product that would be irresistible to black smokers. To maximize the attractiveness of "Uptown" cigarettes, R. J. Reynolds hired the advertising agency of FCB/Leber Katz Partners to create a marketing campaign that would appeal to black smokers in all socioeconomic categories.[52]

Once FCB/Leber Katz Partners finally settled on the theme "Uptown, the place. The taste" and had developed ads stressing the new cigarette's enhanced menthol taste, it appeared that R. J. Reynolds had a potential megahit on its hands.[53] Unfortunately for the company, not everyone in the African American community hailed its pending appearance.

Dr. Louis Sullivan, Secretary of Health and Human Services under President George Bush, was the most prominent African American critic of the proposed Uptown cigarette. Following Sullivan's lead, other black leaders blasted R. J. Reynolds for specifically targeting blacks. Feeling the heat from this protest, R. J. Reynolds subsequently announced that it would withdraw Uptown from market consideration, at a cost of between $5 and $7 million dollars.[54]

By the end of the 1980s, increased black consumer criticism of the marketing campaigns of cigarette and liquor companies revealed the growing sophistication of African American shoppers. Corporate marketers would now have to do more than simply "recognize" blacks and "invite" them to use a particular product. Still, the furor over the black-targeted marketing campaigns of tobacco and liquor companies brought to the surface the powerful influence these companies had in the African American community and particularly their influence over civil rights organizations and black media outlets. As a March 26, 1989, Atlanta *Constitution* article on the marketing presence of liquor and cigarette companies in the black community noted:

Therein lies a dilemma for organizations such as the National Urban League and the National Association of Colored People (NAACP) which have traditionally railed against black exploitation. They have become economically dependent on the very corporations that saturate their communities with billboard ads. In many instances, the same corporations donate millions of dollars each year to financially struggling black organizations.[55]

When asked in 1989 what would happen if black media forsook alcohol and tobacco ads and revenue, the veteran black advertising executive Caroline Jones, of the black-owned Mingo-Jones agency, predicted that "black media would go down the drain tomorrow."[56]

Revelations concerning the pervasive role of liquor and tobacco companies in the black community put African American consumers in a challenging situation. A growing number of blacks, from all classes, were increasingly concerned about the negative impact of legalized drug use, via tobacco and alcohol consumption, in the African American community. Yet, it was also increasingly clear that any sustained consumer movement against liquor and cigarette companies would not include the group's traditional advocates, civil rights organizations and the black press.

If thoughtful African American consumers were troubled about the role of cigarette and alcohol companies in their community, other research, related to the extent of black wealth, created even greater concern. Billy J. Tidwell's 1988 essay "Black Wealth, Facts and Fiction" suggested that increased African American consumerism since the 1960s didn't necessarily reflect substantive economic progress. Tidwell, then director of research for the National Urban League, offered a bleak assessment of contemporary black America in the NUL's *State of Black America 1988.* He asserted:

> Based on current census data, the total net worth* of all U.S. households is approximately $6,830 billion. Blacks account for $192 billion, or a minuscule 2.8 percent of the total. By contrast, the aggregate net worth of white households is $6,498 or 95 percent of the national total. . . . Thus, the net worth estimate for black households is more than eight percent below their proportion of the population, while the net worth of white households exceeds their proportion of the population by a considerable margin. Converted into dollar terms, black households are "undervalued" by some $559 billion, relative to their proportion of the U.S. population.[57]

*Net worth refers to the value of such items as interest-bearing savings accounts, stocks, bonds, real estate, and consumer goods.

Moreover, Tidwell lamented:

On a per-household basis, whites enjoy about 12 times the net worth of blacks. The average net worth of black households is $3,400, compared to $39,000 for white households. Viewed from any perspective, the position of black Americans is very marginal.[58]

As the 1980s drew to a close, notions of substantive African American economic progress had been all but dashed. Although the number of blacks who possessed upper-class status stood at an all-time high, a significant number of African Americans still found themselves at the bottom of the U.S. economic totem pole. Moreover, while collective black spending power had increased, the primary beneficiaries of this phenomenon were not African American consumers but the corporations that sought their relatively limited dollars.

7

Epilogue

The Changing Same: American Corporations and Black Consumers during the 1990s

By 1990 Americans of African descent were a far different people than they had been at the dawn of this century. Once perceived as primarily a rural group with limited disposable income, African Americans, by the last decade of the twentieth century, were a free-spending, pronouncedly urban people. Despite this reality, however, advertising and marketing literature continued to discuss and document an ongoing insensitivity toward black consumers. Even when black consumers were duly recognized, the consequences were often mixed. For instance, the re-emergence of the blaxploitation movie genre, albeit in a different form, captivated a new generation of African American moviegoers. Also, an accelerated interest in black consumers by white purveyors of personal care products and insurance put even greater strain on black-owned businesses operating in these areas. As a result, a growing number of African Americans are questioning the relationship between the black community and white-controlled companies. It remains to be seen if today's black consumers can indeed exert more substantive power in contemporary America.

African American consumers, despite the economic deprivation associated with the urban "underclass," represented a vital part of the U.S. economy by 1990. A study conducted by the Selig Center for Economic Growth at the University of Georgia determined that black buying power would rise from $304 billion in 1990 to $427 billion in 1996, an increase of 40.5 percent, compared to a projected 35.2 percent increase in total U.S. consumer spending during the same period. In addition, the Selig Center predicted that in the same six-year span African Americans' share of the nation's aggregate buying power would rise from 7.5 to 7.8 percent.[1]

Considering the Selig Center's predictions, it seemed contradictory that, in some areas of American marketing, the interests of black consumers re-

mained all but ignored. An important 1991 study of magazine advertisements by the New York City Department of Consumer Affairs illustrated
this situation.

After conducting a random survey of advertisements in twenty-seven national magazines published between July 1988 and July 1991, the Department of Consumer Affairs discovered that:

> Although blacks make up 12 percent of the United States population and
> more than 11 percent of all magazine readers, they appear in only 4.5 percent
> of all magazine advertisements and constitute a little more than 3 percent of
> the characters in those advertisements.[2]

Table 7.1 provides statistics on the presence (or lack thereof) of African
Americans in selected magazine advertisements, as documented by the New
York City Consumer Affairs Department's probe.

Predictably, the advertising industry sought to deflect the implicit charge
of racism associated with the Consumer Affairs Department's findings. For
instance, a July 23, 1991 New York *Times* article entitled "Blacks Are Found
to Be Still Scarce in Advertisements in Major Magazines," quoted John E.
O'Toole, president of the American Association of Advertising Agencies, as
saying marketers tended "to choose the model that reflects the majority of
their constituency, which for most consumer products is white."[3] Still, some
advertising executives, such as Roy J. Bostock, chief executive of the influential D'Arcy Masius Benton & Bowles agency, linked the shortage of blacks
in magazine advertising with white racial attitudes. Bostock, whose agency
represented such clients as General Motors, Proctor & Gamble, and Burger
King, told the New York *Times* that "sensitivity to the representation of minorities in advertising existed in the early and mid-1970s, but that sensitivity waned somewhat for some agencies and advertisers during the Reagan
years."[4]

The widespread publicity given the New York Consumer Affairs research
produced public soul- searching within the advertising industry regarding its
attitudes toward black consumers, black colleagues in the industry, and
African Americans in general. A June 15, 1992, article in *Advertising Age*, titled "The Ad Industry's 'Dirty Little' Secret," provided an especially damn-
ing appraisal of apparent institutional racism within U.S. advertising agencies.

As part of the research for the article, the top twenty-five American advertising agencies were asked, "How many blacks work at your shop?" Only
five agencies responded. This overwhelming lack of compliance, coupled

TABLE 7.1
Use of Black Models in Selected Magazine Ads,
1988–1991

Magazine	% Black Models	% Black Readers
Better Homes & Gardens	2.6	9.3
Business Week	5.1	10.8
Cosmopolitan	2.7	10.1
Esquire	2.4	25.5
Family Circle	2.8	9.2
Fortune	4.3	9.1
GQ	2.9	24.2
House & Garden	1.9	7.9
Life	3.0	13.7
Newsweek	5.0	8.3
New Yorker	2.9	5.9
Seventeen	2.8	12.7
Time	4.8	9.8

SOURCE: New York City Consumer Affairs Department Report, July 23, 1991; Philadelphia *Inquirer,* July 24, 1991, 1F.

with estimates that only 1 percent of the managers at mainstream agencies were black, suggested the existence of antiblack attitudes within the nation's advertising industry.[5]

To its credit, the article highlighted not only industrywide racial bias but racial exclusion within the pages of *Advertising Age*:

> Of the 658 people (excluding celebrities and spouses whose jobs aren't identified) shown so far this year on *Advertising Age's* "Photo Review" page—a weekly snapshot of sorts of the leaders and strivers in media, advertising and marketing—six were black. . . . Only two blacks (not counting a shot of the U.S. Olympic basketball team) have been pictured this year on AA's first three pages: Whoopi Goldberg and Spike Lee.[6]

Lowell Thompson, an African American with decades of experience in the advertising industry, published an even more biting critique of ad agencies's racial attitudes. In a November 16, 1992, *Advertising Age* article titled, "Blacks in Ad Agencies: It Used to Be Better," Thompson offered a bleak assessment of African Americans' role in the advertising industry.

Twenty years earlier, or what Thompson called "1972 B.R." (Before Reagan, Recession, and Retrenchment), black creative professionals were much more visible in major advertising agencies.[7] Moreover, the mind-set of advertising executives in the early 1990s contributed to the dearth of African Americans in the industry. With undisguised sarcasm, Thompson asserted that white advertising executives believed that blacks:

have yet to develop the brain mass and consequently the conceptual capacity necessary to conjure up the high level symbolism of a Mr. Whipple, a Dough-boy, an Energizer Bunny or a Ronald McDonald, not to mention the advanced language and manipulation skills needed to pen such immortal phrases as "It's it and that's that," "We love to fly and it shows," "Tsk, tsk, Wisk, Wisk," and "You got the right one, baby, uh huh!"[8]

Thompson's caustic analysis of the advertising industry was especially powerful in the wake of Revlon's ill-fated 1991 advertising campaign for its new fragrance "Unforgettable," a fiasco that suggested that the reasoning capacity of some white creative professionals could also be questioned.

With no apparent African American input, Revlon's "Unforgettable" commercial featured footage of the legendary Nat King Cole singing his trademark song as well as footage of a group of white models.[9] Ironically, as the *Wall Street Journal* noted in 1993, the only "unforgettable" aspect of this campaign was its omission of any black models:

> The Revlon commercial used a beloved black artist in praise of a parade of "unforgettable" women—all of whom were white. When Revlon later tried to remedy the gaffe, by hastily tacking on a shot of the black model Beverly Johnson to the end of the spot, the effort struck some as clumsy.[10]

The "Unforgettable" debacle, along with other well-publicized instances of insensitivity toward African American consumers, contributed to a growing sense of alienation and frustration within the black community. This potentially volatile situation exploded during the spring of 1992 when the police assailants of Rodney King (black America's most famous motorist) were acquitted by a Simi Valley, California, jury of what seemed to most observers to be obvious wrong-doing. The Simi Valley verdict itself led to violent expressions of outrage by African Americans. Still, many observers of this phenomenon contended that the travesty of justice in Simi Valley represented only one of many grievances blacks had against U.S. society. The advertising industry, in response, intensified its introspection regarding the treatment of African Americans both in agencies and in advertisements.

During the summer of 1992, *Advertising Age* conducted a random survey of 470 marketing and media executives to determine whether there was any link between advertising and racial tension. The vast majority of the respondents were white (93.8 percent); 3.5 percent were black; and the rest were of other races.[11]

When asked, "Has advertising had an influence on the U.S.'s current racial problems?," 56.3 percent answered in the affirmative, while 41.1 percent did not see a connection between advertising and racial tension. Even more illuminating were responses to the question "How many black people in non-clerical positions do you work with on a daily basis?" Nearly 57 percent of the respondents answered "none," and another 16.8 percent answered "one."[12]

This reaffirmation of the "whiteness" of the U.S. advertising industry, especially at its upper levels, prompted a movement among advertisers and corporations to link products with racial tolerance and diversity. For instance, during early 1993, MasterCard cosponsored a teen summit in New York City that focused on racism; McDonald's ran several prominent ads promoting the Dr. Martin Luther King Jr. holiday; and the Hampton, New Hampshire-based Timberland Company began an international print ad campaign featuring one of its products with a large headline urging consumers to "Give Racism the Boot."[13]

This trend toward the aggressive marketing of racial harmony appeared linked to the profit motive. As a January 19, 1993, Los Angeles *Times* article surveying this phenomenon noted:

> Racial harmony will be the advertising cause for 1993—particularly for firms trying to tap into the teenage market, said Marian Salzman, president of the New York research firm BKG Youth Inc. . . . A recent survey of teen-agers conducted by BKG for Eastman Kodak Co. revealed that more than a third of those responding said they had been victims of racial discrimination. Only 15% of the teenagers surveyed said they would "never" date a person of another race. For big marketers, this clearly signals that racial harmony sells.[14]

For many African Americans trying to survive in the increasingly mean streets of urban America, the findings of the BKG survey offered little consolation. In fact, their rage and frustration remained as intense as ever. Many black films produced during the late 1980s and early 1990s were a manifestation of the anger expressed by African Americans in the wake of Simi Valley. Movies such as Spike Lee's *Do The Right Thing*, John Singleton's *Boyz N the Hood*, and Matty Rich's *Straight Out of Brooklyn* graphically chronicled the travails and frustrations of late-twentieth-century black urban life.[15] Critics of these films tended to decry their overtly violent content. In fact, the gang-oriented violence featured in *Boyz N the Hood* and *New Jack City*, another film of this genre, apparently led to gang-oriented violence at movie theaters across America in 1991.[16]

Despite the association of these "new" black films with violence, their supporters asserted that they merely reflected reality, however unpalatable. John Singleton, when interviewed for the July 29, 1991, issue of *Newsweek* about violence at showings of his *Boyz N the Hood* and at black movies in general, responded:

> It wasn't the film [that caused violence]. It was the fact that a whole genera-
> tion [of black men] doesn't respect themselves, it makes it easier for them to
> shoot each other. This is a generation of kids who don't have father figures.
> They're looking for their manhood, and they get a gun. The more of these
> people that get together, the higher potential for violence. . . . Some people
> want black film makers to make films about black people sitting up in
> churches and singing. That's safe to older bourgeois black people, and it's safe
> to some "liberal-minded" white people. But I'm not going to make films like
> that because that's not what I see my friends doing.[17]

Regardless of whether one was a critic or a supporter of such films as *Boyz N the Hood*, one fact that had nothing to do with perceptions of "reality" remained crystal clear. Black movies were made (or not made) on the basis of profitability. The fact that *Boyz N the Hood* grossed more than $60 million from an investment of $6 million clearly indicated a strong market existed for such a product.[18] Moreover, Hollywood investors, with their "bottom-line" mentality, intended to do what was necessary to fully exploit this apparent demand. As Spike Lee, the "dean" of contemporary African American filmmakers, bluntly told *Time* in an June 17, 1991, article about the resurgence of black-oriented films, "Black films will be made as long as they make money."[19]

During the early 1990s, African Americans continued to represent a disproportionately large segment of Hollywood's consumer base. While blacks constituted approximately 12 percent of the U.S. population, their ticket purchases accounted for more than 25 percent of Hollywood's estimated $4.6 billion film revenue in 1990.[20]

Although there were distinct parallels between 1970s "blaxploitation" films and black-oriented films of the 1990s, perhaps the major difference between the two eras was the 1990s' focus on "crossover" marketability. Unlike such earlier films as *Shaft*, *Superfly*, and *The Mack*, which appealed almost exclusively to African American moviegoers, movies like *Do the Right Thing*, *Boyz N the Hood*, and even *Malcolm X* were viewed by a significant number of whites. There were a variety of sociological, psychological, and economic reasons for this phenomenon.

During the 1980s, those African Americans who did not materially benefit from the Civil Rights Movement increasingly attracted the attention of both scholars and the nation's mass media.[21] For many white Americans, the existence of a growing urban black "underclass" seemed startling, especially because the mass media, since the late 1960s, had projected an image of African American "progress" by focusing upon the exploits (and salaries) of various black athletes and entertainers.[22] It was in this setting that Spike Lee, a film director with an admittedly limited grasp of the social, political, and economic nuances of African American life, became what one observer described as an "information conduit" to whites seeking to know more about the urban black experience.[23]

Lee's film *Do the Right Thing*, released in 1989, focused on life in a black Brooklyn neighborhood. It quickly became a major crossover hit. In fact, the entire July 6, 1989, edition of ABC News' *Nightline* program focused on the movie and its impact on the country. As the show's moderator, Forrest Sawyer, noted in the program's introduction, "This film is making America listen and talk, even argue, about one of the most painful problems of our society."[24]

Besides the "educational" nature of films such as *Do the Right Thing*, black films of the late 1980s and early 1990s reached a crossover audience because they accentuated the growing impact of black culture on the psyche of some young whites. During this period, undoubtedly to the consternation of white parents, "hip-hop" or "rap" became the preferred music of millions of white teenagers and young adults. Through rap music videos on such venues as MTV, even suburban whites could get a glimpse of the lifestyle of urban black "homeboys." While some of these inner-city images were, perhaps, contrived to accentuate the marketing appeal of certain groups,* the unique language and clothing associated with hip-hop and rap culture captivated young people of all races.[25]

Because of rap music's crossover appeal, it did not take Hollywood long to discover that this music genre could be profitably melded into the movie industry. As Elvis Mitchell, a noted African American media critic, told the *New York Times Magazine* in a July 14, 1991, article about the black film resurgence:

> When Hollywood realized that white kids were really into rap—and don't kid yourself, that's the audience the studios are really lusting for—a little light went on: "Hey, we can make money from black culture."[26]

---

*Nelson George's hilarious movie *CB4* (1993) offered a satirical look at the world of hip-hop, especially "gangsta" rap. This film insinuated that some gangsta rappers were nothing more than middle-class blacks putting on an act.

It appears more than coincidental that some of the most profitable black movies during this period featured rap artists in prominent roles. Along with the immensely popular *Boyz N the Hood*, which showcased the performer Ice Cube, the film *House Party* (1990), which grossed in excess of $26 million from a $2.5 million investment,[27] starred the rappers Kid & Play.

Ironically, Spike Lee's movie on the black nationalist icon Malcolm X graphically illustrated the importance of the crossover audience to Hollywood producers. It also demonstrated the power of economics over artistic considerations (and historical accuracy).

It has been estimated that a film must make two and one half times its production costs before it breaks even.[28] With this in mind, when Spike Lee demanded $35 million in production costs from Warner Brothers, he perhaps unwittingly set the stage for the subsequent dilution of Malcolm's life on screen. Since black patronage alone would not generate the $90 million needed to make *Malcolm X* profitable, Lee felt compelled to shape the film to reach a crossover audience. To achieve this goal, Lee ultimately muted or deleted many controversial, yet historically accurate, aspects of Malcolm's life.[29]

During the 1990s, thoughtful African American moviegoers found their situation less than enviable. Not only were they being served watered-down versions of history, but many of the films featuring blacks continued to conjure up historical stereotypes. Movies like *Boyz N the Hood* and *House Party* depicted the contemporary African American experience as a modern-day version of *Porgy & Bess*'s "Catfish Row," where the "natives" intermittently spent their time engaging in violence against each other, using drugs (including alcohol), and partying.

White Hollywood's control of African American screen images, despite the presence of more black directors, is evident if we examine the fate of Haile Gerima's critically acclaimed 1994 film, *Sankofa*. *Sankofa*, which depicted the dynamics and consequences of the trans-Atlantic slave trade from the viewpoint of transplanted Africans, created a stir in international film circles, winning major awards at the Milan and Fespaco Film Festivals. Yet, despite the film's enthusiastic overseas reception, U.S. distributors ignored it.[30] When asked about this snub, Kay Shaw, the national distribution manager of Washington, D.C.'s Mypheduh Films, Inc., which produced the film, told *Black Enterprise* in 1994:

> If this was a film about pathology in the black community, it would have been well received [in the States]. . . . *Sankofa* celebrates the story of our resistance

to the enslavement process. In it, black people are not a backdrop to their own story.[31]

Undaunted by mainstream distributors' disinterest in his film, Gerima, a Howard University professor, decided to distribute *Sankofa* independently. After a successful eleven-week run at Washington, D.C.'s Biograph theater, which Gerima personally rented, the film, through Gerima's direct efforts, played to sellout audiences in a number of other urban centers. In fact, by 1995, *Sankofa*, which had become a grass-roots film classic, had grossed more than $2.5 million.[32] Mainstream distributors nevertheless continued to ignore *Sankofa*.

The 1990s African American community, like its 1970s counterpart, has reaped little, if any, monetary benefits from its disproportionately massive patronage of Hollywood productions. Consequently, blaxploitation, in an economic sense, has remained alive and well.

Although many recent black-oriented films have been shot on location in urban African American enclaves and have provided short-term business opportunities for neighborhood entrepreneurs, most of the money associated with the production of these films has ended up in nonblack hands. For instance, in 1995, there were fewer than ten black-owned movie theaters in the United States. Thus, the vast majority of contemporary African American moviegoers, paradoxically, spend their money at downtown and suburban cinema mutiplexes to see films about life in the "hood."[33]

Both the 1970s and the 1990s featured films that appeared to be aimed primarily at black male audiences. Like the 1970's *Shaft* and *Superfly*, movies such as *Boyz N the Hood*, *Do the Right Thing*, and *House Party* viewed the world through the lens of black men. Black women, in both decades, were essentially depicted as auxiliary mother figures or sexual playthings. Although Julia Dash's 1991 film, *Daughters of the Dust*, provided a penetrating depiction of the experiences of black women, its moderate box office performance ($800,000 production cost, $1.8 million gross after thirty-three weeks)[34] apparently convinced Hollywood that movies with such a focus were not profitable. The 1995 screen adaptation of Terry McMillan's novel *Waiting to Exhale*, however, dramatically altered perceptions about the profit potential of movies that specifically targeted African American female consumers.

Before its film adaptation, *Waiting to Exhale*, which chronicled the personal trials and tribulations of a group of black women, was an overwhelming literary success. In 1992, the year of its publication, it ranked ninth on the list of top-selling fiction hardbacks, with 663,333 books sold. In 1993, 1,562,000 paperback copies of *Waiting to Exhale* were sold. Consequently, even before its December 1995 film premiere, there were a significant number of African American women who had read (or heard about) *Waiting to Exhale* and were eager to see how it would play out on screen.[35]

The marketing of *Waiting to Exhale*, before its premiere, further heightened the anticipation of the film by black female consumers. Excerpts from the film were liberally exhibited on such venues as Black Entertainment Television, and the movie's soundtrack appeared a month before the film's initial showing. Featuring such notable African American female performers as Whitney Houston (one of the stars of the movie), Aretha Franklin, Chaka Khan, Patti LaBelle, Toni Braxton, and TLC, the *Waiting to Exhale* soundtrack quickly zoomed to the top of *Billboard* magazine's listing of the two hundred top-selling albums in the United States. Moreover, as late as June 1996, the soundtrack still ranked twenty-fifth, with more than six million units sold.[36]

Besides the standard production of an auxiliary *Waiting to Exhale* soundtrack album to go along with the movie, the novel itself received a facelift that boosted sales in 1995. Despite exceptionally strong sales in 1992 and 1993, *Waiting to Exhale* had not been among the top-selling mass market fiction paperbacks in 1994.[37] However, in 1995, to coincide with the release of the *Waiting to Exhale* movie, the novel's cover was changed to a photograph of the four female stars of the movie. This marketing ploy apparently worked. In 1995 *Waiting to Exhale* once again joined the ranks of best-seller mass market fiction paperbacks, with more than one million books sold.[38]

Considering the preliminary buildup, the premiere of *Waiting to Exhale*, during Christmas weekend 1995, seemed almost anticlimactic. Yet, African American women, primed for this event, came out in droves to see the movie. Between December 22 and 25, *Waiting to Exhale* was the country's top box-office hit, taking in a reported $14,126,927.[39] In its last appearance on *Variety* magazine's weekly listing of the sixty top-grossing U.S. movies, in late April 1996, *Waiting To Exhale* had a reported cumulative worldwide box office of $79,949,594 ($67,012,629 domestic; $12,936,965 foreign).[40]

Although *Waiting to Exhale* dropped off the list of the sixty top-grossing films in late April 1996, that did not signal the end of its profitability. The following month, the movie's home video version appeared in video stores across America. Within a couple of weeks, *Waiting to Exhale* moved to the top of *Billboard* magazine's listing of the forty top-selling videos. As late as July 4, *Waiting to Exhale* still ranked as the seventh best-selling movie video in the United States.[41]

While Hollywood apparently did not realize the profit potential associated with targeting African American women until the mid-1990s, other sectors of the U.S. economy, notably the cosmetic and the personal care products industries, had been acutely aware of black women's consumer clout since the 1970s. During the 1990s, companies in these industries made even greater inroads among black female shoppers.

A watershed event in the wooing of African American female consumers was the Maybelline Company's introduction in 1991 of "Shades of You," a collection of face and lip makeup specifically for black women. This represented the first time a major cosmetic company had created a mass-market line for African American women.[42] Still, Maybelline's historic maneuver appeared to have been primarily motivated by a desire for profit, rather than by a strong commitment to serving the needs of black female consumers. As a December 17, 1990, article in *Advertising Age*, which previewed Maybelline's campaign, reported:

> For Maybelline, its latest move may prove a way to regain lost ground. The company is now the No. 2 cosmetics marketer, with an estimated 17.5% share, trailing No. 1 Cover Girl's 23% but ahead of No. 3 Revlon's 13%. . . . "It's a smart move," said industry consultant Allan Motus of Maybelline's new line. "Instead of going eyeball to eyeball with Cover Girl, they can go for a specific segment for incremental market share. That's shrewd."[43]

Other white-owned cosmetic companies quickly caught on to Maybelline's strategy and launched their own campaigns to reach the black woman of the 1990s. The Estee Lauder Company's creation of "Prescriptives All Skins" in 1991 was especially significant, since Estee Lauder had long been considered one of the premiere cosmetic lines. In fact, before 1991, the company had cultivated an image that linked its products with upper-class white women. Yet, as 1990 census data revealed an African American female population that was growing both in numbers and in affluence, Estee Lauder decided to expand its clientele to include black women. Like Maybelline's "Shades of You" line, which proved to be profitable, Estee Lauder's "Prescriptives All Skins" enhanced the company's financial stature. In fact, "Prescriptives All Skins," which offered more than one hundred custom-blended makeup shades, attracted nearly fifty thousand new black customers during its first year.[44]

The increasing beauty options available to black women in the 1990s generated a mixed reaction in the African American community. A June 1993 *Black Enterprise* article titled "Redefining Beautiful" captured the essence of this debate when it asserted:

> more than a dozen makeup lines and line extensions have been thrust at the black female consumer in the last two years. And there are more on the horizon. Without question, the onslaught of competition in the ethnic cosmetics market is good news for black women, who for the first time have the dizzying array of cosmetic choices that white women have long enjoyed. But it could herald disaster for smaller and some black-owned companies, who lack the deep pockets needed for massive advertising campaigns as well as the financial clout to demand adequate shelf space. . . . There is no way for the beauty industry's major players to hit their sales targets without cutting deeply into consumer bases of smaller, more established ethnic cosmetic companies.[45]

One black-owned cosmetics company that aggressively reacted to increased white competition for black female shoppers was Fashion Fair Cosmetics. Because Fashion Fair Cosmetics was a subsidiary of the Johnson Publishing Company and received extensive advertising space in *Ebony* and *Jet*, it had long been the leading marketer of cosmetics to African American women. Yet, increased competition forced Fashion Fair to both refine and redefine its product line. In 1992 the company redesigned the packaging of its products to enhance their aura of elegance. Also, during the same year, Fashion Fair and Johnson Publishing introduced the new "Ebone" cosmetic line. Unlike Fashion Fair Cosmetics, which were aimed at an upscale black female clientele, "Ebone" sought to attract younger and less affluent black women. In the short term, both of these maneuvers proved profitable.[46]

While Fashion Fair Products represented a continuing black business success story, fate was far less kind to the Johnson Products Company, another Chicago-based African American enterprise. In 1993 Johnson Products, a leading pioneer in the black hair care industry, which once held a phenomenal 80 percent market share, agreed to a buyout by a white-owned Miami holding company. Increased competition from white companies, along with domestic squabbling within this family-owned business, contributed to Johnson Products' demise.[47]

The takeover of Johnson Products by the Ivax Corporation for $67 million created considerable concern among other black-owned hair care companies. As Lafayette Jones, founder of the American Health and Beauty Aids

Institute (an African American trade association), told the *Wall Street Journal* shortly after Ivax announced its acquisition of Johnson Products: "This company [Johnson Products] historically has been a beacon to other black entrepreneurs in the country. There are many people who are saddened by its sale to a general market company."[48]

Increased white competition represented a serious problem for black-owned companies not only in the cosmetics and personal care products industry but also in the insurance industry. In fact, since the 1970s, the collective plight of black-owned insurance companies had grown increasingly desperate.

By the 1990s, black insurance companies, in comparison to the broader industry, were suffering from shrinking total assets, shrinking premium income, and a shrinking workforce.[49] Even more illustrative of African American insurers' woes is the increasing disappearance of individual companies; between 1984 and 1995, the number of black-owned insurance companies decreased by 39 percent, from thirty-six to twenty-two.[50]

Notwithstanding America's implementation of a "one-way" version of racial desegregation, which promoted greater interaction between white companies and black consumers but not the opposite, black insurers' present-day problems can be traced to the related factors of economy of scale and product diversity. Put simply, larger white companies can offer black consumers both more economical policies and a wider array of coverage choices.

Despite the gloomy overall picture, the four largest black insurance companies (North Carolina Mutual, of Durham, North Carolina; Atlanta Life, of Atlanta, Georgia; Golden State Mutual, of Los Angeles, California; and Universal Life, of Memphis, Tennessee) continue to keep their heads slightly above water.[51] Still, it remains to be seen if they (and their smaller counterparts) will survive into the twenty-first century.

Ironically, while an increasing number of black-owned enterprises were disappearing from the landscape of American business, the increasing spending power of their former black clients and customers received center-stage attention in the July 1996 issue of *Black Enterprise*. In what was dubbed the "Consumer Empowerment Issue," readers were told, in an article titled "The Real Black Power":

> While corporate America benefits from the dollars African Americans spend, we haven't done enough to leverage that spending clout. The fact is that, once harnessed, African American dollars can be the difference between profit and

loss for any consumer product on the market today. Even more important: Given our current socio-political climate, aside from our voting power, our buying power is the only major leverage we have left.[52]

Black Enterprise went on to cite the Dallas-based Black Consumer Organization of America (BCOA) as an important contemporary effort to systematically harness African American consumer spending. As BCOA president Darlene Edwards-Beacham told the magazine, "We underestimate the power we do have. We need to figure a way to muscle that power."[53]

The venerable National Association of Market Developers (NAMD), too, in recent years, has intensified its efforts on behalf of African American consumers. This long-time intermediary between corporate America and black shoppers, comprised primarily of African American marketing and advertising professionals, is seeking to use its influence to effect a more reciprocal economic relationship between U.S. corporations and the black community. Individual members have been challenged to urge their respective companies and clients to invest more resources in African American enclaves.[54]

Despite the good intentions of organizations like the National Association of Market Developers and the Black Consumer Organization of America, the task before them seems especially daunting. Contemporary African American consumers, despite their increased collective spending power, appear to have less leverage than their forebears. For instance, during the enormously successful Montgomery Bus Boycott, local African Americans not only withheld their patronage of city buses but increased their patronage of various African American enterprises. This dual strategy ultimately helped them achieve victory. Yet, the ongoing disappearance of historically black-owned businesses leaves today's African American consumers all but totally dependent on white (and other nonblack) enterprises for goods and services. Thus, the July 1996 issue of *Black Enterprise,* which linked black consumer "empowerment" to making purchases that directly or indirectly positively affect black-owned businesses,[55] brings to mind the folk maxim "it's too late to close the barn door when the horse is gone."

One positive development, in the midst of an increasingly disturbing scenario, is a resurgence of interest in African American consumer cooperatives. One such company, Black Heritage Products, Inc., based in Greensboro, North Carolina, offers members a wide variety of black-manufactured products. Moreover, the company seeks to combine the traditional consumer cooperative with multilevel marketing. In its October/November

1996 newsletter, Black Heritage Products offered the following rationale for its existence:

> Presently we only retain in the Black community 7 cents of each dollar made by us. The other 93 cents are spent with people that return no value, no support, no concern. It's madness! Black Heritage Products is in existence to stop this madness. . . . Remember when we stop willingly "giving" our money away, we ALL will start to prosper.[56]

Despite the logic behind Black Heritage Products and similar enterprises, it remains to be seen if they can ultimately attract enough black consumer support to truly compete with white-owned businesses.

As the twentieth century draws to a close, it is clear that, since the passage of the Civil Rights Act of 1964, increased black consumerism has produced some serious negative consequences for the African American community. Individual African Americans possess more consumer goods than ever before. Still, if one were to take a stroll through most urban black enclaves in America, one would be hard pressed to see where increased African American spending has improved the infrastructure and the ambiance of these neighborhoods. Black consumers, who now spend the vast majority of their money in shiny downtown and suburban shopping malls, enhance the economic bases of these outside areas to the detriment of their own enclaves. This self-destructive tendency raises the question "Is the slow, but steady, destruction of urban black America (and its businesses) too steep a price to pay for unrestricted African American consumerism?" For contemporary African Americans who would answer "yes," the future demands the development of strategies that will stimulate more constructive economic activity within the black community. A truly free people possesses the power to produce, as well as to consume.

Appendix

National Negro Business League Black Consumer Questionnaire, 1931

This appendix, a reproduction of the National Negro Business League's aborted 1931 national survey of African American consumers, represents a pioneering attempt to generate detailed information about black shoppers.

The National Negro Business League is making a determined fight for the Negro to gain for him a more secure economic place in American life. The strongest argument we have is the power represented in the dollars we spend through stores of various kinds. The National Association of Colored Women is helping us to make a study of the buying habits of Negroes. It is hoped, therefore, that you will cooperate with us by filling out the enclosed questionnaire.

This is a group study, and we hope that you will not take [it] in the spirit of prying into your personal affairs. For that reason, no signatures are requested, and the facts will be published in totals only.

When you have filled it out, please return it to the president of your association who sent it to you, or you may send it direct to the office of the National Negro Business League, 145 West 41st Street, New York City.

★★★★★★★★★★★★★★★★★★★★★★★★★★★

1. Total number in family____ Adults____ Children____ (Boys____ Girls____)

2. Check the income group in which the family belongs:
   ( ) Under $500 a year   ( ) $2,000–$3,000 a year
   ( ) $500–$1,000 a year   ( ) $3,000–$4,000 a year
   ( ) $1,000–$2,000 a year   ( ) $4,000–$5,000 a year
                                     ( ) Over $5,000 a year

3. What amount do you usually spend each month for:
     a. Food_____ (including groceries____ meat____ bread___)
     b. Clothing_____ (including shoes___)
     c. House furnishings and equipment_____
     d. Uplift_____ (including charities____ church____ lodges___)
     e. Recreation_____
     f. Insurance and Savings_____

4. Does your family have:
     Automobile____ telephone____ electric refrigerator____ radio____
     electric washing machine____ vacuum cleaner____

5. Price for price and grade for grade, which do you find more satisfactory:
     a. Advertised brands of goods___
     b. Unadvertised brands of goods___
     c. Unbranded goods___

6. Number in order of importance the factors which influence your buying:
     Convenient location of store___
     Helpful service of the merchant___
     Confidence in the merchant___
     Habits in asking for special brands___
     Price___
     Attractiveness of packages___
     Quality___
     Neatness of store___

7. If you use any advertising medium as a guide in shopping, please check:
     Daily Newspapers___ magazines___ radio___
     Negro newspapers___ street car cards___ direct letters___
     billboards___ store windows___

8. Check the items or service you purchase from Negroes regularly or occasionally
     Groceries___ clothing___ drugs___ physician___ insurance___
     theatre___ dentist___ shoe repair___ restaurant___ taxicab___
     bank___ laundry___
     a. Are Negro clerks as courteous as white clerks?
          Yes___ No___

Are Negro clerks as efficient as white clerks?

Yes___ No___

b. Do you read Negro newspapers regularly? Yes___ No___

9. Remarks _____

_____

_____

_____

Notes

NOTES TO CHAPTER I

1. *The Social and Economic Status of the Black Population in the United States: An Historical View, 1790–1978* (Washington, D.C.: U.S. Bureau of the Census, 1980), 15.

2. *Negro Population, 1790–1915* (Washington, D.C.: U.S. Bureau of the Census, 1918) p. 92; Charles E. Hall, ed. *Negroes in the United States, 1920–1932* (Washington, D.C.: U.S. Bureau of the Census, 1935), 53.

3. *The Social and Economic Status of the Black Population in the U.S.*, 14.

4. Among the books that examine the economic plight of black southerners after the Civil War are: Pete Daniel, *The Shadow of Slavery: Peonage in the South, 1901–1969* (Urbana: University of Illinois Press, 1990; originally published 1972); Jay R. Mandle, *The Roots of Black Poverty: The Southern Plantation Economy after the Civil War* (Durham: Duke University Press, 1978); Daniel A. Novak, *The Wheel of Servitude: Black Forced Labor after Slavery* (Lexington: University of Kentucky Press, 1978); and William Cohen, *At Freedom's Edge: Black Mobility and the Southern White Quest for Racial Control, 1861–1915* (Baton Rouge: Louisiana State University Press, 1991).

5. Among the books that examine the sociopolitical plight of black southerners after the Civil War are: Rayford W. Logan, *The Betrayal of the Negro from Rutherford B. Hayes to Woodrow Wilson* (New York: Collier Books, 1965; originally published 1954); Forrest G. Wood, *Black Scare: The Racist Response to Emancipation and Reconstruction* (Berkeley: University of California Press, 1968); Allen W. Trelease, *The Ku Klux Klan Conspiracy and Southern Reconstruction* (New York: Harper & Row, 1971); C. Vann Woodward, *The Strange Career of Jim Crow*, 3d ed. (New York: Oxford University Press, 1974); and Eric Foner, *Reconstruction: America's Unfinished Revolution, 1863–1877* (New York: Harper & Row, 1988).

6. Marilyn Kern-Foxworth, *Aunt Jemima, Uncle Ben, and Rastus: Blacks in Advertising, Yesterday, Today, and Tomorrow* (Westport, Conn.: Praeger, 1994), 30–32.

7. Ibid., 31–32.

8. Noliwe M. Rooks, *Hair Raising: Beauty, Culture, and African American Women* (New Brunswick, N.J.: Rutgers University Press, 1996), 26.

9. Booker T. Washington, *The Negro in Business* (New York: AMS Press, 1971; originally published in 1907), 297.

10. Ibid.

11. Ibid.

12. Monroe N. Work, ed., *Negro Year Book and Annual Encyclopedia of the Negro, 1912* (Tuskegee, Ala.: Negro Year Book Company, 1912), 180. Although *The Negro Yearbook* characterized itself as an "annual encyclopedia," it did not appear on a yearly basis. There were eleven editions that covered the years 1912; 1913; 1914–15; 1916–17; 1918–19; 1921–22; 1925–26; 1931–32; 1937–38; 1941–46; and 1952.

13. Ibid.

14. *Negro Year Book and Annual Encyclopedia of the Negro, 1913*, 24.

15. Ibid.

16. *Negro Year Book and Annual Encyclopedia of the Negro, 1916–1917*, 318–320; *Negro Year Book and Annual Encyclopedia of the Negro, 1918–1919*, 358.

17. *Negro Year Book, 1916–1917*, 318; *Negro Year Book, 1918–1919*, 355.

18. "How Negroes Spent Their Incomes, 1920–1943," *Sales Management* 54 (June 15, 1945): 106.

19. Hall, *Negroes in the U.S., 1920–1932*, 55.

20. Emmett J. Scott, *Negro Migration during the War* (New York: Oxford University Press, 1920), 50.

21. Ibid., 102.

22. Ibid., 102–103.

23. Ibid., 123–124; 129–130; 136.

24. Ibid., 86–87.

25. Brian Rust, *The American Record Label Book* (New Rochelle, N.Y.: Arlington House, 1978), 212–213; Arnold Shaw, *Black Popular Music in America: From the Spirituals, Minstrels, and Ragtime to Soul, Disco, and Hip-Hop* (New York: Schirmer Books, 1986), 93–94; Eileen Southern, *The Music of Black Americans: A History*, 2d ed. (New York: Norton, 1983), 365.

26. Rust, *The American Record Label Book*, 214.

27. Ibid.; Shaw, *Black Popular Music*, 96.

28. Southern, *The Music of Black Americans*, 366.

29. Shaw, *Black Popular Music*, 102.

30. Ibid.

31. Ibid.; Rust, *The American Record Label Book*, 226.

32. Frederick G. Detweiler, *The Negro Press in the United States* (Chicago: University of Chicago Press, 1922), 113–114.

33. Guy B. Johnson, "Newspaper Advertisements and Negro Culture," *Journal of Social Forces* 3 (May 1925): 707–708.

34. Detweiler, *The Negro Press*, 116.

35. Ibid., 120.

36. Johnson, "Newspaper Advertisements and Negro Culture," 706.

37. A good starting point to ascertain the sentiment of black business proponents during the 1920s is Ronald W. Bailey, ed., *Black Business Enterprise: Historical*

and Contemporary Perspectives (New York: Basic Books, 1971). Part One of this book, "Recurring Themes: An Historical Overview," includes five essays that discuss the historical dynamics of a "black economy." Scholars who have examined the business and economic consequences of the Great Migration include: Allan H. Spear, *Black Chicago: The Making of a Negro Ghetto, 1890–1920* (Chicago: University of Chicago Press, 1967), 181–185; Florette Henri, *Black Migration: Movement North, 1900–1920* (Garden City, N.Y.: Anchor Press, 1975), 158–164; Kenneth Kusmer, *A Ghetto Takes Shape: Black Cleveland, 1870–1930* (Urbana: University of Illinois Press, 1976), 191–194; and Joe W. Trotter, *Black Milwaukee: The Making of an Industrial Proletariat, 1915–1945* (Urbana: University of Illinois Press, 1985), 80–93. Another important source is John Sibley Butler, *Entrepreneurship and Self-Help among Black Americans: A Reconsideration of Race and Economics* (Albany, N.Y.: SUNY Press, 1991), 71–76. Butler, a sociologist, elaborates on the "economic detour" concept put forward by Merah S. Stuart in 1940. Stuart, who wrote a classic book about black insurance companies, discussed the disadvantageous position of black businesspersons in U.S. society and how they struggled to survive. Finally, Juliet E. K. Walker's *The History of Black Business in America: Capitalism, Race, and Entrepreneurship* (New York: Twayne Publishers, 1998) and her edited *Encyclopedia of African American Business History* (Westport, CT: Greenwood Publishers, 1998) should further enhance our knowledge of historical African American business persons.

38. Albon L. Holsey, "Negro in Business Aided by Racial Appeal," *Forbes* 21 (January 15, 1928): 44.

39. Ibid.; 44–46.

40. Albon L. Holsey, "What the Negro Is Doing in Business," *Forbes* 23 (May 1, 1929), 36; Work, *Negro Year Book, 1931–1932*, 133.

41. Holsey, "What the Negro Is Doing in Business," 38.

42. Ibid.

43. Ibid.

44. Albon L. Holsey, "The C.M.A. Stores Face the Chains," *Opportunity* 7 (July 1929): 210.

45. Ibid.

46. Work, *Negro Year Book, 1931–1932*, 133. For a recent discussion of the C.M.A. see chapter 4 of Winston McDowell, "The Ideology of Black Entrepreneurship and Its Impact on the Development of Black Harlem, 1930–1955" (Ph.D. diss., University of Minnesota, 1996).

47. "Business and Government Leaders to Aid Study of Negro Market," *Sales Management* 28 (January 28, 1931): 78.

48. Ibid.

49. Albon L. Holsey Collection, Box 43, Tuskegee Institute.

50. Ibid.

51. H. A. Haring, "Selling to Harlem," *Advertising & Selling* 11 (October 31, 1928): 17.

52. Ibid., 17–18.

53. Ibid., 50.

54. Ibid.

55. H. A. Haring, "The Negro as Consumer," *Advertising & Selling* 15 (September 3, 1930): 20.

56. Ibid., 21.

57. Ibid.

58. Ibid., 68.

59. Paul K. Edwards, *The Southern Urban Negro as a Consumer* (New York: Prentice-Hall, 1932), ix.

60. Ibid., 32–33.

61. Ibid., 38–39.

62. Ibid.

63. Ibid., 42.

64. Ibid., 46–78.

65. Ibid., 97.

66. Ibid., 97–98. This further corroborates Robin D. G. Kelley's assertions regarding pre–Civil Rights Movement-era black resistance in the South.

67. Ibid., 122–126.

68. Ibid., 132–134.

69. Ibid., 242–245.

70. Ibid., 234.

71. Paul K. Edwards, "Distinctive Characteristics of Urban Negro Consumption" (Ph.D. diss., Harvard University, 1936), 86.

72. Ibid.

73. Ibid.

74. Ibid., 95–96.

75. Ibid., 101.

76. Ibid., 130.

77. Robert B. Settle and Pamela L. Alreck, *Why They Buy: American Consumers Inside and Out* (New York: John Wiley, 1986), 10–29.

78. Edwards, "Urban Negro Consumption," 163.

79. T. Arnold Hill, "The Negro Market," *Opportunity* 10 (October 1932): 318.

80. Ibid.

81. "The Negro Market," *Opportunity* 13 (February 1935): 38.

82. Eugene Kinckle Jones, "Purchasing Power of Negroes in the U.S. Estimated at Two Billion Dollars," *Domestic Commerce* 15 (January 10, 1935): 1.

83. Ibid.

84. *The Urban Negro Worker in the United States 1925–1936*, vol. 1 (Washington, D.C.: U.S. Department of the Interior, 1938), iii.

85. Ibid., 110, 112, 115.

NOTES TO CHAPTER 2

1. Rex R. Campbell and Daniel M. Johnson, *Black Migration in America: A Social Demographic History* (Durham: Duke University Press, 1981), 124.

2. John Hope Franklin and Alfred A. Moss Jr., *From Slavery to Freedom: A History of African Americans*, 7th ed. (New York: McGraw-Hill, 1994), 619.

3. Roi Ottley, *New World A-Coming: Inside Black America* (Boston: Houghton-Mifflin, 1943), 293–302.

4. Campbell and Johnson, *Black Migration in America*, 104.

5. David J. Sullivan, "Don't Do This—If You Want to Sell Your Products to Negroes!" *Sales Management* 52 (March 1, 1943): 48, 50.

6. David J. Sullivan, "The American Negro—An 'Export' Market at Home!" *Printer's Ink* 208 (July 21, 1944): 90.

7. Ibid.

8. Ibid., 94.

9. Claude A. Barnett Papers, Chicago Historical Society, Box 131, Folder 5; Vishnu V. Oak, *The Negro Newspaper* (Yellow Springs, Ohio: Antioch Press, 1948), 113, 116.

10. Linda J. Evans, "Claude A. Barnett and the Associated Negro Press," *Chicago History* 12 (Spring 1983): 44; Claude A. Barnett to Paul K. Edwards, June 13, 1931, Paul K. Edwards to Claude A. Barnett, June 20, 1931, Claude A. Barnett Papers, Box 132, Folder 2. Box 132, Folder 2 of the Claude A. Barnett Papers also contains Barnett's correspondence with individuals and organizations regarding his proposed survey of black Chicago consumers. Among the persons who declined Barnett's invitation were: George A. Sloan, president of the Cotton Textile Institute; Fred Rasmussen, executive director of the International Association of Ice Cream Manufacturers; E. L. Newcomb, secretary of the National Wholesale Druggists' Association; and Walter C. Hughes, secretary of the National Confectioners' Association.

11. Oak, *The Negro Newspaper*, 114.

12. Ibid., 114–115.

13. Ibid., 115.

14. *America's Negroes Live as a "Country Within a Country" in Many Places as "A City Within a City"* (New York: Interstate United Newspapers, Inc., 1944), no pagination, Claude A. Barnett Papers, Box 132, Folder 7.

15. Ibid.

16. "158 Negro Newspapers Study Racial Market," *Printer's Ink* 216 (August 23, 1946): 98.

17. "Food, Clothing Get Most of Negroes' $10 Billion," *Advertising Age* 18 (March 24, 1947): 50.

18. Ibid.

19. Ibid.

20. Ibid.

21. "National Negro Market Study Shows $12,000,000,000 Expenditures," *Publishers Weekly* 152 (July 5, 1947): 34–35; Oak, *The Negro Newspaper*, 116.

22. Oak, *The Negro Newspaper*, 115–117; "Negro Markets," *Tide* 20 (March 15, 1946): 86–88.

23. "Negro Incomes and How They Are Spent," *Sales Management* 54 (June 15, 1945): 106.

24. Jules Tygiel, *Baseball's Great Experiment: Jackie Robinson and His Legacy* (New York: Vintage Books, 1984), 52.

25. Ibid.

26. Ibid.

27. *Baseball: A Film by Ken Burns, Inning Six: The National Pastime* (New York: Baseball Film Project, 1994).

28. Tygiel, *Baseball's Great Experiment*, 189.

29. Ibid., 230.

30. Ibid., 232.

31. Ibid., 233–234.

32. Donn Rogosin, *Invisible Men: Life in Baseball's Negro Leagues* (New York: Kodansha International, 1995; first published 1983), 92–96.

33. Robert E. Weems Jr., *Black Business in the Black Metropolis: The Chicago Metropolitan Assurance Company, 1925–1985* (Bloomington: Indiana University Press, 1996), 57–58.

34. Nelson George, *The Death of Rhythm & Blues* (New York: Pantheon Books, 1988), 11–12.

35. "The Forgotten 15,000,000," *Sponsor* 3 (October 10, 1949): 24ff; "The Forgotten 15,000,000," part 2, *Sponsor* 3 (October 24, 1949): 30ff.

36. "The Negro Market: $15,000,000,000 to Spend," *Sponsor* 6 (July 28, 1952): 31.

37. "The Forgotten 15,000,000 . . . Three Years Later," *Sponsor* 6 (July 28, 1952): 29.

38. "The Negro Market: $15,000,000,000 to Spend," 76.

39. "Negro Radio: 200-Plus Specialty Stations—More Coming," *Sponsor* 6 (July 28, 1952): 80.

40. Ibid., 79.

41. Ibid., 33, 78.

42. "Negro Results Stories: Rich Yields for All Clients," *Sponsor* 6 (July 28, 1952): 39, 84–86.

43. "Highlights of 1955 Negro Radio," *Sponsor* 9 (September 19, 1955): 107.

44. George, *The Death of Rhythm & Blues*, 41.

45. Ibid.

46. Ibid.

47. Ibid., 42.

48. Jane Pinkerton, "The Negro Market: Why Buyers Are Looking Twice," *Sponsor Negro Issue* 11 (September 28, 1957): 35.

49. "The Negro Stations Revolve around the Disk Jockey," *Sponsor Negro Issue* 12 (September 20, 1958): 39; William Barlow, "Commercial and Non-commercial Radio," in *Split Image: African Americans in the Mass Media*, ed. Jannette L. Dates and William Barlow (Washington, D.C.: Howard University Press, 1990), 209, 214.

50. Radio station WBOK advertisement, *Sponsor* 7 (August 24, 1953): 94.

51. "Negro Stations: Over 600 Stations Strong Today," *Sponsor* 9 (September 19, 1955): 144; "Negro Appeal Stations: They Work with and Sell the Community," *Sponsor Negro Issue* 11 (September 28, 1957): 10.

52. Rollins Broadcasting, Inc., advertisement, *Sponsor Negro Issue* 12 (September 20, 1958): 2.

53. Rounsaville Stations advertisement, *Sponsor* 9 (September 19, 1955): 151.

54. Ibid.

55. "Negro Stations: Over 600 Stations Strong," 145.

56. "NNN: Negro Radio's Network," *Sponsor* 8 (September 20, 1954): 54, 150–152.

57. National Negro Network advertisement, *Sponsor* 8 (September 20, 1954): 46.

58. Albert Abarbanel and Alex Haley, "A New Audience for Radio," *Harpers* 212 (February 1956): 59.

59. Horace Clarence Boyer, *How Sweet the Sound: The Golden Age of Gospel* (Washington, D.C.: Elliot & Clark, 1995), 67.

60. Ibid., 52–53.

61. Ibid., 60–61.

62. Martin and Morris Music Company Records, Archives Center, National Museum of American History, Smithsonian Institution, Series 3C, Boxes 6 and 7.

63. Boyer, *How Sweet the Sound*, 64, 74–75; Collection description, Martin and Morris Music Company Records.

64. Martin and Morris Music Company Records, Series 2, Boxes 9 and 10.

65. "The Negro Market: An Appraisal," *Tide* 21 (March 7, 1947): 15; Jesse Parkhurst Guzman, ed., *Negro Year Book: A Review of Events Affecting Negro Life, 1941–1946* (Tuskegee, Ala.: Tuskegee Institute Department of Records and Research, 1947), 195.

66. "The Negro Market: An Appraisal," 15.

67. "Are You Interested in a Market Worth Ten Billion Dollars?" *Pepsi-Cola* 8 (May 1948): 6, Pepsi Collection, Research Files, Box 3 Folder 4, Archives Center, National Museum of American History, Smithsonian Institution.

68. Adrian Hirschorn, "Pepsi-Cola's Campaign to the Negro Market," *Printer's Ink* 228 (September 9, 1949): 40.

69. Pepsi Collection, "Pepsi Generation Oral History Project," Series 2 Interviewee File, Box 13, Archives Center, National Museum of American History, Smithsonian Institution.

70. "Experiment in New Orleans," *Pepsi-Cola World* 14 (September 1954): 3, Pepsi Collection, Research Files, Box 3 Folder 4, Archives Center, National Museum of American History, Smithsonian Institution.

71. Ibid.

72. Ibid.

73. Ibid.

74. Ibid.

75. Interview, James Avery, October 22, 1996. Mr. Avery is a former president of the National Association of Market Developers.

76. Ibid.; Interview, Samuel Whiteman and James "Bud" Ward, September 17, 1994. Mr. Whiteman, now deceased, was one of the acknowledged founders of the National Association of Market Developers. Mr. Ward has held a number of positions within NAMD including president of the Washington, D.C. chapter and vice president, executive director, and chairman of the board of the national organization.

77. "History of NAMD," *Emphasis 95*, official program of the 43rd Meeting of the National Association of Market Developers, May 1995, 9; Interview, James Avery, October 22, 1996; Interview, Miriam Evans, October 5, 1994. Mrs. Evans, who worked in the Public Relations Department of Bell Pennsylvania (now Bell Atlantic), served as NAMD's treasurer for many years.

78. "Monumental Achievements: NAMD," *National Black Monitor* 10 (September 1985): 4.

79. "History of NAMD," *Emphasis 95*, 9; Interview, Samuel Whiteman and James "Bud" Ward, September 17, 1994.

80. "NAMD," *National Black Monitor*, 8; Interview, James Avery, October 22, 1996; Interview, Chuck Smith, May 25, 1995. Mr. Smith served in a variety of capacities within the National Association of Market Developers, including vice president, president, and chairman of the board.

81. Interview, Chuck Smith, May 25, 1995.

82. "History of NAMD," *Emphasis 95*, 9; "NAMD," *National Black Monitor*, 10.

83. "The Negro Market: As Customers and Citizens, Its People Are Still Making Significant Progress," *Tide* 26 (July 25, 1952): 44.

84. Sarita Robinson, ed., *Readers Guide to Periodical Literature Volume 19 April 1953–February 1955* (New York: H. W. Wilson, 1955), 1660.

85. William K. Bell, *15 Million Negroes and 15 Billion Dollars* (New York: William K. Bell, 1958), x–xi.

NOTES TO CHAPTER 3

1. Thomas C. Holt, "The Lonely Warrior: Ida B. Wells-Barnett and the Struggle for Black Leadership," in John Hope Franklin and August Meier, eds., *Black Leaders of the Twentieth Century* (Urbana: University of Illinois Press, 1982), 42.

2. August Meier and Elliott Rudwick, "The Boycott Movement against Jim

Crow Streetcars in the South, 1900–1906," *Journal of American History* 55 (March 1969): 758.

3. Ibid., 761.

4. Ibid., 775.

5. Henry Lee Moon, "The Black Boycott," *Crisis* 73 (May 1966): 249–250. Also see August Meier and Elliott Rudwick, "The Origins of Nonviolent Direct Action in Afro-American Protest: A Note on Historical Discontinuities," in David J. Garrow, ed., *We Shall Overcome: The Civil Rights Movement in the United States in the 1950s and 1960s*, vol. 3 (Brooklyn: Carlson, 1989), 315–316.

6. William Edward Burghardt Du Bois, "The Negro's Industrial Plight," *Crisis* 38 (July 1931): 242.

7. Moon, "The Black Boycott," 253.

8. Darlene Clark Hine et al., eds., *Black Women in America: An Historical Encyclopedia* (Brooklyn: Carlson, 1993), 584–586; Darlene Clark Hine, *Hine Sight: Black Women and the Reconstruction of American History* (Bloomington: Indiana University Press, 1994), 129–145.

9. St. Clair Drake, "Why Not Co-operate?" *Opportunity* 14 (August 1936): 233.

10. Ibid., 234.

11. Bertram B. Fowler, "Miracle in Gary: The Negro Gropes toward Economic Equality," *Forum & Century* 96 (September 1936): 135; Margueritte Harmon Bro, "Up by the Bootstraps," *Christian Century* 53 (April 1, 1936): 492.

12. Fowler, "Miracle in Gary," 136.

13. Ibid.; Joseph A. Pierce, *Negro Business and Business Education* (New York: Plenum Press, 1995; originally published in 1947), 164–178.

14. W. E. B. Du Bois, "A Negro Nation within the Nation," *Current History* 42 (June 1935): 270.

15. Roi Ottley, *New World A-Coming: Inside Black America* (Boston: Houghton-Mifflin, 1943), 287–288.

16. David J. Sullivan, "Don't Do This—If You Want to Sell Your Products to Negroes!" *Sales Management* 52 (March 1, 1943): 46, 50.

17. Martin Luther King Jr., *Stride Toward Freedom: The Montgomery Story* (San Francisco: Harper & Row, 1958), 34–38.

18. Ibid., 70.

19. Ibid., 40–41.

20. David J. Garrow, *Bearing the Cross: Martin Luther King and the Southern Christian Leadership Conference* (New York: Vintage Books, 1988), 77.

21. Norman W. Walton, "The Walking City: A History of the Montgomery Bus Boycott," *Negro History Bulletin* 20 (November 1956): 32.

22. Taylor Branch, *Parting the Waters: America in the King Years, 1954–1963* (New York: Touchstone Books, 1989), 201.

23. Ibid., 198.

24. William Bradford Huie, "The Shocking Story of Approved Killing in Mis-

sissippi," *Look* 20 (January 24, 1956): 46–50. Also see Clenora Hudson-Weems, *Emmett Till: The Sacrificial Lamb of the Civil Rights Movement* (Troy, Mich.: Bedford, 1994).

25. William Bradford Huie, "What's Happened to the Till Killers?" *Look* 21 (January 22, 1957): 65.

26. Ronald Walters, "Standing Up in America's Heartland: Sitting in before Greensboro," *American Visions* 8 (February/March, 1993): 20–23.

27. *Business Week*, February 27, 1960, 26.

28. Ibid.

29. Ibid., 28.

30. Ibid.

31. *Business Week*, April 23, 1960, 31.

32. Ibid.

33. Ibid., 32.

34. Ibid.

35. Ibid.

36. Ibid.

37. *Business Week*, December 17, 1960, 34.

38. *Business Week*, August 5, 1961, 58.

39. Ibid. Also, see Elizabeth Jacoway and David R. Colburn, eds., *Southern Businessmen and Desegregation* (Baton Rouge: Louisiana State University Press, 1982).

40. *Business Week*, August 5, 1961, 58.

41. *Business Week*, May 12, 1962, 130.

42. Ibid., 131.

43. Ibid., 130.

44. Ibid.

45. Garrow, *Bearing the Cross*, 220.

46. Ibid., 226–227.

47. Ibid., 291–292.

48. "Will Negroes Back Christmas Boycott?" *Printer's Ink* 285 (October 4, 1963): 7.

49. Ibid.

50. "Negro Boycott Could Have Serious, Lasting Effect on Sales, Study Shows," *Advertising Age* 34 (September 30, 1963): 3.

51. *Printer's Ink*, October 4, 1963, 7; "No Christmas Boycott," *Crisis* 70 (November 1963): 555–556.

52. John H. Britton, "Negroes Ready to Go for Broke," *Jet*, October 17, 1963, 47–48.

53. Ibid., 49.

54. "Yule Boycott Is Senseless, Johnson Says," *Advertising Age* 34 (October 21, 1963): 3.

55. Robert E. Weems Jr., "The Revolution Will Be Marketed: American Cor-

porations and Black Consumers during the 1960s," *Radical History Review* 59 (Spring 1994): 99–102.

56. Ibid., 96–98.

57. "Smoothing a Way for Rights Law," *Business Week,* June 20, 1964, 32.

58. John Hope Franklin and Alfred A. Moss Jr., *From Slavery to Freedom: A History of African Americans,* 7th ed. (New York: McGraw-Hill, 1994), 624–625.

59. Ibid., 625.

NOTES TO CHAPTER 4

1. Rex R. Campbell and Daniel M. Johnson, *Black Migration in America: A Social Demographic History* (Durham: Duke University Press, 1981), 132.

2. A cross-section of such articles included: C. H. Hall, "Advertisers Guide to Marketing, 1960 Negro Market," *Printer's Ink* 269 (October 30, 1959): 246–247; "Marketing to the Negro Consumer; Special Report," *Sales Management* 84 (March 4, 1960): 36–44; "The Negro Market for Frozen Foods," *Quick Frozen Foods* 22 (April 1960): 106–109; "Combine Media Ads, Displays, Promotions to Reach Negro Market, Panel Tells Adcrafters," *Advertising Age* 32 (November 19, 1962): 52; "The Negro Consumer," *Electrical Merchandising Week* 96 (April 27, 1964): 13–26; Norman W. Spaulding, "Bridging the Color Gap," *Public Relations Journal* 25 (April 1969): 8–11; and Raymond Oladipupo, "The Urban Negro Separate & Distinct," *Mediascope* 13 (July 1969): 18, 76.

3. "Know-How Is Key to Selling Negro Market Today," *Sponsor Negro Issue* 15 (October 9, 1961): 26–27.

4. John H. Johnson and Lerone Bennett Jr., *Succeeding against the Odds* (New York: Warner Books, 1989), 173, 179–180, 229.

5. Ibid., 156–157, 287.

6. Ibid., 277–280.

7. Maurine Christopher, "CORE Seeks More Integrated Ads: CORE Invites 14 Major Advertisers to Discuss Using Negroes in Ads," *Advertising Age* 33 (September 9, 1963): 1, 128; Maurine Christopher, "CORE Intensifies Drive for Negroes in Ads; Zeroes in on Pepsi-Cola Co.," *Advertising Age* 35 (November 9, 1964): 3, 71; "Boycott by Negroes?" *Printer's Ink* 284 (August 23, 1963): 5–6; "Same Ad, Intelligently Done, Can Sell to Both Whites, Negroes: Bullock," *Advertising Age* 31 (June 12, 1961): 23; "Integrated Ads Not Offensive to Whites: Dallas Group Told," *Advertising Age* 38 (October 14, 1968): 31; "Use of Negro Models in Ads Won't Reduce Sales to Whites, [John H.] Johnson Advises Workshop," *Advertising Age* 38 (December 9, 1968): 24; "Use of Black Models in Ads Doesn't Alter Sales Patterns, BofA Reports," *Advertising Age* 40 (November 9, 1970): 52; Lester Guest, "How Negro Models Affect Company Image," *Journal of Advertising Research* 10 (April 1970): 29–33.

8. Johnson and Bennett, *Succeeding against the Odds*, 27.

9. *The Negro Handbook* (Chicago: Johnson Publishing Company, 1966), 214.

10. D. Parke Gibson, "Advertising and the Dual Society: Challenge of the Seventies," *Mediascope* 13 (August 1969): 63.

11. Elsie Archer, "How to Sell Today's Negro Woman," *Sponsor* 20 (July 25, 1966): 49.

12. Lawrence E. Black, "The Negro Market: Growing, Changing, Challenging," *Sales Management* 91 (October 4, 1963): 46.

13. Black advisers to American corporations seemed to be partially responsible for this development. See "Don't Contrive Integrated Ads, Johnson Advises," *Advertising Age* 33 (September 23, 1963): 1, 111; "Help Negro in Image Effort Via Ads, Wilkins Asks," *Advertising Age* 33 (November 11, 1963): 1, 112.

14. "The Soul Market in Black and White," *Sales Management* 102 (June 1, 1969): 37–41.

15. Ibid., 37.

16. Ibid., 40.

17. Ibid.

18. *Zebra Associates: Why We Are . . . What We Are . . . Who We Are*, 1969 company promotional pamphlet, 3–7, Carolyn R. Jones Collection, Box 1, Folder 1, Archives Center, National Museum of History, Smithsonian Institution.

19. "Minority Training Program Part of Zebra's Operation," June 19, 1969 company press release, Carolyn R. Jones Collection, Box 1, Folder 1, Archives Center, National Museum of History, Smithsonian Institution.

20. "Zebra Agency Offers Top Talents to Small Black Advertisers," June 19, 1969 company press release, Carolyn R. Jones Collection, Box 1, Folder 1, Archives Center, National Museum of History, Smithsonian Institution.

NOTES TO CHAPTER 5

1. Curtis Mayfield, "No Thing on Me (Cocaine Song)," *Superfly* (LP record: RSO Records, Inc., RS-1-3046; 1972).

2. *The Social and Economic Status of the Black Population in the United States: An Historical View, 1790–1978* (Washington, D.C.: U.S. Bureau of the Census, 1979), 14.

3. Rex R. Campbell and Daniel M. Johnson, *Black Migration in America: A Social Demographic History* (Durham: Duke University Press, 1981), 152.

4. Cobbett S. Steinberg, *Film Facts* (New York: Facts On File, 1980), 46.

5. James P. Murray, "The Subject Is Money," *Black Creation* 4 (Winter 1973): 26.

6. Ibid.

7. Daniel J. Leab, *From Sambo to Superspade: The Black Experience in Motion Pictures* (Boston: Houghton-Mifflin, 1975), 233; Robert E. Weems Jr., "The Revolution Will Be Marketed: American Corporations and African-American Consumers during the 1960s," *Radical History Review* 59 (Spring 1994): 94–107.

8. Donald Bogle, *Toms, Coons, Mulattoes, Mammies, & Bucks: An Interpretive History of Blacks in American Films* (New York: Continuum, 1989), 215–217.

9. Ed Guerrero, *Framing Blackness: The African-American Image in Film* (Philadelphia: Temple University Press, 1993), 73.

10. Bogle, *Toms, Coons*, 220–223; Guerrero, *Framing Blackness*, 78–79; Leab, *From Sambo to Superspade*, 234–237.

11. Leab, *From Sambo to Superspade*, 234.

12. Bogle, *Toms, Coons*, 238; Fred Beauford, "Black Movies Create Box-Office Magic," *Black Enterprise* 4 (September 1972): 53.

13. Guerrero, *Framing Blackness*, 82.

14. Steinberg, *Film Facts*, 86–87; "Hollywood's New Public," *The Economist* 247 (May 19, 1973): 53.

15. Murray, "The Subject Is Money," 26.

16. Ibid.; "Hollywood's New Public," 53.

17. "Blacks vs. Shaft," *Newsweek* 80 (August 28, 1972): 88.

18. Adam David Miller, "Black Films $$$: A Critique," *Black Scholar* 4, (January 1973): 55.

19. Bogle, *Toms, Coons*, 241–245. Donald Bogle is the originator of the term "Buckmania."

20. Theophilus Green, "The Black Man as Movie Hero," *Ebony* 27 (August 1972): 148; Barbara Morrow Williams, "Filth vs. Lucre: The Black Community's Tough Choice," *Psychology Today* 7 (February 1974): 102; Beauford, "Black Movies," 48.

21. "Hollywood's New Public," 53.

22. Roland F. Jefferson, "The Black Film Boom: Decerebrate, Dangerous and Declining," *Journal of the National Medical Association* 67 (January 1975): 13.

23. Bogle, *Toms, Coons*, 251–252; Guerrero, *Framing Blackness*, 98–100; Nelson George, *Blackface: Reflections on African Americans and the Movies* (New York: Harper-Collins, 1994), 57. The term "Superbadd Supermama," again, is directly derived from Don Bogle's classic work.

24. Beauford, "Black Movies," 48; "Hollywood's New Public," 53; David Graham Du Bois, "Review of *Sounder*," *Black Scholar* 4 (January 1973): 53–54; Bogle, *Toms, Coons,* 246–249.

25. Beauford, "Black Movies," 48; Murray, "The Subject Is Money," 29; Bogle, *Toms, Coons*, 245.

26. "Uptown Saturday Night," *Ebony* 29 (July 1974): 52–53.

27. *Variety* 275 (July 3, 1974): 9; 276 (October 16, 1974): 9.

28. Leab, *From Sambo to Superspade*, 258–260.

29. Pearl Bowser, "History Lesson: The Boom Is Really an Echo," *Black Creation* 4 (Winter 1973): 34.

30. Williams, "Filth vs. Lucre," 98–99.

31. Ibid., 99.

32. Ibid.

33. Ibid.

34. Ibid.

35. "Blacks vs. Shaft," 88.

36. Ibid.

37. Michael Mattox, "The Day Black Movie Stars Got Militant," *Black Creation* 4 (Winter 1973): 40–42.

38. Ibid., 42.

39. Alvin J. Pouissaint, "Blaxploitation Movies: Cheap Thrills That Degrade Blacks," *Psychology Today* 7 (February 1974): 22, 26.

40. *Ibid.*, 98.

41. James P. Murray, *To Find an Image: Black Films from Uncle Tom to Superfly* (Indianapolis: Bobbs-Merrill, 1973), 168.

42. Renee Ward, "Black Films, White Profits," *Black Scholar* 7 (May 1976): 19–22.

43. Murray, *To Find an Image*, 168; "The Black Movie Boom," *Newsweek* 78 (September 6, 1971): 66.

44. Murray, *To Find an Image*, 168–169.

45. Leab, *From Sambo to Superspade*, 259.

46. Ward, "Black Films, White Profits," 21.

47. Jefferson, "The Black Movie Boom," 12; Guerrero, *Framing Blackness,* 97.

48. Leab, *From Sambo to Superspade*, 262; Guerrero, *Framing Blackness*, 105.

49. Guerrero, *Framing Blackness*, 105.

50. George, *Blackface*, 63–64; Bogle, *Toms, Coons*, 262–264.

51. Shirley H. Rhine, "The Economic Status of Black Americans," *Conference Board Record* 9 (August 1972): 27, 29.

52. Ibid., 31.

53. "Beauty Chemicals: The Ethnic Market," *Chemical Marketing Reporter* 203 (June 11, 1973): 36.

54. Ibid.

55. Catherine Ellis Hunter, "Flori Roberts: White Success in Black Cosmetics," *Drug & Cosmetic Industry* 122 (June 1978): 32–36.

56. Charles Marticorena, "Ethnic Market: Biggest Potential for Growth in Cosmetics Industry," *Chemical Marketing Reporter* 207 (June 23, 1975): 38.

57. Ibid.

58. "Selling Black Cosmetics Proves a Tricky Business," *American Druggist* 176 (August 1977): 59–60.

59. Ibid., 61.

60. "Avon Aims New Line, Ad Effort at Fast-Growing Black Market," *Advertising Age* 46 (July 28, 1975): 57.

61. James P. Forkan, "Who's Who in $350,000,000 Black Grooming Market," *Advertising Age* 43 (November 20, 1972): 96–97; "Essence Urges R & D for Blacks," *Product Marketing* 6 (December 1977): 30.

62. "Black Cosmetics: A Beautiful Business," *Chemical Week* 120 (June 8, 1977): 47.

63. Ibid., 47–48.

64. "Essence Urges R & D for Blacks," 1, 30.

65. Ibid., 31.

66. Grayson Mitchell, "Battle of the Rouge," *Black Enterprise* 9 (August 1978): 25.

67. Ibid.

68. Ibid.

69. Ibid., 26.

70. Robert E. Weems Jr., *Black Business in the Black Metropolis* (Bloomington: Indiana University Press, 1996), 103.

71. Jacob M. Duker and Charles E. Hughes, "The Black-Owned Life Insurance Company: Issues and Recommendations," *Journal of Risk and Insurance* 40 (June 1973): 223.

72. Ibid., 225.

73. Ibid., 226.

74. "The Bedrock of Black Wealth," *Black Enterprise* 10, June, 1980, 141.

75. "The Prudential Insurance Company of America" and "Metropolitan Life Insurance Company," *Best's Insurance Reports: Life-Health 1979* (Oldwick, N.J.: A. M. Best Company, 1979), 1580, 1180.

76. Monroe Anderson, "Black Advertising Agencies Are Attempting to Get the Black Market," *National Observer* (November 13, 1971): 11; Ted Angelus, "Black Film Explosion Uncovers an Untapped, Rich Market," *Advertising Age* 43 (July 24, 1972: 51, 53.

77. "Black Media Less Efficient, Y & R Says," *Advertising Age* 43 (April 3, 1972): 1.

78. Ibid.

79. "Our Longevity Shows We've Been Efficient: [John H.] Johnson," *Advertising Age* 43 (May 29, 1972): 50.

80. John H. Johnson, "Black Media Fill Needs Not Recognized Elsewhere," *Advertising Age* 50 (April 16, 1979): S-25.

81. Anderson, "Black Advertising Agencies," 11.

82. Bob Donath, "Black-Owned Shops Still Seeking Identity," *Advertising Age* 48 (May 16, 1977): 3.

83. Ibid., 98.

84. Ibid., 96.

85. Ibid., 3.

NOTES TO CHAPTER 6

1. Charles Dickens, *A Tale of Two Cities* (New York: Bantam Books, 1981; originally published in 1859), 1.

2. David H. Swinton, "Economic Status of Black Americans during the 1980s: A Decade of Limited Progress," in *The State of Black America 1990*, ed. Janet Dewart (New York: National Urban League, 1990), 25–52. Other published works that survey the economic status of African Americans during the 1980s include Andrew Brimmer, "Economic Outlook: Reaganomics and the Black Community," *Black Enterprise* 12 (December 1981): 43–44; Timothy Bates, "The Declining Relative Incomes of Urban Black Households," *Challenge* 26 (May–June 1983): 48–49; Reynolds Farley and Suzanne M. Bianchi, "The Growing Gap between Blacks," *American Demographics* 5 (July 1983): 15–18; "America's Underclass," *Economist* 298 (March 15, 1986): 29–32.

3. Robert B. Hill, "The Economic Status of Black Americans," in *The State of Black America 1981*, ed. James D. Williams (New York: National Urban League, 1981), 7; David H. Swinton, "The Economic Status of the Black Population," in *The State of Black America 1983*, ed. James D. Williams (New York: National Urban League, 1983), 45.

4. Denys Vaughn-Cooke, "The Economic State of Black America—Is There a Recovery?," *The State of Black America 1984*, ed. James D. Williams (New York: National Urban League, 1984), 18.

5. Ibid., 14–15.

6. Swinton, "Economic Status of Black Americans during the 1980s," 47.

7. Ibid., 34–35.

8. Jerome D. Williams and William J. Qualls, "Middle-Class Black Consumers and Intensity of Ethnic Identification," *Psychology & Marketing* 6 (Winter 1989): 267.

9. Robert B. Hill, "The Black Middle Class: Past, Present and Future," *The State of Black America 1986* (New York: National Urban League, 1986), 43–44.

10. Ibid., 48.

11. Ibid., 48–49.

12. Ibid., 50–52.

13. Ibid., 52, 56.

14. William O'Hare, "In the Black," *American Demographics* 11 (November 1989): 25.

15. Ibid., 26.

16. Ibid., 26–27.

17. Ibid., 27.

18. Herbert Allen, "Product Appeal: No Class Barrier," *Advertising Age* 52 (May 18, 1981): S-4.

19. Ibid.

20. Ibid.

21. Ibid.

22. Ibid.

23. B. Drake Stelle, "Publishers See Segmentation in Black Market," *Advertising Age* 52 (May 18, 1981): S-6.

24. Williams and Qualls, "Middle Class Black Consumers," 270, 272.

25. James C. Lawson, "Financial Services Target Segment within a Segment," *Advertising Age* 57 (August 25, 1986): S-1, S-2.

26. Ibid., S-2.

27. George A. Hacker, Ronald Collins, and Michael Jacobson, *Marketing Booze to Blacks* (Washington, D.C.: Center for Science in the Public Interest, 1987), 6; "Black Figures to Be Bigger," *Advertising Age* 52 (July 27, 1981): S-12.

28. Ibid.

29. Hacker, Collins, and Jacobson, *Marketing Booze to Blacks*, 3.

30. Ibid., 12–13.

31. Ibid., 13–14.

32. Ibid., 14.

33. Ibid., 18.

34. Ibid., 18, 20.

35. Ibid., 20.

36. Ibid., 15–17.

37. Ibid., 11.

38. Ibid., 12.

39. Ibid., 11–12.

40. Ibid., 22.

41. Ibid., 23.

42. Cynthia Durcanin: "Sign of the Times: 'Sin' Ads Target Blacks," Atlanta *Constitution*, March 26, 1989, 14A.

43. Ibid., 1,5.

44. Ibid., 31.

45. Ibid., 33.

46. Ibid., 34.

47. Ibid., 32.

48. Ibid., 34–35.

49. Ibid., 37.

50. Djata, "The Marketing of Vices to Black Consumers," *Business and Society Review* 62 (Summer 1987): 49.

51. Gail Baker Woods, *Advertising and Marketing to the New Majority* (Belmont, Calif.: Wadsworth, 1995), 110; Judann Dagnoli, "RJR's Uptown Targets Blacks," *Advertising Age* 60 (December 16, 1989): 44.

52. Baker Woods, *Advertising and Marketing to the New Majority*, 111.

53. Ibid.

54. Ibid.

55. Durcanin, "Sign of the Times,": 'Sin' Ads Target Blacks," 1A.

56. Patricia Edmonds, "Are Tobacco, Alcohol Industries Friends or Foes of Minorities?" Miami *Herald*, August 13, 1989, 5G.

57. Billy J. Tidwell, "Black Wealth: Facts and Fiction," in *The State of Black America 1988*, ed. Janet Dewart (New York: National Urban League, 1988), 195.

58. Ibid.

NOTES TO CHAPTER 7

1. Jeffrey M. Humphreys, "Black Buying Power by Place of Residence: 1990–1996," *Georgia Business and Economic Conditions* 55 (July–August 1995): 2.

2. Randall Rothenberg, "Blacks Are Found to Be Still Scarce in Advertisements in Major Magazines," *New York Times*, July 23, 1991, A–7.

3. Ibid.

4. Ibid.

5. Joseph M. Winski, "The Ad Industry's 'Dirty Little Secret'," *Advertising Age* 63 (June 15, 1992): 16, 38.

6. Ibid., 16.

7. Lowell Thompson, "Blacks in Ad Agencies: It Used to be Better," *Advertising Age* 63 (November 16, 1992): 22.

8. Ibid.

9. "African-Americans," *Adweek's Marketing Week* 32 (January 21, 1991): 19.

10. Laura Bird, "Marketers Miss Out by Alienating Blacks," *Wall Street Journal*, April 9, 1993, B8.

11. Adrienne Ward, "What Role Do Ads Play in Racial Tension," *Advertising Age* 63 (August 10, 1992): 1.

12. Ibid.

13. Bruce Horovitz, "Harmonic Convergence: Racial Tolerance Is Suddenly a Hot Topic in Advertising," Los Angeles *Times*, January 19, 1993, D1.

14. Ibid., D6.

15. Richard Corliss, "Boyz of New Black City," *Time* 137 (June 17, 1991): 64–68.

16. John Leland and Donna Foote, "A Bad Omen for Black Movies?" *Newsweek* 118 (July 29, 1991): 48.

17. Ibid., 48–49.

18. Mark Lowery and Nadirah Z. Sabir, "The Making of 'Hollywood,'" *Black Enterprise* 25 (December 1994): 108.

19. Corliss, "Boyz of New Black City," 68.

20. Jesse A. Rhines, *Black Film/White Money* (New Brunswick, N.J.: Rutgers University Press, 1996), 7.

21. A cross-section of contemporary articles focusing on continuing economic deprivation in the African American community includes: "Black Americans: Still Trailing Behind," *Economist* 314 (March 3, 1990): 17–19; "America's Blacks: A World Apart," *Economist* 318 (March 30, 1991): 17–18; Henry Louis Gates Jr., "Two Nations . . . Both Black," *Forbes* 150 (September 14, 1992): 132–135. Perhaps the most debated scholarly study of the underclass is William Julius Wilson, *The Truly Disadvantaged: The Inner City, the Underclass, and Public Policy* (Chicago: University of Chicago Press, 1987). Among a number of other studies of the urban black poor are Michael B. Katz, ed., *The Underclass Debate: Views from History* (Princeton: Princeton

University Press, 1993), and Douglas S. Massey and Nancy A. Denton, *American Apartheid: Segregation and the Making of the Underclass* (Cambridge, Mass.: Harvard University Press, 1993).

22. Robert E. Weems Jr., "Black America during the 1960s: What Really Happened?" *Western Journal of Black Studies* 14 (Fall 1990): 155.

23. Rhines, *Black Film/White Money*, 106, 112,

24. Ibid., 110–111.

25. Karen Grigsby Bates, "They've Gotta Have Us: Hollywood's Black Directors," *New York Times Magazine*, July 14, 1991, 18.

26. Ibid.

27. Ibid.

28. Rhines, *Black Film/White Money*, 69.

29. Ibid., 72–73.

30. Lowery and Sabir, *"Hollywood,"* 112.

31. Ibid.

32. Rhines, *Black Film/White Money*, 171–172.

33. Ibid., 7.

34. Ibid., 96.

35. *The Bowker Annual: Library and Book Trade Almanac*, 38th ed. (New Providence, N.J.: R. R. Bowker, 1993), 567; *The Bowker Annual*, 39th ed. (1994), 625.

36. *Billboard*, June 8, 1996, 118.

37. *The Bowker Annual*, 40th ed. (1995), 599–600.

38. *The Bowker Annual*, 41st ed. (1996), 638.

39. *Variety* 361 (January 1–7, 1996): 12.

40. Ibid., 362 (April 29–May 5, 1996): 12.

41. *Billboard*, May 11, 1996, 60; May 18, 1996, 65; May 25, 1996, 80; June 1, 1996, 81; July 6, 1996, 82.

42. Pat Sloan, "New Maybelline Line Targets Blacks," *Advertising Age* 61 (December 17, 1991): 1.

43. Ibid., 36.

44. Caroline V. Clarke, "Redefining Beautiful," *Black Enterprise* 23 (June 1993): 243, 246, 248.

45. Ibid., 244.

46. Ibid., 248.

47. Brett Pulley, "Johnson Products Agrees to $67 Million Ivax Buyout," *Wall Street Journal*, June 15, 1993, B3.

48. Ibid.

49. Matthew S. Scott, "B.E. Financials Overview," *Black Enterprise* 26 (June 1996): 164; Robert E. Weems Jr., "A Crumbling Legacy: The Decline of African American Insurance Companies in Contemporary America," *Review of Black Political Economy* 23 (Fall 1994): 25–37.

50. Scott, "B.E. Financials Overview," 164; Weems, "A Crumbling Legacy," 31.

51. Weems, "A Crumbling Legacy," 31–32.

52. Marjorie Whigham-Desir, "The Real Black Power," *Black Enterprise* 26 (July 1996): 62.

53. Ibid.

54. Claudia M. Abercrumbie, "Corporate America: It's Your Move!" *Emphasis 94* (official program of the 42d meeting of the National Association of Market Developers, Dallas, Texas, 1994): 12.

55. Whigham-Desir, "The Real Black Power," 62.

56. "We Must Stop the MADNESS!!!," *Black Heritage Products, Inc., Newsletter* 22 (October/November 1996): 1.

Selected Bibliography

PRIMARY SOURCES

Collections of Papers

Barnett, Claude A. Papers. Chicago Historical Society, Chicago, Illinois.

Holsey, Albon L. Papers. Tuskegee Institute, Tuskegee, Alabama.

Jones, Carolyn R. Papers. Archives Center, National Museum of History, Washington, D.C.

Martin and Morris Music Company. Papers. Archives Center, National Museum of History, Washington, D.C.

Pepsi-Cola. Papers. Archives Center, National Museum of History, Washington, D.C.

Government Publications

U.S. Bureau of the Census. *Negroes in the United States, 1920–1932*. Washington, D.C.: Government Printing Office, 1935.

———. *Negro Population, 1790–1915*. Washington, D.C.: Government Printing Office, 1918.

———. *The Social and Economic Status of the Black Population in the United States: An Historical View, 1790–1978*. Washington, D.C.: Government Printing Office, 1979.

U.S. Department of Commerce. *Guide to Negro Marketing Information*. Washington, D.C.: Government Printing Office, 1966.

U.S. Department of the Interior. *The Urban Negro Worker in the United States: 1925–1936*. Washington, D.C.: Government Printing Office, 1938.

U.S. Department of Labor. *Negroes in the United States: Their Employment and Economic Status*. Washington, D.C.: Government Printing Office, 1952.

SECONDARY SOURCES

Books and Articles

Abarbanel, Albert, and Alex Haley. "A New Audience for Radio." *Harper's* 212 (February 1956): 57–59.

Abercrumbie, Claudia M. "Corporate America: It's Your Move!" *Emphasis* 94 (official program of the 42d meeting of the National Association of Market Developers, Dallas, Texas, 1994).

"Adman's Guide to Negro Media." *Sponsor (Negro Market Supplement)* 21 (July 1967): 42–45, 48–51.

"Ads in Negro-Market Media Do Double Duty with Negro Buyers, Zimmer Says." *Advertising Age* 35 (13 January 1964): 72.

"Ads Progress in Portraying Blacks but Still Fall Short, Study Finds." *Advertising Age* 40 (3 February 1969): 87.

"Ads Sans Minorities Distort U.S. Image, Says N.Y. Committee." *Advertising Age* 34 (4 March 1963): 28.

"Advice on the Negro." *Business Week* (13 April 1940): 47–48.

"African-Americans." *Adweek's Marketing Week* 32 (21 January 1991): 18–21.

Alexis, Marcus. "Pathways to the Negro Market." *Journal of Negro Education* 28 (Spring 1959): 114–27.

———. "Patterns of Black Consumption, 1935–1960." *Journal of Black Studies* 1 (September 1970): 55–74.

Allen, Bonnie. "The Macho Men: What Ever Happened to Them?" *Essence* 9 (February 1979): 62, 90–98.

Allen, Herbert. "Product Appeal: No Class Barrier." *Advertising Age* 52 (18 May 1981): S-4, S-14.

———. "Black Media's Low Profile Poses a Problem." *Advertising Age* 52 (19 October 1981): S-52.

Allen, Joe. "Ethnic Skin/Hair Products Up 12–20% in '79; Misconceptions Still Cause Lost Millions in Sales." *Supermarket Business* 35 (May 1980): 26.

"America's Blacks: A World Apart." *Economist* 318 (30 March 1991): 17–19.

"America's Underclass: Doomed to Fail in the Land of Opportunity." *Economist* 298 (15 March 1988): 29–32.

Anderson, Al. "White Agencies Should Use Black Shops as Consultants." *Advertising Age* 50 (16 April 1979): S-18.

Anderson, Hayward S. "Competition in the Face of Integration." *Negro Educational Review* 15 (April 1964): 51–59.

Anderson, Monroe. "Black Advertising Agencies Are Attempting to Get the Black Market." *National Observer* (13 November 1971): 11.

Andreason, Alan R. *Improving Inner-City Marketing.* Chicago: American Marketing Association, 1972.

———. *The Disadvantaged Consumer.* New York: Free Press, 1975.

———. "The Differing Nature of Consumerism in the Ghetto." *Journal of Consumer Affairs* 10 (Winter 1976): 179–90.

Angelus, Ted. "Black Film Explosion Uncovers an Untapped, Rich Market." *Advertising Age* 43 (24 July 1972): 51–53.

Aptheker, Herbert, ed. *A Documentary History of the Negro People in the United States, 1933–1945.* Vol. 3. Secaucus, N.J.: Citadel Press, 1974.

"Are You Interested in a Market Worth Ten Billion Dollars." *Pepsi Cola* 8 (May 1948): 6, 15.

Atwan, Robert, Donald McQuade, and John W. Wright. *Edsels, Luckies, and Frigidaires: Advertising the American Way.* New York: Dell, 1979.

"Avon Aims New Line, Ad Effort at Fast-Growing Black Market." *Advertising Age* 46 (28 July 1975): 57.

Bailey, Ronald W., ed. *Black Business Enterprise: Historical and Contemporary Perspectives.* New York: Basic Books, 1971.

Banner, Lois. *American Beauty.* Chicago: University of Chicago Press, 1983.

Barry, Thomas E., and Michael G. Harvey. "Marketing to Heterogenous Black Consumers." *California Management Review* 17 (Winter 1974): 50–57.

Barthel, Diane. *Putting on Appearances: Gender and Advertising.* Philadelphia: Temple University Press, 1987.

Bates, Karen Grigsby. "They've Gotta Have Us: Hollywood's Black Directors." *New York Times Magazine* (14 July 1991): 15–19, 38–40, 44.

Bates, Timothy M. *Black Capitalism: A Quantitative Analysis.* New York: Praeger, 1973.

———. "The Declining Relative Incomes of Urban Black Households." *Challenge* 26 (May–June 1983): 48–49.

"Battle of the Lunch Counters: Latest Drive for Integration." *U.S. News & World Report* 48 (7 March 1960): 44–46.

Bauer, Raymond A., and Scott M. Cunningham. "The Negro Market." *Journal of Advertising Research* 10 (April 1970): 3–13.

Bauer, Raymond A., Scott M. Cunningham, and Lawrence H. Wortzel. "The Marketing Dilemma of Negroes." *Journal of Marketing* 29 (July 1965): 1–6.

Beauford, Fred. "Black Movies Create Box-Office Magic." *Black Enterprise* 4 (September 1972): 47–53.

"Beauty Chemicals: The Ethnic Market." *Chemical Marketing Reporter* 203 (11 June 1973): 35–36.

"Be Honest in Ads Addressed to Negro Market, Adclub Told." *Advertising Age* 39 (30 September 1968): 64.

Bell, William K. *15 Million Negroes and 15 Billion Dollars.* New York: William K. Bell, 1958.

"Be Sure Negroes Featured in Ads Are Identified with Civil Rights Effort: Robinson." *Advertising Age* 38 (10 April 1967): 12.

Bird, Laura. "Marketers Miss Out by Alienating Blacks." *Wall Street Journal* (9 April 1993): B8.

Black, Lawrence E. "The Negro Market: Growing, Changing, Challenging." *Sales Management* 91 (4 October 1963): 42–47.

"Black Agencies Should Be Used to Reach Black Markets, Wright Says." *Advertising Age* 40 (3 February 1969): 87.

"Black Americans: Still Trailing Behind." *Economist* 314 (3 March 1990): 17–19.

"The Black Consumer: A Major New Force in the American Economy." *Black Enterprise* 4 (November 1973): 17–21.

"Black Cosmetics: A Beautiful Business." *Chemical Week* (8 June 1977): 47–49.

"Black Cosmetics Market Continues to Expand." *American Druggist* 179 (April 1979): 55–56.

"*Black Enterprise* Plans Research on Black Consumer." *Advertising Age* 43 (17 July 1972): 20.

"Black [Alcohol Consumption] Figures to be Bigger." *Advertising Age* 52 (27 July 1981): S-12.

"Black Is." *Sales Management* 103 (15 September 1969): 64–68.

"Black Look in Beauty." *Time* 93 (11 April 1969): 72–74.

"Black Market." *Time* 99 (10 April 1972): 53.

"Black Media Less Efficient, Y & R Says." *Advertising Age* 43 (3 April 1972): 1, 68.

"The Black Movie Boom." *Newsweek* 78 (6 September 1971): 66.

"Black Music Formats Found Good as Gold in Pulling Audiences." *Television/Radio Age* 35 (21 March 1988): A10–A20.

"Black Power in the Marketplace." *Sales Management* 97 (15 September 1966): 36.

"Blacks vs. Shaft." *Newsweek* 80 (28 August 1972): 88.

Blake, Rick. "Reaching the World's Ninth Largest Market." *Public Relations Journal* 41 (June 1985): 30–31.

Bogle, Donald. *Toms, Coons, Mulattoes, Mammies & Bucks: An Interpretive History of Blacks in American Films.* New York: Continuum, 1989.

Bowser, Pearl. "History Lesson: The Boom Is Really an Echo." *Black Creation* 4 (Winter 1973): 32–34.

"Boycott by Negroes?" *Printer's Ink* 284 (23 August 1963): 5–6.

Boyd, Dale E. "Black Radio: A Direct and Personal Invitation." *Media-scope* 26 (August 1969): 14–15.

Boyenton, William H. "The Negro Turns to Advertising." *Journalism Quarterly* 42 (Spring 1965): 227–35.

Boyer, Horace Clarence. *How Sweet the Sound: The Golden Age of Gospel.* Washington, D.C.: Elliott & Clark, 1995.

Branch, Taylor. *Parting the Waters: America in the King Years, 1954–1963.* New York: Touchstone Books, 1988.

Brimmer, Andrew F. "The Negro in the National Economy." In *The American Negro Reference Book*, edited by John P. Davis, 251–336. Englewood Cliffs, N.J.: Prentice-Hall, 1966.

———. "Economic Outlook: Reaganomics and the Black Community." *Black Enterprise* 12 (December 1981): 43–44.

Britton, John H. "Negroes Ready to Go for Broke." *Jet* (17 October 1963): 46–50.

Bro, Margueritte Harmon. "Up by the Bootstraps." *Christian Century* 53 (1 April 1936): 492–94.

Brown, J. Clinton. "Which Black Is Beautiful?" *Advertising Age* 64 (1 February 1993): 19.

Bryant Jr., Keith L., and Henry C. Dethloff. *A History of American Business.* Englewood Cliffs, N.J.: Prentice-Hall, 1983.

Bullock, Henry Allen. *Pathways to the Houston Negro Market.* Ann Arbor, Mich.: J.W. Edwards, 1957.

———. "Consumer Motivations in Black and White—I." *Harvard Business Review* 39 (May 1961): 89–104.

———. "Consumer Motivations in Black and White—II." *Harvard Business Review* 39 (July 1961): 110–24.

Buni, Robert. *Robert L. Vann of the Pittsburgh Courier.* Pittsburgh: University of Pittsburgh Press, 1974.

"Burgeoning Middle Class Boosting Negro Buying Power." *Sales Management* 93 (20 November 1964): 77–78.

Burrows Jr., Felix A. "More Research $ Needed to Reach Black Consumer." *Advertising Age* 50 (16 April 1979): S-18.

"Business and Government Leaders to Aid Study of Negro Market." *Sales Management* 28 (10 January 1931): 78.

Butler, John S. *Entrepreneurship and Self-Help among Black Americans.* Albany: State University of New York Press, 1991.

Cayton, Horace C., and St. Clair Drake. *Black Metropolis: A Study of Negro Life in a Northern City.* New York: Harcourt, Brace, 1945, 1970.

Chinyelu, Mamadou. "No Color in Magazine Ads." *Black Enterprise* 22 (December 1991): 11.

Choudhury, Pravat, and Lawrence Schmid. "Black Models in Advertising to Blacks." *Journal of Advertising Research* 14 (June 1974): 19–23.

Choudhury, Pravat K. "Marketing Bank Services to Blacks." *Journal of Bank Research* 8 (Spring 1978): 52–57.

Christopher, Maurine. "Desegregate Ads, TV, Lever Tells Agencies." *Advertising Age* 34 (12 August 1963): 1, 8.

———. "P&G Is Next CORE Target: Agencies Later." *Advertising Age* 34 (26 August 1963): 3, 251.

———. "CORE Seeks More Integrated Ads: CORE Invites 14 Major Advertisers to Discuss Using Negroes in Ads." *Advertising Age* 33 (9 September 1963).

———. "CORE Seeks More Integrated Ads; NAACP Tells 4A's of 5-Point Program." *Advertising Age* 34 (9 September 1963): 1, 128.

———. "CORE Intensifies Drive for Negroes in Ads; Zeroes in on Pepsi-Cola Co." *Advertising Age* 35 (9 November 1964): 3, 71.

———. "TV: Negroes Break into Commercials, Shows." *Advertising Age* 39 (30 December 1968): 3.

———. "Integrated TV Ads Draw Praise of Admen." *Advertising Age* 40 (3 February 1969): 3, 108.

"Civil Rights Bill: No Limits on the Customers." *Business Week* (29 June 1963): 95.

Clarke, Caroline V. "Redefining Beautiful." *Black Enterprise* 23 (June 1993): 243–52.

Claspy, Jane. "Johnson Products: Black Is Still Beautiful." *Drug & Cosmetic Industry* 141 (December 1987): 24–25, 72–73.

"Clients Seek Advice on Negro Market." *Sponsor (Negro Market Supplement)* 20 (25 July 1966): 40–43.

Coates, Colby. "Arbitron Studies Ways to Track Black Audience." *Advertising Age* 49 (5 June 1978): 95.

Cohen, Dorothy. "Advertising and the Black Community." *Journal of Marketing* 34 (October (1970): 3–11.

Cohen, Laurie P. "Slowdown in Advertising to Blacks Strains Black Ad Firms and Media." *Wall Street Journal* (23 March 1988): 2-1.

Cohen, William. *At Freedom's Edge: Black Mobility and the Southern White Quest for Racial Control, 1861–1915.* Baton Rouge: Louisiana State University Press, 1991.

Coles Jr., Flournoy A. *Black Economic Development.* Chicago: Nelson-Hall, 1975.

Colfax, J. David, and Susan Frankel Sternberg. "The Perpetuation of Racial Stereotypes: Blacks in Mass-Circulation Magazine Advertisements." *Public Opinion Quarterly* 36 (Spring 1972): 8–18.

Colford, Steven W. "Black Boycott of Advertisers Mulled." *Advertising Age* 57 (13 October 1986): 24.

Colle, Royal. "Negro Image in the Mass Media: A Case in Social Change." *Journalism Quarterly* 45 (Spring 1968): 55–60.

"Combine Media Ads, Displays, Promotions to Reach Negro Market, Panel tells Adcrafters." *Advertising Age* 32 (19 November 1962): 52.

"Consumers' Cooperation among Negroes in Gary, Ind." *Monthly Labor Review* 42 (February 1936): 369–71.

Cook, Marvin K. "Modern Negro Cosmetics II." *Drug & Cosmetic Industry* 106 (May 1970): 42–44.

"CORE, Pepsi End Flareup Based on Misunderstanding." *Advertising Age* 35 (16 November 1964): 143.

"CORE Pleased with Advertisers' Attitude in Latest Meeting." *Advertising Age* 35 (30 November 1964): 46.

Corliss, Richard. "Boyz of New Black City." *Time* 137 (17 June 1991): 64–68.

"Cosmetic Makers Explore Underdeveloped Black Market." *Product Marketing and Cosmetic & Fragrance Retailing* 10 (December 1981): 1, 21, 26.

"Courting the Black Billionaire." *Media-scope* 13 (August 1969): 41–42, 66–70, 82.

Cox, Keith K. "Social Effects of Integrated Advertising." *Journal of Advertising Research* 10 (April 1970): 41–44.

Culley, James, and Rex Bennett. "Selling Women, Selling Blacks." *Journal of Communications* 26 (Autumn 1976): 160–74.

Dagnoli, Judann. "RJR's Uptown Targets Blacks." *Advertising Age* 60 (16 December 1989): 4, 44.

Daniel, Pete. *The Shadow of Slavery: Peonage in the South, 1901–1969.* Urbana: University of Illinois Press, 1972, 1990.

Darity Jr., William J. "Illusions of Black Economic Progress." *Review of Black Political Economy* 10 (Winter 1980): 153–68.

Dates, Jannette L., and William Barlow, eds. *Split Image: African Americans in the Mass Media*. Washington, D.C.: Howard University Press, 1990.

Davis, Donald A. "Ethnic Cosmetics: What Are We Waiting For?" *Drug & Cosmetic Industry* 139 (October 1986): 32–36, 90.

———. "Black Cosmetics: Affront Costs Revlon." *Drug & Cosmetic Industry* 140 (February 1987): 42–46.

Davis, Riccardo A. "Advertisers Boost Minority Efforts." *Advertising Age* 64 (16 August 1993): 12.

Delener, Nejdet. "Cosmetics & HBAs for Black Consumers: A Growing, Profitable—But Ignored—Market." *Marketing News* 20 (15 March 1986): 32.

Detweiler, Frederick G. *The Negro Press in America*. Chicago: University of Chicago Press22.

Dietrich, Robert F. "Know Your Black Shopper: Race May Be One of Your Least Important Clues." *Progressive Grocer* 54 (June 1975): 45–46.

Dillingham, McKinley. "To Hike Profit Margins, Learn to Tap Black Market." *Advertising Age* 50 (16 April 1979): S-29.

Djata. "The Marketing of Vices to Black Consumers." *Business and Society Review* (Summer 1987): 47–49.

Dominick, Joseph R., and Bradley S. Greenburg. "Three Seasons of Blacks on Television." *Journal of Advertising Research* 10 (April 1970): 21–27.

Donaton, Scott. "Census May Mean Minority Media Jackpot." *Advertising Age* 62 (5 August 1991): 12.

"Don't Contrive 'Integrated' Ads, Johnson Advises." *Advertising Age* 34 (23 September 1963): 1, 111.

Drake, J. G. St. Clair. "Why Not Co-operate?" *Opportunity* 14 (August 1936): 231–34, 251.

Dubey, Sumati N. "Blacks' Preference for Black Professionals, Businessmen, and Religious Leaders." *Public Opinion Quarterly* 34 (Spring 1970): 113–16.

Du Bois, William Edward Burghardt. *Economic Cooperation among Negroes*. Atlanta: Atlanta University Press, 1907.

———. "Georgia Negroes and Their Fifty Millions of Savings." *World's Work* 18 (May 1909): 11550–54.

———. "The Negro's Industrial Plight." *Crisis* 38 (July 1931): 241–42.

———. "A Negro Nation within the Nation." *Current History* 42 (June 1935): 265–70.

Dugas, Christine, and Kenneth Dreyfack. "A Gaffe at Revlon Has the Black Community Seething." *Business Week* (9 February 1987): 36–37.

Duker, Jacob M., and Charles E. Hughes. "The Black-Owned Life Insurance Company: Issues and Recommendations." *Journal of Risk and Insurance* 40 (June 1973): 221–30.

Durcanin, Cynthia. "Sign of the Times: 'Sin' Ads Target Blacks." *Atlanta Constitution* (26 March 1989): 1A, 14A.

"*Ebony* Survey Reveals Negro Buying Habits." *Advertising Age* 21 (28 July 1950): 16–17.

"Economically the Negro Gains, But He's Still the Low Man." *Business Week* (18 December 1954): 76–96.

"The Economic Future of the Negro." *The Outlook* 82 (20 January 1906): 102–3.

"Economic Pressure of Negro Consumer Expanding." *Advertising Age* 32 (28 August 1961): 32.

Edmonds, Patricia. "Are Tobacco, Alcohol Industries Friends or Foes of Minorities?" *Miami Herald* (13 August 1989): 4G–5G.

———. "Who Donates What to Minority Groups." *Miami Herald* (13 August 1989): 3G.

Edwards, Paul K. *The Southern Urban Negro as a Consumer.* New York: Prentice-Hall, 1932.

Elie, L. Eric. "Black History: Corporate Image Ads Abound." *Atlanta Constitution* (15 February 1989): 1B.

Epstein, Edwin M., and David R. Hampton. *Black Americans and White Business.* Encino, Calif.: Dickenson, 1971.

"*Essence* Urges R&D for Blacks." *Product Marketing and Cosmetic & Fragrance Retailing* 6 (December 1977): 1, 30–31.

"Ethnic Market Wants Better Products/Service." *Product Marketing and Cosmetic & Fragrance Retailing* 9 (March 1980): S4–S6.

Evans Jr., W. Leonard, and H. Naylor Fitzhugh. "The Negro Market—Two Viewpoints." *Media-scope* 11 (November 1967): 70–78.

Evans, Linda J. "Claude A. Barnett and the Associated Negro Press." *Chicago History* 12 (Summer 1983): 44–56.

Ewen, Stuart. *Captains of Consciousness: Advertising and the Social Roots of Consumer Culture.* New York: McGraw-Hill, 1976.

"Experiment in New Orleans." *Pepsi-Cola World* 14 (September 1954): 3–4.

"The Far-Flowing Negro Tide." *Newsweek* 50 (23 December 1957): 21–27.

Farley, Reynolds, and Suzanne M. Bianchi. "The Growing Gap Between Blacks." *American Demographics* 5 (July 1983): 15–18.

Favrot, Leo M. "How Chambers of Commerce Can Help Solve the Negro Problem." *American City Magazine* 33 (August 1925): 194–96.

Feehery, John. "Purex Launches Ads in *Ebony* in Test of 'Subtleties' of Negro Marketing." *Advertising Age* 36 (1 February 1965): 4, 46.

———. "Negro Market Sought Because of Hard-Headed Economics: Johnson." *Advertising Age* 36 (29 November 1965): 3, 14.

"The 15 Billion Dollar Market." *The Negro History Bulletin* 18 (October 1954): 12.

Finley, Skip. "12% Market Share is 12%—No Matter What the Source." *Advertising Age* 50 (16 April 1979): S-26.

Fisher, Christy. "Ethnics Gain Market Clout." *Advertising Age* 62 (5 August 1991): 3.

Fisher, Paul, and Ralph Lowenstein, eds. *Race and the Mass Media.* New York: Praeger, 1967.

Fletcher, Linda P. *The Negro in the Insurance Industry.* Philadelphia: University of Pennsylvania Press, 1970.

———. "The Black-Owned Insurance Company: Further Comments." *Journal of Risk and Insurance* 42 (June 1975): 351–54.

Foner, Eric. *Reconstruction: America's Unfinished Revolution, 1863–1877.* New York: Harper & Row, 1988.

"Food, Clothing Get Most of Negroes' 10 Billion." *Advertising Age* 18 (24 March 1947): 50.

Forkan, James P. "Black Ownership of Radio Grows—Slowly." *Advertising Age* 41 (9 February 1970): 10.

———. "Who's Who in $350,000,000 Black Grooming Market." *Advertising Age* 43 (20 November 1972): 96–97.

Fowler, Bertram B. "Miracle in Gary: The Negro Gropes toward Economic Equality." *Forum & Century* 96 (September 1936): 134–37.

Fox, Stephen. *The Mirror Makers: A History of American Advertisers and Its Creators.* New York: Vintage Books, 1985.

Franklin, John Hope, and Alfred A. Moss Jr. *From Slavery to Freedom: A History of African Americans.* 7th ed. New York: McGraw-Hill, 1994.

Frazier, Edward Franklin. *Black Bourgeoisie: The Rise of a New Middle Class in America.* New York: Collier, 1957, 1962.

Freeman, Laurie. "Big Marketers Move in on Ethnic Haircare." *Advertising Age* 57 (12 May 1987): 24, 28.

Friend, Irwin, and Irving B. Kravis. "New Light on the Consumer Market." *Harvard Business Review* 35 (January–February 1957): 105–16.

"Frozen 'Soul Foods' in Ghetto Market Require New Selling Technique." *Quick Frozen Foods* 31 (November 1969): 109–10, 131.

Furman, Phyllis. "Ethnic Haircare Marketers Battling for Share." *Advertising Age* 158 (2 March 1987): S-2.

Gadsden, Sheila. "Seeking the Right Tack in Talking to Blacks." *Advertising Age* 56 (12 September 1985): 18, 21.

———. "Toyota Taps Black Buying Power." *Advertising Age* 58 (14 December 1987): S-5–S-6.

Garfield, Bob. "Colt 45 Ads a Black Day for Blacks." *Advertising Age* 57 (10 November 1986): 84.

Gates Jr. Henry Louis. "Two Nations . . . Both Black." *Forbes* 150 (14 September 1992): 132–35.

George, Nelson. *The Death of Rhythm & Blues.* New York: Pantheon Books, 1988.

———. *Blackface: Reflections on African-Americans and the Movies.* New York: Harper-Collins, 1994.

Gibson, D. Parke. "How to Plan a Negro Market Campaign." *Sales Management* (15 April 1969): 55–72.

———. "Advertising and the Dual Society: Challenge of the Seventies." *Media-scope* 13 (August 1969): 62–63.

———. *The $30 Billion Negro.* New York: Macmillan, 1969.

———. *$70 Billion in the Black: America's Black Consumers.* New York: Macmillan, 1978.

———. "Black Middle Class Emerges as Dominant Consumer Force." *Advertising Age* 50 (16 April 1979): S-24.

Glasgow, Douglas G. *The Black Underclass.* San Francisco: Jossey-Bass, 1980.

Glaxton, Robert. "The Black Cosmetics Market." *Drug & Cosmetic Industry* 124 (May 1979): 78, 146–48.

Goodall, Kenneth. "Blacks in Advertisements in the Post-Mammy Era." *Psychology Today* 6 (October 1972): 138.

Goodwin, E. Marvin. *Black Migration in America from 1915–1960: An Uneasy Exodus.* Lewiston, N.Y.: E. Mellen Press, 1990.

Gould, John W., Norman B. Sigband, and Cyril E. Zoerner Jr. "Black Consumer Reactions to 'Integrated' Advertising: An Exploratory Study." *Journal of Marketing* 34 (July 1970): 20–26.

Graves, Earl G. "Black Media Success Is Bittersweet." *Advertising Age* 50 (16 April 1979): S-2.

———. "Are We Better Off Now?" *Black Enterprise* 15, no. January (1985): 11.

———. "Figures Show African Americans Not Well Represented in Adland." *Advertising Age* 64 (15 March 1993): 24.

Grayson, William P. "What the $20 Billion Negro Market Means to You." *Negro Digest* 12 (January 1962): 62–67.

Green, Richard L. "Black Buying Patterns Are Revealing." *Advertising Age* 50 (16 April 1979): S-34.

Green, Theophilus. "The Black Man as Movie Hero." *Ebony* 27 (August 1972): 144–48.

Groh, George W. *The Black Migration: The Journey to Urban America.* New York: Weybright and Talley, 1972.

"Growing Black Consumer Income Stirring Ad Interest." *Television/Radio Age* 32 (18 February 1985): B-3–B-6.

"Growing Retail Market Seen in Joint Survey of Nation's Minorities." *Commerce Today* 1 (23 August 1971): 18–20.

Guerrero, Ed. *Framing Blackness: The African American Image in Film.* Philadelphia: Temple University Press, 1993.

"Guess Who's Coming to Market?" *Sales Management* 100 (1 May 1968): 44–46.

Guest, Lester. "How Negro Models Affect Company Image." *Journal of Advertising Research* 10 (April 1970): 29–33.

Gupta, Udayan. "Black Radio's Lost Monopoly." *Madison Avenue* 27 (May 1985): 110–17.

Guzman, Jessie Parkhurst, Vera Chandler Foster, and W. Hardin Hughes, eds. *Negro Year Book: A Review of Events Affecting Negro Life, 1941–1946*. Tuskegee, Ala.: Tuskegee Department of Records and Research, 1947.

Hacker, George A., Ronald Collins, and Michael Jacobson. *Marketing Booze to Blacks*. Washington, D.C.: Center for Science in the Public Interest, 1987.

Hairston, Deborah. "The Battle of the Curls." *Black Enterprise* 15 (June 1985): 169–74.

Hall, Claude H. "Advertisers Guide to Marketing, 1960 Negro Market." *Printer's Ink* 269 (30 October 1959): 246–47.

———. "The Negro Market: A Compact Sales Target." *Printer's Ink* 284 (1 September 1961): 287–88.

Hare, Nathan. "How and Why Negroes Spend Their Money." *Negro Digest* 14 (May 1965): 4–11.

Haring, H. A. "Selling to Harlem." *Advertising & Selling* 11 (31 October 1928): 17–18, 50–53.

———. "The Negro as Consumer." *Advertising & Selling* 15 (3 September 1930): 20–21, 67–68.

Harmon, J. H., Arnett G. Lindsey, and Carter G. Woodson. *The Negro as a Businessman*. College Park, Md.: McGrath, 1929.

Harris, Abram L. *The Negro as Capitalist: A Study of Banking and Business among American Negroes*. Philadelphia: American Academy of Political and Social Science, 1936.

Harris, Michael W. *The Rise of Gospel Blues: The Music of Thomas Andrew Dorsey in the Urban Church*. New York: Oxford University Press, 1992.

Hartt, Rollin Lynde. "I'd Like to Show You Harlem!" *Independent and Weekly Review* 105 (2 April 1921): 334–35, 357–58.

Hayes, Marion. "A Century of Change: Negroes in the U.S. Economy, 1860–1960." *Monthly Labor Review* 85 (December 1962): 1359–65.

Heilbut, Anthony. *The Gospel Sound: Good News and Bad Times*. 4th ed. New York: Limelight Editions, 1992.

"Help Negro in Image Effort via Ads, Wilkins Asks." *Advertising Age* 34 (11 November 1963): 1, 112.

Henderson, Alexa Benson. *Atlanta Life Insurance Company: Guardian of Black Economic Dignity*. Tuscaloosa: University of Alabama Press, 1990.

Henderson, William L., and Larry C. Ledebur. *Economic Disparity: Problems and Strategies for Black America*. New York: Free Press, 1970.

Henri, Florette. *Black Migration: Movement North, 1900–1920*. 1st ed. Garden City, N.Y.: Anchor Press, 1975.

Higgs, Robert. *Competition and Coercion: Blacks in the American Economy, 1865–1914*. Cambridge: Cambridge University Press, 1977.

Hill, Robert B. "The Economic Status of Black Americans." In *The State of Black America 1981*, edited by James D. Williams, 1–59. New York, N.Y.: National Urban League, 1981.

———. "The Black Middle Class: Past, Present, and Future." In *The State of Black America 1986*, edited by James D. Williams, 43–61. New York: National Urban League, 1986.

Hill, T. Arnold. "The Negro Market." *Opportunity* (October 1932): 318–19.

Hills, Gerald E. "The Black-Owned Life Insurance Company: Comment." *Journal of Risk and Insurance* 42 (June 1975): 346–51.

Hillsman, Joan R. *Gospel Music: An African American Art Form.* Washington, D.C.: Middle Atlantic Regional Press, 1990.

Hine, Darlene Clark. "Housewives' League of Detroit." In *Black Women in America: An Historical Encyclopedia*, edited by Darlene Clark Hine, Elsa Barkley Brown, and Rosalyn Terborg-Penn, 584–86. Vol. I. Brooklyn, N.Y.: Carlson, Inc, 1993.

———. *Hine Sight: Black Women and the Reconstruction of American History.* Bloomington: Indiana University Press, 1994.

Hirschhorn, Adrian. "Pepsi-Cola's Campaign to the Negro Market." *Printer's Ink* 228 (9 September 1949): 38–40.

"History of NAMD." *Emphasis 95.* Program of the 43d meeting of the National Association of Market Developers, May 1995.

"Hollywood's New Public." *The Economist* 247 (19 May 1973): 53.

Holsey, Albon L. "Negro in Business Aided by Racial Appeal." *Forbes* 21 (15 January 1928): 42–48.

———. "The C.M.A. Stores Face the Chains." *Opportunity* 7 (July 1929): 210–13.

———. "What the Negro Is Doing in Business." *Forbes* 23 (1 May 1929): 36–39.

Holte, Clarence L. "The Negro Market: To Profit from It, Recognize It and Service Its Needs." *Printer's Ink* 263 (4 April 1958): 29–32.

Horovitz, Bruce. "Harmonic Convergence: Racial Tolerance Is Suddenly a Hot Topic in Advertising." *Los Angeles Times* (19 January 1993): D1, D6.

Hudson-Weems, Clenora. *Emmett Till: The Sacrificial Lamb of the Civil Rights Movement.* Troy, Mich.: Bedford, 1994.

Hughes, Emmett John. "The Negro's New Economic Life." *Fortune* 54 (September 1956): 127–31, 248–62.

Huie, William Bradford. "The Shocking Story of Approved Killing in Mississippi." *Look* 20 (24 January 1956): 46–50.

———. "What's Happened to the Emmett Till Killers?" *Look* 21 (22 January 1957): 63–68.

Humphrey, Ronald, and Howard Schuman. "The Portrayal of Blacks in Magazine Advertisements: 1950–1982." *Public Opinion Quarterly* 48 (Fall 1984): 551–63.

Humphreys, Jeffrey M. "Black Buying Power by Place of Residence: 1990–1996." *Georgia Business and Economic Conditions* 55 (July–August 1995): 1–15.

Hunter, Catherine Ellis. "Flori Roberts: White Success in Black Cosmetics." *Drug & Cosmetic Industry* 122 (June 1978): 32–35, 190.

Hyatt, Marshall, ed. *The Afro-American Cinematic Experience: An Annotated Bibliography & Filmography.* Wilmington, Del.: Scholarly Resources, 1983.

Ijere, Martin O. *Survey of Afro-American Experience in the U.S. Economy.* Hicksville, N.Y.: Exposition Press, 1978.

"The Impact of Inflation: As Prices have Risen, Black Economic Progress has Slowed Down." *Black Enterprise* 9 (June 1979): 213–15.

"Integrated Ads Misfire in White-Only Media, John Johnson Tells WSAAA." *Advertising Age* 35 (27 April 1964): 2, 61.

"Integration: Not Only in School." *Business Week* (6 September 1958): 38–39.

Jacoway, Elizabeth, and David R. Colburn, eds. *Southern Businessmen and Desegregation.* Baton Rouge: Louisiana State University Press, 1982.

Jaffe, Alfred J. "The Negro Market Is Getting Bigger in Two Directions." *Sponsor (Negro Market Supplement)* 12 (20 September 1958): 3–5, 32–34.

Jefferson, Roland S. "The Black Film Boom: Decerebrate, Dangerous, and Declining." *Journal of the National Medical Association* 67 (January 1975): 11–15.

Jeffries, LeRoy W., ed. *Facts about Blacks.* Vol. 8. Los Angeles: LeRoy W. Jeffries & Associates, 1986.

Jencks, Christopher, and Paul E. Paterson, eds. *The Urban Underclass.* Washington, D.C.: Brookings Institution, 1991.

Johnson, Charles S. "The Changing Economic Status of the Negro." *Annals* 140 (November 1928): 128–37.

Johnson, Daniel M., and Rex R. Campbell. *Black Migration in America: A Social Demographic History.* Durham: Duke University Press, 1981.

Johnson, Guy B. "Newspaper Advertisements and Negro Culture." *Journal of Social Forces* 3 (May 1925): 706–9.

Johnson, John H. "Does Your Sales Force Know How to Sell the Negro Trade? Some Do's and Don'ts." *Advertising Age* 23 (17 March 1952): 73–74.

———. "Negro Market Will Be Controlling Factor in Profit Margins of Big U.S. Companies in 15 Years." *Advertising Age* 35 (21 September 1964): 119–20.

———. "Big-City Negro Market No. 1 Insurance Opportunity." *National Underwriter* 70 (19 March 1966): 2, 18–20.

———. "The Greening of the Black Consumer Market." *Crisis* 83 (March 1976): 92–95.

———. "Black Media Fill Needs Not Recognized Elsewhere." *Advertising Age* 50 (16 April 1979): S-19, S-25.

Johnson, John H., and Lerone Bennent Jr. *Succeeding against the Odds.* New York: Warner Books, 1989.

Johnson, Joseph T. *The Potential Negro Market.* New York: Pageant Press, 1952.

Jones, Eugene Kinckle. "Purchasing Power of Negroes in the U.S. Estimated at Two Billion Dollars." *Domestic Commerce* 15 (10 January 1935): 1.

Jordan, Vernon E. "Black-Aimed Advertising—Some Pluses, Some Minuses." *Advertising Age* 50 (16 April 1979): S-29.

Joseph, W. F. "Promotions Play Well with Blacks." *Advertising Age* 58 (14 December 1987): S-1–S-2.

Joyce, George, and Norman Govoni, eds. *The Black Consumer: Dimensions of Behavior and Strategy.* New York: Random House, 1971.

Kassarjian, Harold H. "The Negro and American Advertising, 1946–1965." *Journal of Marketing Research* 6 (February 1969): 29–39.

———. "Evidence on the Changing Image of Black People." In *Emerging Issues in Black Economic Development,* edited by Benjamin F. Bobo and Alfred E. Osborne, 167–87. Lexington, Mass.: Lexington Books, 1976.

Katz, Michael B., ed. *The Underclass Debate: Views from History.* Princeton, N.J.: Princeton University Press, 1993.

Kauffman, Stanley. "Stanley Kauffmann on Films." *New Republic* 168 (28 April 1973): 20, 33–34.

"Keep Militancy against Madison Ave. 'Oppressors,' Black Adfolk Are Told." *Advertising Age* 41 (9 March 1970): 3.

Kelley, Robin D. G. *Race Rebels: Culture, Politics and the Black Working Class.* New York: Free Press, 1994.

Kelley, Thomas E. "Johnson Products Makes Radio Ads via 'Mini-Concerts'." *Advertising Age* 42 (15 March 1971): 40.

Kennedy, Louise Venable. *The Negro Peasant Turns Cityward.* New York: AMS Press, 1930, 1968.

Kern, Richard. "Of Minorities and Metros: A Few Surprises." *Sales & Marketing Management* 141 (September 1989): 14.

Kern-Foxworth, Marilyn. *Aunt Jemima, Uncle Ben, and Rastus: Blacks in Advertising, Yesterday, Today, and Tomorrow.* Westport, Conn.: Praeger, 1994.

King Jr., Martin Luther. *Stride toward Freedom: The Montgomery Story.* 1st ed. New York: Harper, 1958.

King Jr., Martin Luther, and Grover C. Hall Jr. "Alabama's Bus Boycott: What It's All About, Pro and Con." *U.S. News & World Report* 41 (3 August 1956): 82–89.

Kinzer, Robert H., and Edward Sagarin. *The Negro in American Business: The Conflict Between Separatism and Integration.* New York: Greenberg, 1950.

"Know-How Is Key to Selling Negro Today." *Sponsor (Negro Market Supplement)* 15 (9 October 1961): 9–10, 26–27.

Kronus, Sidney. *The Black Middle Class.* Columbus, Ohio: Charles E. Merrill, 1971.

Krzysik, Duane G., and Sheri A. Gatto. "Black Hair Care Products: New Formulating Concepts With Silicones." *Drug & Cosmetic Industry* 141 (November 1987): 28–38.

Kusmer, Kenneth L. *A Ghetto Takes Shape: Black Cleveland, 1870–1930.* Urbana: University of Illinois Press, 1976.

Landry, Ron. "'Disrespect' Hurts City Stores." *Supermarketing* 33 (October 1978): 1, 32–33.

Lawson, Bill E., ed. *The Underclass Question.* Philadelphia: Temple University Press, 1992.

Lawson, James C. "Minority Celebs Reach beyond Target Market." *Advertising Age* 50 (30 July 1979): S-4.

———. "Financial Services Target Segment within a Segment." *Advertising Age* 57 (25 August 1986): S-1–S-2.

Leab, Daniel J. *From Sambo to Superspade: The Black Experience in Motion Pictures.* Boston: Houghton-Mifflin Company, 1975.

Leland, John, and Donna Foote. "A Bad Omen for Black Movies?" *Newsweek* 118 (29 July 1991): 48–49.

Leland, John, Andrew Murr, Mark Miller, Farai Chideya, and Abigail Kuflik. "New Jack Cinema Enters Screening." *Newsweek* 117 (10 June 1991): 50–52.

Lemmons, Stanley J. "Black Stereotypes as Reflected in Popular Culture." *American Quarterly* 21 (Spring 1977): 103–6.

Levin, Gary. "Honoring [Martin Luther] King: Marketers Woo Blacks in Holiday Promotions." *Advertising Age* 59 (18 January 1988): 80.

Lewis, Claude. "Where Are Black Models in Ads?" *Philadelphia Inquirer* (7 August 1991): 12A.

Lewis, Earl. *In Their Own Interests: Race, Class, and Power in Twentieth-Century Norfolk, Virginia.* Berkeley: University of California Press, 1991.

"Libra: New Line of Negro Cosmetics." *Drug & Cosmetic Industry* 105 (December 1969): 44–46.

Lipman, Joanne. "Sports Marketers See Evidence of Racism." *Advertising Age* 59 (18 October 1988): B1.

Logan, Rayford W. *The Betrayal of the Negro from Rutherford B. Hayes to Woodrow Wilson.* New York: Collier Books, 1954, 1965.

Logan, Rayford W., and Michael R. Winston, eds. *Dictionary of American Negro Biography.* New York: Norton, 1982.

Lowery, Mark, and Nadirah Z. Sabir. "The Making of 'Hollywood'." *Black Enterprise* 25 (December 1994): 104–12.

Lum, Sarah. "Ethnic Hair Care—A Growing Market." *Madison Avenue* 25 (May 1983): 72.

Mabry, Marcus, Daniel Glick, and Shawn D. Lewis. "Fighting Ads in the Inner City." *Newsweek* 115 (5 February 1990): 46.

MacDonald, J. Fred. "Stereotypes Fall in TV Ad Portrayals." *Advertising Age* 55 (19 November 1984): 44.

Madhubuti, Haki R., ed. *Why L.A. Happened: Implications of the '92 Los Angeles Rebellion.* Chicago: Third World Press, 1993.

"Madison Avenue Looks at Negro Radio." *Sponsor (Negro Market Supplement)* 19 (26 July 1965): 44–47.

Maggard, John P. "Negro Market—Fact or Fiction?" *California Management Review* 14 (Fall 1971): 71–80.

Magiera, Marcy. "Lee: Black Films Get Less Support." *Advertising Age* 62 (1 April 1991): 38.

"Major Breakthrough in Integrated Ads, N.Y. Committee Says." *Advertising Age* 35 (17 February 1964): 58.

Mandle, Jay R. *The Roots of Black Poverty: The Southern Plantation Economy after the Civil War.* Durham: Duke University Press, 1978.

Marable, Manning. *How Capitalism Underdeveloped Black America: Problems in Race, Political Economy, and Society.* 1st ed. Boston: South End Press, 1983.

Marchand, Roland. *Advertising the American Dream: Making Way for Modernity.* Berkeley: University of California Press, 1985.

"Marketers Go Outside to Get Inside New Segments." *Beverage World* 103 (August 1984): 30–33.

"Marketing to Blacks Still Mystifies Whites, Speakers Advise Conference." *Advertising Age* 40 (2 June 1969): 19.

"Marketing to Negro Isn't Segregation in Reverse: Gibson." *Advertising Age* 36 (27 September 1965): 27.

"Marketing to the Negro Consumer." *Sales Management* 84 (4 March 1960): 36–44.

Markham, Clarence M. "Black Conventions Mean Big Money." *Advertising Age* 50 (23 April 1979): S-12–S-13.

Marks, Carole. *Farewell—We're Good and Gone: The Great Black Migration.* Bloomington: Indiana University Press, 1989.

Marshall, Robert A., and Eli A. Zubay. *The Debit System of Marketing Life and Health Insurance.* Englewood Cliffs, N.J.: Prentice-Hall, 1975.

Marticorena, Charles. "Ethnic Market: Biggest Potential for Growth in Cosmetics Industry." *Chemical Marketing Reporter* 207 (23 June 1975): 37–39.

Martin, Joel P. "Segmenting the Black Market." *Marketing/Communications* 10, July (1985): 17–19, 69.

Massey, Douglas, and Nancy Denton. *American Apartheid: Segregation and the Making of the Underclass.* Cambridge, Mass.: Harvard University Press, 1993.

Mattox, Michael. "The Day Black Movie Stars Got Militant." *Black Creation* 4 (Winter 1973): 40–42.

McKelvey, Blake. *The Emergence of Metropolitan America.* New Brunswick, N.J.: Rutgers University Press, 1968.

Meier, August, and Elliott Rudwick. "The Boycott Movement against Jim Crow Streetcars in the South, 1900–1906." *Journal of American History* 55 (March 1969): 756–75.

———. "The Origins of Nonviolent Direct Action in Afro-American Protest: A Note on Historical Discontinuities." In *We Shall Overcome: The Civil Rights Movement in the United States in the 1950s and 1960s,* vol. 3, edited by David J. Garrow. Brooklyn: Carlson, 1989.

Miller, Adam David. "Black Films $$$: A Critique." *Black Scholar* 4 (January 1973): 54–55.

Mingo, Frank. "Black Middle Class Calls for Marketing Adjustment." *Advertising Age* 50 (16 April 1979): S-29.

Mingo, Frank, and Caroline Jones. "Good Minority-Oriented Advertising Is Just Good Advertising." *Broadcasting* (30 November 1981): 14.

Mitchell, George S., and Anna Holden. "Money Income of Negroes in the United States." *Journal of Negro Education* 22 (Summer 1953): 333–42.

Mitchell, Grayson. "Battle of the Rouge." *Black Enterprise* 9 (August 1978): 23–29.

Mitchell, Ivor S. "Cultural Dimensions of Marketing Strategies." *Review of Black Political Economy* 10 (Spring 1980): 247–61.

"Monumental Achievement: NAMD." *National Black Monitor* 10 (September 1985): 4, 8, 10, 12, 14–15.

Moon, Henry Lee. "The Black Boycott." *Crisis* 73 (May 1966): 249–54, 278.

"More Race Pressure on Business." *Business Week* (12 May 1962): 130–32.

Morrow, J. J. "American Negroes—A Wasted Resource." *Harvard Business Review* 35 (January–February 1957): 65–74.

Murray, Florence, ed. *The Negro Handbook.* New York: Wendell Malliet, 1942.

———, ed. *The Negro Handbook, 1946–1947.* New York: A.A. Wyn, 1947.

———, ed. *The Negro Handbook, 1949.* New York: Macmillan, 1949.

Murray, James P. "The Subject Is Money." *Black Creation* 4 (Winter 1973): 26–30.

———. *To Find an Image: Black Films from Uncle Tom to Super Fly.* Indianapolis: Bobbs-Merrill, 1973.

"Must Project More Realistic Image of Negro, Admen Told." *Advertising Age* 35 (27 July 1964): 84.

Navarro, Mireya. "Tobacco and Alcohol Manufacturers Find Minorities are Growing Wary." *New York Times* (8 August 1990): A13.

"Negro Boycott." *Business Week* (23 July 1960): 30.

"Negro Boycott Could Have Serious, Lasting Effect on Sales, Study Shows." *Advertising Age* 34 (30 September 1963): 3, 110.

"Negro Brand Preferences: They Are Different." *Sponsor (Negro Market Supplement)* 21 (July 1967): 38–41.

"Negro Business Pressure Grows." *Business Week* (23 April 1960): 31–33.

"The Negro Consumer." *Electrical Merchandising Week* 96 (27 April 1964): 13–26.

"Negro Cosmetics: Seminar Assesses Special Needs." *Drug & Cosmetic Industry* 105 (October 1969): 66, 150–51.

"The Negro-Directed Advertiser Gets a Plus from Negro Radio." *Sponsor (Negro Market Supplement)* 12 (20 September 1958): 6–7, 34–37.

"Negro Family Is Better Market for Luxuries Than White with Same Income, Study Says." *Advertising Age* 30 (16 March 1959): 56.

"Negro Groups Put the Economic Pressure On." *Business Week* (27 February 1960): 26–28.

"Negro Incomes and How They Are Spent." *Sales Management* 54 (15 June 1945): 106.

"Negro Is Basic Market, *Ebony* Publisher Says." *Advertising Age* 32 (18 December 1961): 92.

"Negro Market: Buying Power Changes Market Place." *Printer's Ink* 284 (30 August 1963): 9.

"Negro Markets." *Tide* 20 (15 March 1946): 86–88.

"Negro Market Data: Still Inadequate But Starting to Flow." *Sponsor (Negro Market Supplement)* 13 (26 September 1959): 12–13

"Negro Radio Attracts Madison Ave. Attention." *Sponsor (Negro Market Supplement)* 20 (25 July 1966): 32–39.

"Negro Radio Comes of Age." *Sponsor (Negro Market Supplement)* 8 (20 September 1954): 49–50, 149–50.

"Negro Radio: Keystone of Community Life." *Sponsor (Negro Market Supplement)* 7 (24 August 1953): 68–69, 72–73, 78–84.

"Negro Radio: Over 600 Stations Strong Today." *Sponsor (Negro Market Supplement)* 9 (19 September 1955): 112–13, 143–52.

"Negro Radio Results: No Product Limitations." *Sponsor (Negro Market Supplement)* 7 (24 August 1953): 74–75, 96.

"Negro Radio's 1965-Style 'New Sound'." *Sponsor (Negro Market Supplement)* 19 (26 July 1965): 52–57.

"Negro Radio's Prosperous Market." *Sponsor (Negro Market Supplement)* 14 (26 September 1960): 6–10, 47–49.

"Negro Radio: 200 Plus Specialist Stations—More Coming." *Sponsor (Negro Market Supplement)* 6 (28 July 1952): 32–33, 78–84.

"Negro Results Stories: Rich Yield for All Clients." *Sponsor (Negro Market Supplement)* 6 (28 July 1952): 38–39, 84–86.

"Negroes: Big Advances in Jobs, Wealth, Status." *U.S. News & World Report* 45 (28 November 1958): 90–92.

"Negroes' Favorite Brands Differ from Whites in Half of Categories, RKO Finds." *Advertising Age* 40 (10 February 1969): 44–45.

"Negroes Get More 'Brand Conscious' as Incomes Rise." *Advertising Age* (18 March 1946): 30–31.

"Negroes Go North, West." *U.S. News & World Report* 31 (16 November 1951): 50–53.

"Negroes in Chicago Market Like Tide, Pepsi, Study Shows." *Advertising Age* 38 (24 April 1967): 33.

"The Negro's Force in the Marketplace." *Business Week* (26 May 1962): 76–84.

The Negro Handbook. Chicago: Johnson, 1966.

"The Negro Market: As Customers and Citizens, Its People Are Still Making Significant Progress." *Tide* 26 (25 July 1952): 43–49.

"The Negro Market." *Time* 68 (13 August 1956): 62–63.

"The Negro Market: An Appraisal." *Tide* 21 (7 March 1947): 15–18

"The Negro Market: $15 Billion to Spend." *Sponsor (Negro Market Supplement)* 6 (28 July 1952): 30–31, 72, 76–78.

"The Negro Market for Frozen Foods." *Quick Frozen Foods* 22 (April 1960): 106–9.

"The Negro Market: How to Tap 15 Billion in Sales." *Time* 64 (5 July 1954): 70.

"The Negro Market: 23 Million Consumers Make a $30 Billion Market Segment." *Marketing Insights* 2 (29 January 1969): 9–12.

"The Negro Moves." *Time* 58 (19 November 1951): 26.

"The Negro Stations Revolve around the Disk Jockey." *Sponsor (Negro Market Supplement)* 12 (20 September 1958): 8–9, 37–40.

"The Negro Woman Goes to Market." *Brown American* 1 (April 1936): 13.

Nelson, Havelock, and Michael A. Gonzales. *Bring the Noise: A Guide to Rap Music and Hip Hop Culture.* New York: Harmony Books, 1991.

"New Business Ways in the South." *Business Week* (5 August 1961): 56–58, 63.

Newman, Mark. "On the Air With Jack L. Cooper: The Beginnings of Black Appeal Radio." *Chicago History* 12 (Summer 1983): 51–58.

"New Marketing Profile of U.S. Negro Emerges." *Sponsor (Negro Market Supplement)* 19 (26 July 1965): 38–43.

"New Starch Study Shows Blacks Have Fewer Misgivings about Advertising." *Advertising Age* 44 (16 April 1973): 30.

"NNN: Negro Radio's Network." *Sponsor (Negro Market Supplement)* 8 (20 September 1954): 54, 150–52.

Nobles, Wade, and Lawford L. Goddard. "Drugs in the African-American Community: A Clear and Present Danger." In *The State of Black America 1989*, edited by Janet Dewart, 161–81. New York: National Urban League, 1989.

"No Christmas Boycott." *Crisis* 70 (November 1963): 555–56.

Novak, Daniel A. *The Wheel of Servitude: Black Forced Labor after Slavery.* Lexington: University of Kentucky Press, 1978.

Oak, Vishnu V. *The Negro Newspaper.* Yellow Springs, Ohio: Antioch Press, 1948.

———. *The Negro's Adventure in General Business.* Yellow Springs, Ohio: Antioch Press, 1949.

O'Dell, Jack H. "The Negro People in the Southern Economy." *Freedomways* (Fall 1963): 526–48.

O'Hare, William P. "In the Black." *American Demographics* 11 (November 1989): 24–29.

O'Hare, William P., and William H. Frey. "Booming, Suburban and Black." *American Demographics* 14 (September 1992): 30–38.

Oladipupo, Raymond. "The Urban Negro: Separate & Distinct." *Media-scope* 13 (July 1969): 18, 76.

———. *How Distinct Is the Negro Market?* New York: Ogilvy & Mather, 1970.

"Old Taylor Drive Aimed at Negro Market Honors Little-Known 'Ingenious American'." *Advertising Age* 38 (11 December 1967): 12.

Ottley, Roi. *New World A-Coming: Inside Black America.* Boston: Houghton-Mifflin, 1943.

Peterson, Robert. *Only the Ball Was White.* New York: McGraw-Hill, 1970, 1984.

Petrof, John. "The Effects of Student Boycotts Upon the Purchasing Habits of Negro Families in Atlanta, Georgia." *Phylon* 24 (Fall 1963): 266–70.

———. "Customer Strategy for Negro Retailers." *Journal of Retailing* 43, no. Fall (1967): 30–38.

———. "Reaching the Negro Market: A Segregated vs. a General Newspaper." *Journal of Advertising Research* 8 (June 1968): 40–43.

Pierce, Joseph A. *Negro Business and Business Education.* New York: Plenum Press, 1947, 1995.

"Pillsbury Aims Enriched Flour at Negro Areas." *Advertising Age* 40 (15 September 1969): 26.

Pinkerton, Jane. "The Negro Market: Why Buyers Are Looking Twice." *Sponsor (Negro Market Supplement)* 11 (28 September 1957): 3–5, 33–36.

Pitts, Robert E., D. Joel Whalen, Robert O'Keefe, and Vernon Murray. "Black and White Response to Culturally Targeted Television Commercials: A Values-Based Approach." *Psychology & Marketing* 6 (Winter 1989): 311–28.

Ploski, Harry A., and Warren Marr, eds. *The Negro Almanac: A Reference Work on the Afro-American.* 1776 Bicentennial Edition. New York: Bellwether, 1976.

Ponder, Henry. "An Example of the Alternative Cost Doctrine Applied to Racial Discrimination." *Journal of Negro Education* 35 (Winter 1966): 42–47.

Poussaint, Alvin F. "Blaxploitation Movies: Cheap Thrills That Degrade Blacks." *Psychology Today* 7 (February 1974): 22, 26–27, 30–32, 98.

Price, Daniel O. *Changing Characteristics of the Negro Population: A 1960 Census Monograph.* Washington, D.C.: U.S. Department of Commerce/Bureau of the Census, 1969.

Primm, Beny J. "Drug Use: Special Implications for Black America." In *The State of Black America 1987,* edited by Janet Dewart, 145–58. New York: National Urban League, 1987.

Proctor, Barbara. "Black, It's Beautiful!" *Media Decisions* 12 (April 1977): 72–75.

Pulley, Brett. "Johnson Products Agrees to $67 Million Ivax Buyout." *Wall Street Journal* (15 June 1993): B3.

"Radio: Major Medium for Reaching U.S. Negroes." *Sponsor (Negro Market Supplement)* 18 (17 August 1964): 36–43.

Randall, Iris W. "Needs, Wants & Whims in Ethnic Hair Care." *Drug & Cosmetic Industry* 139 (October 1986): 38–40, 88–90.

Reichly, A. James. "How John Johnson Made It." *Fortune* 77 (January 1968): 152–53, 178–80.

Reiss, Craig. "Black Media Assn. Cites Offensive Ads." *Advertising Age* 54 (19 September 1983): 78.

Rhine, Shirley H. "The Economic Status of Black Americans." *Conference Board Record* 9 (August 1972): 27–36.

Rhines, Jesse Algeron. *Black Film / White Money.* New Brunswick, N.J.: Rutgers University Press, 1996.

"RJR Cancels Test of 'Black' Cigarette." *Marketing News* 24 (19 February 1990): 10.

Rogosin, Donn. *Invisible Men: Life in Baseball's Negro Leagues.* New York: Kodansha International, 1995; first published in 1983.

Rooks, Noliwe M. *Hair Raising: Beauty, Culture, and African American Women.* New Brunswick, N.J.: Rutgers University Press, 1996.

Rothenberg, Randall. "Blacks Are Found to Be Still Scarce in Advertisements in Major Magazines." *New York Times* (23 July 1991): A-7.

Rozen, Leah. "Black Publisher 'Sells Her People' to Advertisers." *Advertising Age* 48 (12 September 1977): 44–45.

Rust, Brian. *The American Record Label Book.* New Rochelle, N.Y.: Arlington House, 1978.

"Same Ad, Intelligently Done, Can Sell Both Whites, Negroes: Bullock." *Advertising Age* 32 (12 June 1961): 23.

Samuels, Allison, and Jerry Adler. "One for the Sistas." *Newsweek* 127 (8 January 1996): 66–68.

Sawyer, Broadus E. "An Examination of Race as a Factor in Negro-White Consumption Patterns." *Review of Economics and Statistics* 44 (May 1962): 217–20.

Schlinger, Mary Jane, and Joseph T. Plummer. "Advertising in Black and White." *Journal of Marketing Research* 9 (May 1972): 149–53.

Schmidt, David, and Ivan Preston. "How NAACP Leaders View Integrated Advertising." *Journal of Advertising Research* 9 (September 1969): 13–16.

Schoenberg, Tom, and Joseph Jordan. "Formulating Mild Ethnic Shampoos & Conditioners." *Drug & Cosmetic Industry* 141 (November 1987): 40–48, 76.

Schultz, Ellen. "Bad Times for Black Business." *Adweek* 27 (5 May 1986): 16–17.

Scott, Emmett J. *Negro Migration during the War.* New York: Oxford University Press, 1920.

Sederberg, Kathryn. "Syndicated 'Soul Train' Heads Down TV Track to Young, Black Market." *Advertising Age* 42 (7 February 1972): 34.

"Selling Black Cosmetics Proves a Tricky Business." *American Druggist* 176 (August 1977): 59–61.

"Selling the Negro Market." *Tide* 25 (20 July 1951): 37–44.

"Selling to Negroes: Don't Talk Down." *Sponsor (Negro Market Supplement)* 6 (28 July 1952): 36–37, 86–87.

"Selling to the Black Consumer." *Black Enterprise* 4 (November 1973): 31–33, 58–60.

Settle, Robert B., and Pamela L. Alreck. *Why They Buy: American Consumers Inside and Out.* New York: John Wiley, 1986.

Shaw, Arnold. *Black Popular Music in America: From the Spirituals, Minstrels, and Ragtime to Soul, Disco, and Hip-Hop.* New York: Schirmer Books, 1986.

Shepard, Juanita M. "The Portrayal of Black Women in the Ads of Popular Magazines." *Western Journal of Black Studies* 4 (Fall 1980): 179–82.

Sherman, Richard B., ed. *The Negro and the City.* Englewood Cliffs, N.J.: Prentice-Hall, 1970.

Sinha, Jessica. "Ethnic Marketing: Is It Worth an Extra Effort?" *Product Marketing and Cosmetic & Fragrance Retailing* 6 (June 1977): 29–34.

Sloan, Pat. "Revlon Fights Back: PR Efforts Aimed at Black Boycott." *Advertising Age* 58 (9 February 1987): 71.

———. "New Maybelline Line Targets Blacks." *Advertising Age* 61 (17 December 1990): 1, 36.

Smikle, Ken. *The Buying Power of Black America*. Chicago: Target Market News Group, 1992.

Smith, Clarence O. "Black Market? It's Virtually Untapped." *Advertising Age* 50 (16 April 1979): S-14–S-16.

Smith, Sid. "Black Dollars Lost Because Agencies Fear 'to Rock Boat'." *Advertising Age* 50 (16 April 1979): S-18.

"Smoothing a Way for Rights Law." *Business Week* (20 June 1964): 32.

Smythe, Mabel M. "The Black Role in the Economy." In *The Black American Reference Book*, edited by Mabel M. Smythe, 207–50. Englewood Cliffs, N.J.: Prentice-Hall, 1976.

Snyder, Glenn H. "'Black Is Beautiful' Market Bringing New Dollars to Supers." *Progressive Grocer* 51 (April 1972): 142–50.

———. "A Way to Win Black Customers." *Progressive Grocer* 55 (November 1976): 83–86.

———. "When Ethnic Merchandising Is Not Just a Sideline." *Progressive Grocer* 68 (December 1989): 109–12.

Solomon, Paul J., Ronald F. Bush, and Joseph F. Hair Jr. "White and Black Consumer Sales Response to Black Models." *Journal of Marketing Research* 13 (November 1976): 431–34.

"The Soul Market in Black and White." *Sales Management* 102 (1 June 1969): 37–42.

Southern, Eileen. *The Music of Black Americans: A History*. 2d ed. New York: Norton, 1983.

"South's Race Disputes Involve Businessman." *Business Week* (17 December 1960): 32–33.

Spaulding, Norman W. "Bridging the Color Gap." *Public Relations Journal* 25 (April 1969): 8–11.

Spear, Allan H. *Black Chicago: The Making of a Negro Ghetto, 1890–1920*. Chicago: University of Chicago Press, 1967.

"Stations Beamed at Negro Market Form Negro Radio Association." *Advertising Age* 31 (15 August 1960): 81.

Steele, Edgar A. "Some Aspects of the Negro Market." *Journal of Marketing* 11 (April 1947): 399–401.

Steinback, Robert L. "Smoke Screen? Selling Tobacco, Alcohol to Minorities." *Miami Herald* (13 August 1989): 1G.

Steinberg, Cobbett S., ed. *Film Facts*. New York: Facts on File, 1980.

Stelle, B. Drake. "Publishers See Segmentation in Black Market." *Advertising Age* 52 (18 May 1981): S-6, S-16.

Sterner, Richard, Lenore A. Epstein, Ellen Winston, et al. *The Negro's Share: A Study of Income, Consumption, Housing and Public Assistance.* New York: Harper & Brothers, 1943.

Stith, Melvin T., and Ronald E. Goldsmith. "Race, Sex, and Fashion Innovativeness: A Replication." *Psychology & Marketing* 6 (Winter 1989): 249–62.

Sturdivant, Frederick D. "Better Deal for Ghetto Shoppers." *Harvard Business Review* 46 (March–April 1968): 130–39.

Sturdivant, Frederick D., and Walter T. Wilhelm. "Poverty, Minorities, and Consumer Exploitation." *Social Science Quarterly* 49 (December 1968): 643–50.

"Suburban Blacks—Tomorrow's Hot Prospect." *Sales & Marketing Management* 122 (9 April 1979): 96.

Sullivan, David J. "Don't Do This—If You Want to Sell Your Products to Negroes!" *Sales Management* 52 (1 March 1943): 46–50.

———. "The American Negro—an "Export" Market at Home!" *Printer's Ink* 208 (21 July 1944): 90–94.

———. "Why a Handful of Advertisers Dominate Negro Markets." *Sales Management* 65 (15 September 1950): 154–60.

———. "Why Change the Rules When You Hire Negro Salesmen?" *Sales Management* 71 (10 November 1953): 158–60.

Swinton, David H. "The Economic Status of the Black Population." In *The State of Black America 1983*, edited by James D. Williams, 45–114. New York: National Urban League, 1983.

———. "Economic Status of Black Americans." In *The State of Black America 1989*, edited by Janet Dewart, 9–40. New York: National Urban League, 1989.

———. "Economic Status of Black Americans during the 1980s: A Decade of Limited Progress." In *State of Black America 1990*, edited by Janet Dewart, 25–52. New York: National Urban League, 1990.

Swinton, David H., and Julian Ellison. *Aggregate Personal Income of the Black Population in the USA: 1947–1980.* New York: Black Economic Research Center, 1973.

Swisshelm, George. "Widening Economic Gap Reported among Black Consumers." *Television/Radio Age* 34 (16 February 1987): A3–A8.

———. "General Economy Sets Pattern for Black Marketplace." *Television/Radio Age* 35 (21 March 1988): A3–A8.

Taylor, Thayer C. "Black Middle Class: Earn, Baby, Earn." *Sales Management* 113 (8 July 1974): A5–A28.

———. "Blacks: Two Distinct Markets in One." *Sales & Marketing Management* 119 (12 December 1977): 34–35.

Thomas, Jesse O. "The Negro Industrialist." *Proceedings of the National Conference of Social Work* (1928): 455–66.

Thompson, Lowell. "Blacks in Ad Agencies: It Used to Be Better." *Advertising Age* 63 (16 November 1992): 22.

Tidwell, Billy J. "Black Wealth: Facts and Fiction." In *The State of Black America 1988*, edited by Janet Dewart, 193–210. New York: National Urban League, 1988.

"Tips on How to Get Most Out of Negro Radio." *Sponsor (Negro Market Supplement)* 7 (24 August 1953): 76–77, 93–95.

"Tips on Selling via Negro Radio." *Sponsor (Negro Market Supplement)* 8 (20 September 1954): 56, 146–48.

"To Sell in Negro Market, Advertiser Must Communicate Respect for People: Fitzhugh." *Advertising Age* 38 (24 July 1967): 89.

"Treat Negro Equally to Get His Business, Marketing Men Told." Advertising Age 34 (23 September 1963): 1, 111.

Trelease, Allen W. *The Ku Klux Klan Conspiracy and Southern Reconstruction.* New York: Harper & Row, 1971.

Trotter, Joe W. *Black Milwaukee: The Making of an Industrial Proletariat, 1915–1945.* Urbana: University of Illinois Press, 1985.

"TV: A 'New Force' in Selling to U.S. Negroes." *Sponsor (Negro Market Supplement)* 18 (17 August 1964): 44–49.

"TV Ads, Shows Still Lag in Use of Negro, Other Races: ACLU." *Advertising Age* 37 (11 April 1966): 128.

"20% of Negro Families Plan '58 Car Buys: *Ebony.*" *Advertising Age* 29 (28 July 1959): 56.

"$2 Billion Negro Furnishings Market Seen by *Ebony.*" *Advertising Age* 34 (25 March 1963): 88.

Tygiel, Jules. *Baseball's Great Experiment: Jackie Robinson and His Legacy.* New York: Vintage Books, 1984.

Vaughn-Cooke, Denys. "The Economic State of Black America—Is There a Recovery?" In *The State of Black America 1984,* edited by James D. Williams, 1–24. New York: National Urban League, 1984.

Wall, Kelvin A. "The Great Waste: Ignoring Blacks." *Marketing/Communications* 298 (February 1970): 42–50.

———. "Trying to Reach Blacks? Beware of Marketing Myopia." *Advertising Age* 50 (21 May 1979): 59–60.

Walters, Ronald. "Standing Up in America's Heartland: Sitting in before Greensboro." *American Visions* 8 (February/March 1993): 20–23.

Walton, Norman W. "The Walking City, A History of the Montgomery Boycott Part I." *Negro History Bulletin* 20 (October 1956): 17–20.

———. "The Walking City, A History of the Montgomery Boycott Part II." *Negro History Bulletin* 20 (November 1956): 27–33.

Wander, Brandon. "Black Dreams: The Fantasy and Ritual of Black Films." *Film Quarterly* 29 (Fall 1975): 2–11.

Wang, Penelope, and Maggie Malone. "Targeting Black Dollars." *Newsweek* 108 (13 October 1986): 54–55.

———. "Can Revlon Repair Its Image?: Black Leaders Accuse the Cosmetic Giant of Racism." *Newsweek* 109 (23 February 1987): 53.

Ward, Adrienne. "What Role Do Ads Play in Racial Tension?" *Advertising Age* 63 (10 August 1992): 1.

Ward, Renee. "Black Films, White Profits." *Black Scholar* 7 (May 1976): 13–24.

Washington, Booker T. *The Negro in Business.* New York: AMS Press, 1906, 1971.

Washington, Forrester B. "The Effect of Changed Economic Conditions upon the Living Standards of Negroes." *Proceedings of the National Conference of Social Work, 1928* (1928): 466–78.

Weare, Walter B. *Black Business in the New South: A Social History of the North Carolina Mutual Insurance Company.* Durham: Duke University Press, 1973, 1993.

Weems Jr., Robert E. "The Revolution Will Be Marketed: American Corporations and African-American Consumers during the 1960s." *Radical History Review* 59 (Spring 1994): 94–107.

————. "A Crumbling Legacy: The Decline of African American Insurance Companies in Contemporary America." *Review of Black Political Economy* 23 (Fall 1994): 25–37.

————. *Black Business in the Black Metropolis: The Chicago Metropolitan Assurance Company, 1925–1985.* Bloomington: Indiana University Press, 1996.

"We Must Stop the MADNESS!!!" *Black Heritage Products, Inc., Newsletter* 22 (October/November 1966): 1.

Wendt, Elliot. "Reaching the Unreachable Market." *Beverage World* 96 (February 1978): 22.

West, William K. "Building a Lifeline to Ghetto Super Markets." *Progressive Grocer* 58 (January 1979): 101–4.

"Where Race Issue Hits the Pocketbook." *U.S. News & World Report* 41 (23 March 1956): 42–47.

Whigham-Desir, Marjorie. "The New Black Power." *Black Enterprise* 26 (July 1996): 60–68.

Whittler, Tommy E. "Viewers' Processing of Actor's Race and Message Claims in Advertising Stimuli." *Psychology & Marketing* 6 (Winter 1989): 287–309.

"Why the Negro Market Counts." *Business Week* (2 September 1967): 64–70.

Wilkinson, Deborrah M. "Afrocentric Marketing: Not Just a Niche." *Black Enterprise* 26 (July 1996): 72–80.

Williams, Barbara Morrow. "Filth vs. Lucre: The Black Community's Tough Choice." *Psychology Today* 7 February (1974): 98–99, 102.

Williams, Jerome D., and William J. Qualls. "Middle-Class Black Consumers and Intensity of Ethnic Identification." *Psychology & Marketing* 6 Winter (1989): 263–86.

"Will Negroes Back Christmas Boycott?" *Printer's Ink* 285 (4 October 1963): 7–8.

Wilson, William Julius. *The Truly Disadvantaged: The Inner City, the Underclass, and Public Policy.* Chicago: University of Chicago Press, 1987.

Winski, Joseph M. "The Ad Industry's 'Dirty Little Secret.'" *Advertising Age* 63 (15 June 1992): 16, 38.

Wood, Forrest G. *Black Scare: The Racist Response to Emancipation and Reconstruction.* Berkeley: University of California Press, 1968.

Woods, Gail Baker. *Advertising and Marketing to the New Majority.* Belmont, Calif.: Wadsworth, 1995.

Woodson, Carter G. *The Negro Professional Man and the Community.* New York: Negro Universities Press, 1934, 1969.

Woodward, C. Vann. *The Strange Career of Jim Crow.* 3d ed. New York: Oxford University Press, 1974.

Woofter Jr., T. J. "Economic Status of the Negro." *Monthly Labor Review* 32 (April 1931): 847–51.

Work, Monroe N. "A Half Century of Progress: The Negro in America in 1866 and in 1922." *Missionary Review of the World* 45 (June 1922): 430–40.

———, ed. *Negro Year Book and Annual Encyclopedia of the Negro.* Vol. 1. Tuskegee, Ala.: Negro Year Book Company, 1912.

———, ed. *Negro Year Book and Annual Encyclopedia of the Negro.* Vol. 2. Tuskegee, Ala.: Negro Year Book Company, 1913.

———, ed. *The Negro Yearbook, 1916–1917.* Vol. 4. Tuskegee, Ala.: Negro Year Book Company, 1916.

———, ed. *Negro Year Book, 1918–1919: An Annual Encyclopedia of the Negro.* Vol. 5. Tuskegee, Ala.: Negro Year Book Company, 1918.

———, ed. *Negro Year Book: An Annual Encyclopedia of the Negro, 1925–1926.* Vol. 7. Tuskegee, Ala.: Negro Year Book Publishing Company, 1925.

———, ed. *Negro Year Book: An Annual Encyclopedia of the Negro, 1931–1932.* Vol. 8. Tuskegee, Ala.: Negro Year Book Publishing Company, 1931.

———, ed. *Negro Year Book: An Annual Encyclopedia of the Negro, 1937–1938.* Vol. 9. Tuskegee, Ala.: Negro Year Book Publishing Company, 1937.

"Y & R Black Media Report Stirs Furor." *Advertising Age* 43 (10 April 1972): 1, 8.

Zikmund, William G. "A Taxonomy of Black Shopping Behavior." *Journal of Retailing* 53 (Spring 1977): 61–72.

Zinkham, George M., William J. Qualls, and Abhijit Biswas. "The Use of Blacks in Magazine and Television Advertising: 1946 to 1986." *Journalism Quarterly* 67 (Autumn 1990): 547–53.

Dissertations and Theses

Alexis, Marcus. "Racial Differences in Consumption and Automobile Ownership." Ph.D. diss., University of Minnesota, 1959.

Brooks, Dwight. "Consumer Markets and Consumer Magazines: Black America and the Culture of Consumption, 1920–1960." Ph.D. diss. University of Iowa, 1991.

Burrows, John H. "The Necessity of Myth: A History of the National Negro Business League, 1900–1945." Ph.D. diss. Auburn University, 1977.

Davis, Ralph. "Negro Newspapers in Chicago." M.A. thesis, University of Chicago, 1939.

Dowdy, George T. "An Economic Analysis of Consumer Food Buying Habits of Negro Households in Columbus, Ohio." Ph.D. diss. Ohio State University (Columbus), 1952.

Edwards, Paul K. "Distinctive Characteristics of Urban Negro Consumption." Ph.D. diss. Harvard University, 1936.

Kern, Marilyn L. "A Comparative Analysis of the Portrayals of Blacks and Whites in White-Oriented Mass Circulation Advertisements during 1959, 1969, and 1979." Ph.D. diss. University of Wisconsin-Madison, 1979.

McDowell, Winston. "The Ideology of Black Entrepreneurship and its Impact on the Development of Black Harlem, 1930–1955." Ph.D. diss. University of Minnesota (Minneapolis), 1996.

Mock, Wayne L. "Negro-White Differences in the Purchase of Automobiles and Household Durable Goods." Ph.D. diss. University of Michigan (Ann Arbor), 1965.

Newman, Mark. "Capturing the 15-Billion-Dollar Market: The Emergence of Black-Oriented Radio." Ph.D. diss. Northwestern University (Evanston), 1984.

Spaulding, Norman W. "History of Black-Oriented Radio in Chicago, 1929–1963." Ph.D. diss. University of Illinois at Urbana-Champaign, 1981.

Index

About the Author

Robert E. Weems Jr. is an associate professor of history at the University of Missouri-Columbia. He received his P.h.D. from the University of Wisconsin-Madison. His publications include articles in the *Journal of American History*, the *Illinois Historical Journal*, the *Journal of Negro History*, *Radical History Review*, *Business and Economic History*, the *Western Journal of Black Studies*, and the *Review of Black Political Economy*. He is also the author of *Black Business in the Black Metropolis: The Chicago Metropolitan Assurance Company, 1925–1985* (1996).